Management as Deliberation

On How to Get Things Done

By

Sten Jönsson

Management as Deliberation: On How to Get Things Done

By Sten Jönsson

This book first published 2023

Ethics International Press Ltd, UK

British Library Cataloguing in Publication Data

A catalogue record for this book is available from the British Library

Print Book ISBN: 978-1-80441-298-5

eBook ISBN: 978-1-80441-299-2

Table of Contents

Preface vii

Part I. Preliminaries

Chapter 1: Management in context 1

Chapter 2: Plan of attack 21

Chapter 3: Illustrations from the life story interviews 24

Chapter 4: My own experience in researching complexity and time 52

Part II. Reflections on the role of moments of truth in managerial deliberation

Chapter 5: Two main dimensions – complexity and lack of time 73

Chapter 6: Management as deliberation – when context matters ... 76

Chapter 7: Inside the corporation looking out 124

Chapter 8: Coherence and inference to the best explanation 132

Chapter 9: Working with words for a greater good – a new understanding of rationality required 146

Chapter 10: The "system" that selected the respondents for promotion to top jobs 160

Chapter 11: Is "management culture" possible? 175

Chapter 12: What can culture do? Achieving ambidexterity 180

Chapter 13: Mentorship, control structures, and changing contexts 190

Chapter 14: Pragmatism: The essence of getting things done 200

Part III. Concluding remarks

Chapter 15: What does this mean for management as deliberation? 225

Chapter 16: Life stories and their "moments-of-truth" – on the validity of these findings 234

References 248

Preface

This is a book about the complexities of getting things done in large corporations. The better "normal" operational routines function with their standards, performance measures, compliances, and complacencies, the more difficult it is to initiate and implement improvement work. Even to discover that there is a need - that an assumption on which those routines are based no longer is valid may be well-nigh impossible, since so much information is filtered through all-encompassing "integrated information systems". One should spend some time philosophizing about the difference between "data" (represented in "0"s and "1"s in computers) and "information" (given meaning by responsible members of organizations in changing contexts). Managers give meaning to data, whether it comes from attentive observations of contexts or from printouts from computers.

We are witnessing yet another historical rupture in the dominating view of society and its management. We have known since centuries that markets as well as democracy hold in them the seeds of crisis and even self-destruction. Wise men have been preoccupied with the design of remedies since Plato condemning the inroads of democracy in Athens proposed a Republic governed by "Philosopher Kings". As a counter argument to Mercantilism and the Berlin School's focus on making effective use of the nation's resources Carl Menger (1871) proposed that economic judgement should start from the individual's desires and beliefs and focus on utility maximization. This gave rise to the Austrian School in economics. It moved from Vienna to Chicago in the 1960s, supported by a growing group of economists moving out from the private seminars at the Vienna Chamber of Commerce under Ludwig von Mises' leadership, via Mont Pelerin, to Geneva and other places where world trade and the free movement of capital is regulated. They are called neo-liberals nowadays - derogatorily. But they were driven by the best intentions of protecting trade, economic progress, and the well-being of everyman from destructive interventions by imperialists and monopolists. Slobodian (2018) writes about the ambition to "encase" international trade and capital by supranational regulation to protect those activities from short-sighted politics. None-the-less Margaret Thatcher, with her "Big Bang" tried to restore London at its former glory as the centre of the financial world in 1986. We cannot say that this "caused" the financial crisis of 2008, but it certainly did not help to prevent it. Again, a rhetoric about owners ("the market") could govern large corporations toward efficiency, quality (and sustainability?) evolved. Economic growth would benefit everybody as it "seeps down" to the less wealthy – if anything it "seeps up" Piketty (2014) tells us.

And that rhetoric has been very successful! The regulation of economic affairs has increasingly been transferred to supranational institutions, economic and legal arguments complement each other as actors in financial markets find new tax havens and channels to transfer money to places where there is profit to be made outside the reach of national governments. More than half of the world's largest economies are corporations today. (60 out of 100 Fleurbaey, et al. (2018) tell us). Most nations of the world are smaller than the largest corporations. Chandler (1977) told us that we have had a "managerial revolution" – the "invisible hand" (the market) of Adam Smith (1776) has been replaced by the "visible hand" of professional managers. One might wonder what kind of people are placed in these positions, and how they go about doing their jobs as "visible hands"?

How are these business leaders selected for such jobs with more responsibility for the welfare of others than most politicians? What (and when) do they learn as they progress through the ranks? What principles of management do they cherish today? What are the most difficult problems? It is difficult also for the researcher to even get an appointment for an interview, and much less an open-hearted account of how they got promoted and what they have learnt. These top managers are public figures, and any leakage of information will be picked up by media. This makes things somewhat difficult for a management researcher, but interviews with the selected few that I have carried out (sometimes together with others, like Anders Källström and Richard Jönsson) have in general been very agreeable. Top managers like to talk about principles and their roots in practical experience.

This preoccupation with practical facts I initially took as a method they used to persuade me, an academic who has only seen the inside of libraries (they thought) or as a concession to my request to focus their "life story" account on "learning events". But after having spent many hours trying to trace the 'logics-in-use' in the about 1600 accounts of such events that I collected – with little success – I have found another approach to the drawing inferences to "the best explanation" from "surprising observations" that was so frequent features of the accounts of learning events in the interviews. Pursuing the roots of pragmatism, praxeology, even neoliberalism I found myself confronted with "founding fathers" of those thought models in, first Vienna, and then in Eastern Europe not least L'viv in current Ukraine.

"Thinking in orders" as one current historian of Neo-liberalism (Slobodian, 2018) labelled it, is a natural way of approaching a problematic situation with extreme uncertainty. How can some (new) order be restored from this chaos? Slobodian maps how neoliberalism emerged from and adapted to three 'ruptures' in social organization in the 20th century (First World War – demise of some empires; the Economic Depression after the financial crisis of

1929, and the 'revolt of the Global South with the oil crisis of the early 1970s). This was the important "ruptures" that cleared the way for neoliberal thinking as we know it today, but there were important roots earlier in Eastern Europe dominated as it was since centuries of landed aristocrats with enormous latifundia and slave-like labour producing grain for a growing Europe. A growing bourgeoisie in the Polish-Lithuanian Commonwealth (Butterworth, 2020) managed to get a decision through the Sejm on the new constitution of May 3, 1795. It was an enlightened "rule-of-law" codex that was considered an embodiment of the spirit of the Polish nation. Catherine the Great of the Russian Empire would have none of it and set the 3d Partitioning of Poland in motion, thereby eliminating a nation (for a while).

The First World War eliminated two empires (Russia and Austria-Hungary) and that "rupture" faced economists with the unsolvable task of proposing how small German-speaking rest-Austria could be made competitive in a post-war world economy. The Austrian School economist following their ideologue Ludwig von Mises, several of them educated in Law and Economics, used praxeology and deduction rather than empirical studies to define economic (design) principles. Watch the practice of efficient action, the praxeologists said – when humans engage in action it implies that they have preferences, and that is true for anyone who exhibits intentional behaviour. True that markets were "unknowable", but institutes of business cycle research were set up in most countries between the two World Wars. The "invisible hand" could be traced, just like the weather, the "barometer" metaphor came into general use - with the right indices that only economists could understand properly. Mises, Hayek, Kotarbinski, and Lange all stemmed from Eastern Poland and Ukraine (L'viv) where uncertainty about future economic conditions were maximal. You had to rely on praxeology and deduction to solve the complex design issues (after ruptures), and economists should give policy advice to governments. That was in my opinion, and that of Slobodian (2018), the roots of neoliberalism, which has such strong currency today. I will deal with this issue of "clarity-of-thought" in complex circumstances extensively in this text (about how to get things done in large organizations). But already at the end of the 1930s neoliberal economists had started to abandon the idea of prediction and focused on regulation of the markets to save them from the volatile interventions from elected governments.

One might wonder whether there has been another "rupture" between the two series of interviews (1990) and (2020) on which this text is based. There has been extensive digitalization of much of the information provision for managers (several of the 2020 respondents complained that they have little use for the outputs of "integrated information systems", and there is a debate on machines can be made to think like us (Larson, 2021; Zuboff, 2019)). The EU has established an "inner market" and increased its regulation ambitions, and there was a financial crisis 2008, just to name a few. The context is more complex now and there is less time to ponder governance issues while corporate raiders and a variety of finance market actors take "positions" in shareholdings and other financial instruments. And then there is the strong political pressure to demonstrate care for "sustainability". Under such complex circumstances it would not be surprising, would it, to find that leaders of large corporations tend to start their deliberations about improvement initiatives from observed facts ("surprising" or not) and communicate their "inferences to the Best Explanation" to the organization at large, just like the Pragmatists that were established in Cambridge at the same time (Misak, 2016) between the wars. In this way the world views current at the time are present in deliberations on the meanings (rather than the "truth") of current events and on what is the best action now.

It has been a long, roundabout, path to arrive at the conclusion that "my" leaders of large corporations are "meaning-givers" and communicators of new ways of understanding their business in changing contexts. That means that **their business is deliberation**. Since they must assume responsibility for the practical consequences of what they work with, conceptions rather than concepts emerge in accounts. Deliberation understood as an activity of giving meaning in context.

As an academic it comes natural for me to think in terms of **concepts**. "Return-on-investment" is a concept that is defined by the way it is calculated. Since I know how it is calculated I can be sure that 12 % is better than 6 %. The practicing manager judging a proposal to build a production plant in Indonesia must base his judgment about whether to go ahead on a **conception** of the project in many more dimensions, some important others less so. Calculations can only cater for part of the assessment. To justify the final decision the manager – or rather the team of managers – will have to produce a narrative describing the role of that plant in the entire system of production units, supply chains, development options, sustainability concerns and political contexts. (The academic will say: Of Course! All those aspects are included in the calculated 12 %! My response will be: Show me how!)

A conception is a conglomerate of facts, aspects, values, and reasons that, together (since they "make sense") justify setting this singular project in motion by a formal decision (in context). Frequently managers do not have enough time to produce a complete "sense" of the project. It might even be an advantage to have an "open-ended" narrative that presents the project to others so they may complement the description themselves, to makes sense for them. Some of my respondents have told me how the complexity of a project made them hesitate over the best way to present it to the board. If it is too complex, they might reject it. After all, it is a reasonable principle for board members to only accept projects they understand. Better present it in digestible parcels!

Time is problematic. Of course, one can "extend" time by prioritizing and deal with the most important issues first. But 'getting things done' has an automatic focus on "now". Picasso supposedly said that the only reality is "now", and that life is an extended "now". He has a point!

The main problem with this text has been how to present the complexity in a simple way. I have arrived at the conclusion that the best solution is to present it as a number of "reflections" introduced by an "ingress" that gives an illustration from the "life stories" I have recorded. I am not sure that my arguments are right – I remember the good old days when I did mathematical modelling and was quite sure of my conclusions – so I leave it to the reader so connect the dots. For me it seems right to conclude that management consists of two parts; the one we always talk about decision making and management control to see to it that plans are followed, and targets met, and the other that attends to those occasions when expectations (based in beliefs) fail – surprising observations - and must be explained and repaired by improvement work. (The second form must be prioritized with increasing complexity).

The text is structured into an introductory part where the interview material is presented and my own approach to managerial studies over the last few decades is described. Then comes a set of "reflections" on aspects of management that make it difficult. A final part draws conclusions about what this means to the nature of management as deliberation.

I am indebted to many people for help with this, seemingly, last book in my academic career. Anders Källström was an important partner in the 1990 interview series. Richard Jönsson helped with the

2020 one. I am grateful to the members of our little seminar group at GRI, Airi Rovio-Johansson, Gunnar Wahlström, Mikael Wickelgren, Roy Liff, that allowed me to bring up "semi-confusing" thoughts again and again and gave constructive suggestions.

I am grateful for the support I have enjoyed in the form of grants from the Handelsbanken Research Foundation (the Jan Wallander and Tom Hedelius Foundation) over many years. That support continued as I got the idea to repeat the 1990 study 30 years later and applied as emeritus. Thanks!

Thomas Polesie has encouraged me with many extended phone conversations about all kinds of "surprising observations" of the world situations and the correct way to evaluate company performance.

Help with getting the final manuscript into more readable shape by Marion Shirley Söderström is greatly appreciated!

Sten Jönsson
Göteborg, 2023

Part I

Preliminaries

Chapter 1
Management in context

I believe I have discovered some extra dimensions of organizational culture that follow from the need to deal with increased complexity and shorter time for deliberation. Beside the normal management control with regard to performance according to plan or budget, there is a different logic at play when managers in large companies detect a "surprising fact" that starts a process of improvement. The logic in these cases (most of the learning events in my empirical material) is of the kind introduced by Peirce (1903) – one of the fathers of pragmatism – as "abduction":

"The surprising fact, C, is observed.
But if A were true, C would be a matter of course.
Hence there is reason to suspect that A is true"

Think about it. In this case, deliberation starts from a fact … to be explained. Our usual logics have other starting points (Induction, in historical data; Deduction, in assumptions – as in syllogism). The stories I have been told about successful improvement initiatives all start with a fact, not with a hypothesis to be tested. Top managers in our largest corporations seem to apply this way of approaching uncertainty – reasoning that starts with a surprising fact – throughout their career. Having analyzed all the interviews again and again, I believe that this kind of reasoning characterizes management deliberation under conditions of complexity and lack of time. This book is an argument showing how I have arrived at this belief.

We cannot even "explain" consciousness (scientifically)!

To illustrate the sense of this claim let me borrow from Searle (2001, p. 97f.) on the mystery of consciousness. He is debating Edelman's (1983) speculations about what it would take for the biological matter of the brain (neurons firing, storing memories, distinguishing self from non-self, etc.) to produce something called "consciousness", and invites the reader to pinch the left forearm with the right thumb and forefinger. He describes how a signal goes from the receptor nerves of the skin via the spine to a region called the tract of Lissauer, and then into the thalamus and so on. Then what happens? We feel a slight, uncomfortable pain. That feeling is called qualia, and according to Edelman and Searle it is not possible to explain how it comes about by scientific methods. The feeling of pain, the joy of scoring a birdie in golf, or the shame of forgetting Mum's birthday – consciousness is an emergent property of the nerve system that humankind cannot explain, yet. But we all know it is there! Qualia! The issue of how matter becomes imagination (Edelman & Tononi, 2000) evades us.

There is not much point in going into detail. Edelman & Tononi (2000) summarize how the structure of groupings of neurons are selected (somatic selectionism) at an early age for specialized functions and claim that a primary consciousness requires a large volume of re-entry between these functions to emerge. Then there is the binding problem of how these functionally specialized neuronal groups interact – some more strongly than others – (multiple drafts?) to form an attention-directing and integrating dynamic core that generates the sense of redness (if a red object is observed). This is a controversial theory that cannot, according to Edelman himself (Searle, 2001, p. 49) yet be proven or disproven. But it speaks to my imagination. Just think about it. (Organizational culture?)

- The brain/body selects the neuronal groups that "work" (Find the right people.).
- These groups interact intensely (a large simulation) to direct attention and integrate findings through re-entry processes (I think of multiple drafts).
- But then there remains the problem of when to stop iterating. Could that be by way of social sanction? (Talk to your mentor?)

As I said, this is a controversial theory that is debated within its academic discipline, and so should not be transferred lightly to another discipline – like organizational studies – and with the unreliable data that I have, in the form of accounts of learning experiences; I have no proof.

Still, it does not seem too far-fetched to transfer Edelman's conception of what is required for the billions of neurons in the brain to produce something that we call "consciousness" (and they do!) in an organization. In both cases, the key factor is communication – re-entrance. Not only does a signal enter different destinations, it also initiates resonance signals, which Edelman stresses is not feed-back; the signal does not necessarily return to the originating source, which means that it may have effects on other neuron groups, etc. Processing of signals takes place in many places and there is resonance in many places.

A first necessary condition for such a transfer would be that the organization is organic, as opposed to hierarchical. Information or signals would have to be able to travel criss-cross over the structure. The discipline and predictability (for which we usually have hierarchy as a tool) then needs to be located in the individual member of the organization (individual ethics, and membership). That individual member also needs to be true to their "practical identity" (as competent in a certain area) as well as be loyal to the organization's aims. Further, most signals need to be given meaning (in context), which requires interpretation, which in turn, genders uncertainty. Deliberation is called for to reduce uncertainty and work out a plan of action. Then it is a good thing to have someone with whom to bring up the matter of the uncertain observation ("Do you see what I see?"), to discuss relevance and possible action, before going public with a proposal or warning. This trusted person is someone who has earned your trust in earlier conversations – a mentor. With the mentor in focus, we can calibrate our practical identity (Korsgaard, 1996) as a contributing member of our organization.

	TRUST	
INDIVIDUALISM	MENTORSHIP	LOYALTY
	MEMBERSHIP	

Figure 1. *Dimensions of Practical Identity*

Comment: There is little purpose in drawing all the possible connections between these aspects of practical identity.

Going public with an observation or proposal is a major event for the individual member, who hopes for praise, but risks failure, ridicule or criticism

We manage our organizational responsibilities by giving "accounts".

- Accounts – a diversified research area.

Buttny (1993) gives an overview of the literature on accounts research. The academic study of accounts as a phenomenon can be said to have started with Scott & Lyman (1968), who defined the concept as "talk to bridge the gap between actions and expectations". Buttny finds other understandings of the concept in different literatures:

- As descriptions or ordinary explanations
- As part of attribution theory (not only descriptions of what happened but also what caused it)
- As part of ethnomethodology (how persons present their activities to render them sensible or normal)

In much of the analysis, the use of accounts serves as excuses or justifications. But, possibly after Wittgenstein's (1953) language-games gave rise to a linguistic turn in several social science disciplines, narratives came into focus as tools for (ongoing) constructing and re-constructing social relationships, or even a life story (Fisher, 1987; Sarbin, 1986; Gergen & Gergen, 1983)). Buttny (1993) describes his own approach as a "Constructionist Analytic Constructionist Perspective" and gives advice on methods.[1] A subtitle in the Introduction is "Accounts as a Re-presentation of Action" (p. 4). It should be noted that what Buttny describes is a gradual shift, also in methods, from capturing "the truth" towards a focus on "meaning".

In my analyses of the life stories of prominent industrial leaders, I have arrived at a focus on accounts of surprising observations that led to improvement initiatives that the respondents claim they learned something from. This fits well with the Scott & Lyman (1968) focus on the "repair" perspective in accounts; accounts explain problematic situations. Such explanations are required to maintain the social bonds of organizations or society.

[1] I have applied some of them myself in Jönsson (2004) in analyzing recordings of debates in a car development project.

Throughout this text I have used the label "narratives" and claimed that narratives have a typical structure (Manipulation, Competence, Performance, Sanction) that also serves as a template when we try to understand each other in communication (Cooren, 2000). This understanding of the nature of narratives is helpful when coding accounts of learning events inside life stories, for example on logics-in-use or in the development of practical identity.

In sum: My aim in this text has been to analyze the life stories of our most respected industrial leaders with a focus on learning events (narratives about situations where they learnt something about good management), and how they reasoned that this was a significant situation. But a warning is required! The stories as they are told are always greatly simplified narratives about a complex situation and how they were resolved. I think it is a good idea to return to the case of the firewall insulation in Chapter 4 here (again a narrative) for illustration:

The nature of complexity and lack of time

The case concerns a team charged with developing a new automobile model.(More details will be given in chapter 4.)

Spain had changed its tax regulations in a way that could be expected to favour diesel engines, which were considered more environmentally friendly at the time. This was expected to have the greatest effects on leasing and company cars. The Quality department had started a project to maintain the premium standard of its cars by reducing the level of noise that reached the passenger compartment through improved insulation of the firewall (between the engine bay and the interior). John, a member of Bill's group (Interior Design), had picked up the news from the Quality department. He had proposed that the new firewall insulation for diesel varieties of the model should be extended to all engine versions – it would just be a matter of ordering the required CAD work from the supplier. Reduced noise has a value for all cars in the premium segment. John had proposed this to the project leader and been given the go ahead. The cost was outside the project budget, but John (obviously?) knew that Quality had agreed to take the cost in their budget. But he did not inform Bill about this when he briefed him just before the PMG (Project Management Group) meeting. It had all been cleared, Bill was told. It was just a matter of recording the decision in the minutes – a formality. "It's all on this overhead film," he said. "If we take the decision today it will save weeks."

Then, at the meeting, all hell broke loose.

First, the person taking the minutes asked if this was the first time this issue had been brought up. (That was an easy one for Bill; "Yes, it's the first time.")

But then the Project Controller asked who was going to pay, and Bill realized that he had not been properly briefed. So he asked who wanted this information and who had ordered it. (It was Quality, but the Quality department's representative was not present at the meeting.) The meeting lost its direction, and participants started talking to their neighbours about possible explanations.

When the video clip from this incident was played back to the participants individually, most put it down either to Bill's inexperience (he had been appointed as the responsible engineer for Interior Design a few weeks earlier), or to procedural issues. There was also mention of the fact that the presentation did not include any indication of how much the noise level would be reduced.

Fred, who was representing Production Control, and was a sworn enemy of late changes in projects since they tended to disrupt supply plans, not to mention the design of the production process (tooling, etc.), saw this as yet another example of the development team's laxity when it came to the actual consequences of design changes. This was an opportunity to teach them proper project management – how to keep to the task of realizing the design given by the pilot study. The commotion served as a "key" (Goffman, 1974) for him.

Greg, the deputy project leader, who was chairing the meeting (the project leader and Quality representative were at a strategy meeting at HQ) argued that he had not known about this firewall extension beforehand (the project leader had not told him, and this was his first time as chair; he had also been appointed relatively recently). He claimed that there was not much he could do but adjourn the matter.

When the matter was brought up again at the next meeting, two weeks later, it took just seconds. "Agreed! Agreed!" The formal decision was taken ex post. The project leader had already placed the order with the supplier. There was no time to lose.

What does this illustrate?

1. There was a surprising observation (the Spanish tax legislation had been changed to favour diesel engines) the consequences of which needed an explanation.
2. Initiatives were taken to reduce noise levels quickly. Part of this would be to include the change in this project, even if it was not in the pilot study or budget.
3. Bill was briefed about the need for a formal decision to include the change in the project. Although it had been cleared with the project leader, it had to be recorded in the minutes, since it meant a new cost (payment to the supplier).
4. Several members of the project group started to ask questions from the perspective of their competence, which Bill could not answer.

5. The starting points of the narratives of explanation (accounts) given when members were shown the video clip were Bill's competence, new procedures, the view that a premium brand must reduce noise, and other circumstances.
6. In retrospect, one wonders if Greg could have adjourned the meeting, made a phone call to the project leader, and cleared the matter in a few minutes. But Greg did not mention that option; perhaps he did not want to risk being seen as incompetent. Adjourning the request was the correct thing to do.

This illustrates how many dimensions are aroused by a "fuzzy" presentation and how members of the project grapple for keys and apply their specific competence to clarify issues that emerge as they assess the situation. It also illustrates how key people in an organization (in this case Quality, project leader) hold information that is not readily available to others. Greg was right in judging that further communication between those present in the meeting could not have clarified matters.

Is this a normal situation for a team trying to solve complex (or simple) problems? This is hard to prove, but it has certainly been a common characteristic in the university committee meetings I have attended in different capacities during my 40 years there. Now and then debate or deliberation was stopped in order to exert power, usually with reference to a lack of time. Sometimes the person leading the meeting had such authority that questions and debate were postponed until more intimate meetings (gossiping).

On being a constructivist

Consider the research traditions on accounts (Buttny,1993), where a new start comes with the article by Scott & Lyman (1968). The main conception of the phenomenon is that it is a matter of "repair of a problematic situation".[2] The field of study of accounts diversified and found expressions in several disciplines, due particularly to the fundamental influence of Wittgenstein's (1953) introduction of the contextual positioning of accounts into language-games and "forms of life", generating a linguistic turn in the social and humanistic sciences.

We now know (?) that the only way to find out who we are (Grice, 1989; Cooren, 2000) is to act (or just talk) and "read" the reactions of others to our action. To avoid a negative reaction, we feel that we need to give an account that may justify our actions. It is problematic that we are dependent on others in this way. But we must work on our practical identity all the time. We do that by communication and deliberation.

- Deliberation includes constructing accounts – before acting or communicating – of what the situation is and what action is proposed. This requires statements of facts, competences and reasons that fit together. This means that statements of facts need to be related to normative statements. It also means that statements must be persuasive for others as well as for the speaker. A first requirement for a proposed action is that there is a fit between action, facts and competences (including resources), but there must also be a fit between the intended consequences and the aims of the organization. Here it is useful to remind ourselves of the "desire-independent rationality" proposed by Searle (2001).

[2] Never mind that accounts have ancient roots. The Clay Tablets (from 2000 BCE) found in Mesopotamia were mainly accounts, the Hammurabi code (about 1700 BCE) regulated accounting among other things, and ancient Egyptian accounting records go even further back in history (Ezzamel, 2012), not to speak of Paciolo's (1494) presentation of double-entry bookkeeping.

- Speech acts have a direction of fit, either word-to-world or world-to-word. The word-to-world fit concerns the truth of the statement. When I say "It's raining," the other person can look out of the window and check whether my word agrees with the state of the world – that my word fits the world. Boltanski (2011) would do a truth test in this case.

When I make a promise, I commit myself to changing the world to fit my word. "I'll see you outside the cinema at 7 o'clock," means that I commit myself to changing the world (moving my body to the cinema) so that it fits my word. This commitment, which is included in every statement, binding the speaker to the receiver of the message, is the centre piece of Searle's rationality concept. We should take it seriously, because for organizations to prosper it is essential for members to trust each other's commitments. That commitment enables us to build social capital as well as practical identities. Note that the meaning of fit in the "direction-of-fit" used in speech act theory differs. If Carl claims that it is raining and I look out the window to check and find this to be true, the statement is categorized as a fact. But if Carl promised to meet me outside the cinema at 19.00 and turned up at that time, it means that Carl is someone I can trust. In deliberation, the fit might be to a whole frame of reference (Goffman, 1974). But note what Russel (Misak, 2016) claimed about beliefs: many of our beliefs are not available to us until the expectations they give rise to fail. We have made a "surprising observation" (pragmatism) and need to work out an explanation, which may require "repair" of the frame of reference.

This is done chiefly by asking questions: "Do you see what I see?" When the child points out that the small otter is attacking the big one at the Zoo and is told that it is all right because they are "playing", a re-framing takes place. The key (Goffman, 1974), playing, helps the child to a new, enjoyable understanding of the situation. But most of the time an observation is dismissed because it does not fit the current frame. It is not "relevant" (If it is relevant but problematic, there is a difference between the "is" and the "ought".) This is determined by Boltanski's (2011) reality test. Boltanski distinguishes between reality, which is that part of the world that we can deal with rationally using our current definitions, variables, vocabularies and rules of logic, and the rest, non-reality, because we don't have the words to describe and analyze it, is "the world".

The problem, when we realize that an observation as important but irrelevant given the current frame of reference, is that it seems we can only use non-rational arguments – rationality only exists inside a frame – to import the observation into "reality". So we need non-rational arguments: ideological arguments (Geertz, 1973) or emotional arguments. This must be included in our deliberations. Before we start using emotional or ideological arguments publicly, it is a good idea to have a mentor who is willing to listen and ask pertinent questions to build an argument that can persuade the organization at large. Boltanski (2011) calls this kind of test an existential test. The importation of a variable from "the world" to "reality" (to be included in rational deliberation) takes some effort because a re-arrangement of variables is required (Goffman's (1974) "re-framing").[3]

Comparison after 30 years

One might wonder what the point of comparing the life stories of two different generations of leaders is. Everything has changed – contexts, technologies, institutions, education – and therefore comparison is not relevant. To a certain degree I am ready to accept that argument, but I also believe that social structures and codes of conduct change more slowly, and chiefly through deliberation and

---

[3] Remember that a promise is a commitment to change the world to fit the statement. (Show up at the cinema at 19.00)

communication about current issues. Accumulated experiences play a role in that deliberation. (We all know what Germans or Americans are like, don't we?) Furthermore, careers stretch over decades. Some of the senior respondents in 2020 were up and coming juniors in 1990.

Since Swedish industry is concentrated to both large firms (as measured by the Herfindahl-Hirschman Index, among others) and highly internationalized (more than 90% of the sales and employment of most firms in the samples occur abroad), we might expect influences from other cultures to eliminate any Swedishness in organizational culture. Any specific Swedish influences on the leaders would be diluted as they are promoted through the ranks. But that seems not to have been the case. Many firms are very old – the oldest one in the sample was founded in the 13th century – and their leaders have to a large extent made their career inside the same company, or at least inside the same sphere,[4] which grants long-term exposure to company cultures. This would partly insulate people who are stationed abroad during critical periods of their career from a Swedish industrial culture. But then one must remember that the core of industry is of the B2B (business-to-business) kind, deeply rooted in the leading technical universities – at least in the 1990 sample of leaders; a majority in the 2020 sample had a business education. Further, we have the tradition of central wage negotiations, which caters for close coordination of standpoints between representatives of the major firm (so too in dealings with the state). So there is some space for Swedishness. One respondent (1990) told me about his sojourn in South Africa, where there was an understanding that rich white people should have servants for every conceivable task at home; my respondent accepted that as a social

[4] After the First World War, Swedish industry grew rapidly (especially after the Second War, due to its undamaged production facilities) under the umbrella of one or the other of the big banks, in much the same way as the Hausbanks in Germany and Japan functioned.

duty to help local families. But over time he noticed that this tended to make him lazy, so he asked for a transfer in order not to lose his Swedish/company work ethics.

There are some accounts of how the respondents escaped from problematic situations, but the overwhelming majority describe being thrown into a new situation and trying to make sense of it by observing and explaining (accounting for) surprising facts. An advantage here, from a learning perspective, might be that the respondent is made aware of his own (inadequate) beliefs when expectations fail. The surprising observation initiates deliberation, including listening to others (a virtue that several respondents brought up as an explanation for the international success of many Swedish corporations).

The surprises tended to be somewhat different in the two samples (1990 and 2020), even if similar patterns can be seen in how accounts were structured. One might expect that the dramatic changes in contexts that have occurred over the 30 years between 1990 and 2020 (the EU's Single Market, the end of the Soviet Union, digitalization, supply lines from China, among others) would generate different surprises to be explained. Certainly, these are fundamental changes of context, and comparisons between accounts will yield little but impressions.

The overall impressions, however, are that the context of management has grown more complex and that time has become "shorter". The principal marker of this is the increased emphasis on sustainability. There is also an increased sense of lack of time. This is not easy to verify, but it seems reasonable that complexity compresses time, since many more variables have to be considered – and this in a time when financial actors argue that judgement on complex issues should be left to the market. They seem to have persuaded politicians (with the state behaving differently now), but

I was not persuaded in the 1990s and much less so after the collective failure of the financial sector (and academic economists) to foresee the financial crisis of 2007/8. Perhaps complexity generates a sense of urgency to reduce the problem to one of financial outcomes and away from causes and interactions. One age-old method of dealing with lack of time is to extend time by prioritizing – deal with the most urgent problem first – but that would tend to fail more often with increasing complexity.

My current explanation is that complexity requires several competence areas to cooperate (across language and conceptual borders), which has significant effects on the conduct of deliberation in management. It increasingly becomes a matter of communication.

One of the signs of the manner of dealing with complexity is the more frequent mention in 2020 than in 1990 of mentors as participants in these uncertain situations.

So what have I done that justifies this kind of vague reasoning?

I have studied, in some detail, the emergence of what is jokingly referred to as Sweden's "negotiated economy" from the early 1900s. I have also read, carefully, six company biographies. I reported the results of those studies in Jönsson (1995) together with an analysis of the 1990 interviews. I have made a comparative history study of bank failures, and compared recent failures (Barings, Royal Bank of Scotland, Icelandic banks) with those from hundreds of years ago (Medici, Fugger, Sevillian banks). I reported that study in Jönsson (2019). I held a second series of interviews in 2020 (30 years later) and analyzed them to see the use of logics in accounts, which largely failed to provide a basis for understanding. Tracing the linguistic turn in social sciences back to Wittgenstein and the debates in Cambridge in the early 1900s on rationality under uncertainty, I have concluded that pragmatism, with its focus on "Inference to the

Best Explanation", is probably the best basis for reasoning on the deliberation of managers in large organizations. I reported much of this reasoning in Jönsson (2021). The "clarity of thought" that the earliest pragmatist (Peirce) argued for comes from deliberation on the practical consequences that would follow if a certain proposition held true. I believe that is the best description of good management seen as deliberation in a complex context under time pressure. I am reporting that now.

In the two series of interviews on life stories with their focus on learning events, in 1990 and 2020, I found a shift towards increased **complexity and lack of time** in the accounts of top managers. That makes sense! might be one's first reaction. We have digitalization, increased world trade, supply chains.... Of course, the managerial task is more complex, and time is short; tell me something new! Luckily, we have free markets and competition to manage that. Charles Darwin and Adam Smith provided the explanation: it is only natural that some firms will fail, but the fittest will survive. Charles Darwin did not have an explanation for how a successful struggle for life was carried over to the next generation – you know, the "variation, selection, retention" sequence. He did not know about genes, or that pigeons could teach each other, but he knew that the careful selection of parents could generate promising breeding results.

Adam Smith argued for free trade (and competition) at a time when Britain had been party to a peace treaty in Utrecht (1713) under which the South Sea Company (a company set up by the British government) was given a virtual monopoly on the slave trade between Africa and America for 30 years. When he talked about competition, he talked about pin manufacturers and farmers bringing their produce to the market, as was the case when Carl Menger (1871) introduced individual utility maximization as the (so far very successful) explanation for how markets work. Now

Deirdre N. McCloskey (2016) tells us that it was ideas, not capital or institutions, that caused the remarkable economic growth in the late 19th century. What ideas? How did they go from ideas to growth? The obvious link is management!

When my first doctoral student, Nils Brunsson (1976), came to me with his first formulation of the problem for his thesis, he said, "Why can't big companies do something else?" The background was that our city's shipyards were in serious trouble. Government support and technical innovation did not seem to be helping. "Why can't all these metal workers do something else, without one company going bankrupt and a new one being built from scratch?" Good question, but there seemed to be too many variables to deal with, so the discussion filtered it down to a study of how companies go about deciding to invest in the development of products that are new to them. He found (Brunsson, 1976) a company that said, "All new ideas are welcome," and kept to a strict economic calculation regime that was less successful in finding radically new products. Another company that specified more narrowly what kind of product they wanted (rubber, price range, size, etc.) was quite successful in innovation. (Ideas, not capital or institutions? Was it the management approaches to innovation that made the difference?)

Let me pursue this line of thought – management, not capital or institutions. It seems promising, not least because most stories about learning events in the interviews were about singular cases of initiating and carrying through changes. They would be, wouldn't they, since I asked them about learning events; but they talked about getting things done. But the stories do not prove anything, except that the managers who tend to be promoted to the top seem to be masters in discerning opportunities and carrying out organizational changes. This implies that the context– rather than management control in terms of deviations from budgets and corrective measures

– is very much in focus. So a history of managerial context might look like this:

1. Chandler (1962) tells us that up to the end of the 19th century, industrial companies were small, with rarely more than 1,000 employees.[5] This meant that the company was led by an entrepreneur/owner who often assumed responsibility for the local community and the welfare of employees' families. The owner was at the centre, had all the necessary information, and made most of the decisions. There was little complexity and plenty of time.
2. From around the turn of the century, engineers came to dominate thinking about the management of industry, since the application of engineering knowledge allowed firms to harvest economies of scale by rationalizing production systems. (Scientific Management, Taylor, 1911). Now it was the rational ordering of operational processes that was in focus. This way of thinking has had a long life, in part supported by the needs of the two World Wars. It introduced a natural science world view into management and allowed (reluctantly) Business Administration to be introduced as a subject of study at universities.
3. From the 1980s, as part of neoliberal de-regulation, Finance became a model of thought that gained influence on the management of large corporations. This brought the problem of (absent) owners and their relations to the complexity of operations. The ability of owners to control the operations of large companies had been questioned back in 1932 by Berle & Means (1932) and Chandler (1977), but the scientific view of management survived by developing a duality in the leadership of corporations: a principal with power and an

[5] A recent article (Khalili, 2022) informs us that the consultancy firm Accenture has some 721,000 employees worldwide today.

agent with knowledge (Jensen & Meckling, 1976). Both may be assumed to behave egoistically, which is acceptable for principals since they serve the market. The problem now becomes how the owners/the market can control management, which is likely to deceive the owners due to their vast superiority in knowledge about operations. It was widely held that more frequent reporting and regulation of the content of reports would make the market, represented by principals, more efficient in asserting its will.

4. Since regulation is formulated in a legal language for the general case, and applications are set in specific circumstances, a wide area of cheating within the limits of compliance opened up. The excesses of tricks-of-the-trade in financial instruments led to a severe financial crisis in 2007-2008, the effects of which are still with us. At the same time, digitalization has conquered the world. This worked fine in systems ruled by the laws of Nature (like sensors monitoring a complex piece of machinery to indicate when it is time for maintenance) but it is not able to replace human intelligence.[6] In my 2020 interviews, all the respondents who touched on the topic of integrated information systems made statements to the effect that these were of little help in the managerial work they do – spotting surprising facts that offer or require improvements that will change the assumptions on which the integrated information systems are built. Artificial Intelligence can only work with historical data and the machine-like programming that is installed in computers. Such control is based on the historical behaviour of the system. Dealing with surprising facts and designing

[6] There are great hopes now that Artificial Intelligence will save us. All we must do is to accumulate huge amounts of data and apply inductive models. But, as Larson (2021) shows, machines cannot think like humans. I will come back to this issue.

> improvements requires another approach; we can call it intuition (pragmatists will call it abduction).

Frustrated by the frequent mix of logics, the narrative form of accounts, and the start of the managerial processes described in some kind of "new" situation, I have tried to go back to where our academic management ideas stem from and what new challenges managers of large corporations confront. I have also searched for alternative approaches to the management of complexity and lack of time in a changing context and I think I have found reasons to consider modern top management work as "management by deliberation". This essay aims to present the arguments to back up this claim.

Chapter 2
Plan of attack

My ambition is to persuade by reasoning – not by calculation. Calculation, as we all know, is a matter of applying deductive rules to propositional statements. If we do it right and the initial propositions are true, then the conclusion is true. But in my case, and in most of the accounts given by the prominent industrial leaders I have talked to, there is no way of knowing whether the initial propositions, or even the surprising observations, are true. One must construct a plausible explanation and judge whether it is prudent to act on that premise. Complexity and lack of time provide constraints that are intimidating. A manager may retreat into inaction or avoidance, arguing that this situation does not provide for professional management. But most of my respondents did not. In the same way, a prudent academic might avoid analytical work with those life story data. They are not fit for "professional" research. But I have no current academic career to care about, so I will have a go at finding a way to understand what these prominent industrial leaders do when they work through complex problems (obviously they did not talk much about failures – these life stories are about successful management at the top of large corporations). This is how I will structure my argument:

1. First, I will give the reader a sense of the material by means of condensed descriptions of four of the forty+ interviews: two from the 1990 series and two from the 2020 series.
2. Then, I will illustrate my own views of what management is by giving an account of a project I was involved in during the late 1990s, which included video filming the project management team in charge of the development of a new car

model, playing back excerpts to the participants with the question "What is going on here?" and showing how members of the team understood the same scene differently. (The model still turned out to be successful.)

3. Third, I will turn to context. There are two kinds to consider: the emergence of ideas about the subject matter of social sciences (and the proper conduct of management), particularly economics and management, and the increasing complexity and instability of the competitive environment that large, international corporations face today. I conclude that the major difference between the 1990 and 2020 contexts for managers is the increased complexity of the task and the lack of time for deliberation.
4. Finally, I will discuss the implications of these observations for management. I will argue that the form of deliberation when facing complexity and a need to act (now) can be anchored in a philosophy called "pragmatism" which invaded Cambridge (from the US) in the early 1900s, with Frank Ramsey and Ludwig Wittgenstein the prominent receptors. (Keynes and Russel were also there.) The kind of reasoning that it enhanced, nowadays described as "Inference to the Best Explanation", seems to fit what my respondents told me about important moments in their career. It should be placed at the beginning of a venture process; in research, it is where hypotheses are formulated. The researcher must then design severe tests to eliminate false hypotheses ("falsificationism", according to Popper, 1963). For managers, the severe test is to launch the improvement in the market. (The role of mentorship, how to achieve agility, and other aspects will come up here.)
5. I will borrow heavily across disciplines that I am not as well versed in as in management studies. As I said, I don't think I

can "prove" anything – it is not part of the kind of social science I hereby endorse – but I hope I can provide a good argument.

Chapter 3
Illustrations from the life story interviews

I have chosen four life stories from the interviews to illustrate the aspects of management deliberation I believe are particularly relevant in times of complexity and lack of time. Two are from the 1990 interviews, Lennart Johansson (SKF) and Jan Carlzon (SAS) and two, Hasse Johansson (Scania) and Dan Sten Olsson (Stena) from the 2020 interviews. The choice is, of course, somewhat arbitrary, but both pairs represent production and service in some sense. The criterion has been that the chosen examples represent the complexities of adapting to large scale changes in context. I have promised the respondents not to divulge any secrets told in confidence. So I will try to keep my accounts to facts that are generally known.

Lennart Johansson – commitment and practical identity (1990 interview)

What distinguishes Lennart Johansson (LJ), the legendary leader of SKF (ball bearings), is how detailed his accounts about the practical aspects of his work are. His life story starts with convincing descriptions of how his father (his best pal) involved him in building gadgets like radio receivers and steam engines and getting parts for them at a price his father could not really afford. Learning experiences abound in his account, like when they tried to repair a transformer's winding using too little of a thinner thread, which resulted in a shaking transformer that soon started to emit smoke. Pull the plug, put a wet towel over it, put it outside the door on the staircase, and take the scolding from Mum.

Lennart did well at school but could not afford to continue his studies after technical high school. His military training was as a field technician, and during the war he taught a lot of car salesmen about what is under the hood of a military truck. He followed in his father's steps by involving his sons (Lars and Leif) in technical hobby work.

At work, once he was employed by SKF, LJ was soon engaged in automation and technical problem solving. During and after the war there were a lot of women working in production, often with monotone movements and heavy lifting. LJ liked to watch the work process and find solutions: for this lift-and-turn procedure we could use the same solution as the one we have on machine X (with minor modifications.). LJ stressed several times that he preferred to work in direct interaction with the processes to be improved and the people involved ("you have to get a feeling for what it is like to stand there on the shop floor and do the routine work"). His two favourite principles of management were: "management is stumbling over problems and solving them", and "management is selling ideas".

LJ embarked on a string of automation projects in the early 50s and caught the eye of top management. He claimed he learned a lot from starting up the new D plant in Gothenburg in stages. He planned to take a university degree in engineering while working half-time, but his boss could not do without him. LJ recounts that, after receiving an honorary doctorate in technology in 1979, he visited his old boss in hospital, who said that he regretted that decision, but was glad that LJ had done all right anyway. LJ was noticeably emotional when telling the story.

A new CEO called in consultants to evaluate the new D plant where LJ was now the manager. They found nothing to complain about (as LJ noted with pleasure). This CEO sent LJ on missions to England and Italy. In Italy, he was to evaluate the RIV production system (which was about to be taken over). In England, there was a "smart" stipulation concerning patents – your patent is only valid if you start production in the UK within 2 years – so a couple of plants had to be started. That same CEO took the step of making English the corporate language in the mid-60s. LJ describes this as a prerequisite for his great achievement, which was to come.

When a new CEO was appointed in 1971, LJ did not believe he stood a chance, not having a university degree, but he got the job. His first task was to do something about the over-expanded HQ. The American consultants employed by the former CEO had designed an organization where all the subsidiaries reported to him – a centralized solution. LJ tells the story of how the necessary cuts were achieved: they (HQ) were asked to make a list ranking the members of HQ according to how indispensable they were and then LJ would draw the line. He went through that process over a period of three years before the subordinates tired and asked him to simply announce the number that had to go. (The way he told this story indicates that his intention was to make everybody aware of the pain involved in sacking people you know well.)

But the bigger challenge was advancing, with Sweden's negotiations for EU entry (from 1994). SKF had traditionally worked with autonomous production units, each one catering for its local market. Now, increasing automation, which increased set-up times and therefore required larger volumes, together with the prospect of joining the European customs union, provided a different context. Short production runs, many set-ups, and a resulting inventory build-up in the autonomous production units, was no longer tenable for the group. LJ had to focus on this; he mentions good co-workers by name again and again as the story unfolds. During his two years as deputy CEO, he had gathered the facts about the extra cost that comes from producing smaller batches of the same ball bearing in five different places. The task was now to sell the idea that much could be gained by concentrating production volumes to efficient units. This is LJ's hobby horse – management is selling ideas.

But there was a problem. The Sverker Åström of Foreign Office in charge of entry negotiations to the EU for Sweden called him about the risk of negotiations with Brussels leading to "*plafonds*" for steel. ("Plafonds" meant that tariffs for steel would not be reduced in a single step but tapered off slowly.) SKF's main competitor, German VAG, had argued that this would apply to ball bearings as well. LJ explained to Åström that he should convince the EU official in charge of this (Ferdinand Brown) that this must not happen. It would wreck the main mechanism of the Global Forecasting and Supply System (GFSS), which was soon to be launched. Åström said, "You must educate me on this," and then … "Why don't you talk to him yourself?" So, he set up a meeting over lunch and LJ and his colleagues prepared a set of leaflets to support their argument. The argument was that this was about VAG wanting protection, but wasn't the European project all about how Europe was to organize an inner market that could compete with the US? The next day Åström phoned and said, "I don't know what you said to him, but this morning he told me that *plafonds* is not such a good idea."

Another prerequisite for the transformation to GFSS was to have module-based machines that could be adapted as volumes gradually increased – and they should be maintenance-free. LJ sat down with the owner/manager of a trusted machine supplier to work out solutions for production lines. (LJ had helped set up a development lab at that supplier. He was still working on improved machine design with this old partner at the time of the interview – when LJ was in retirement.)

Then LJ started "preaching" about GFSS in Germany, France, England, etc. Resistance was formidable. People would not give up hard-earned orders to other facilities; the idea of GFSS was that production plants would specialize in certain sizes and leave the odd orders to other (specialized) facilities. The coordination/allocation of orders would be done by a centre in Belgium and be based on forecasts (an added information flow would be necessary). LJ's basic belief was that every volume has its own specific, optimal technology, and that GFSS would help stabilize volumes and promote further technological improvement. In the end, preaching and negotiating would not help the major markets in Europe. LJ believed that it was the institutionalized autonomy of the subsidiaries that lay behind the opposition's reasoning. (Seemingly, the reporting by the subsidiaries introduced by the previous CEO, on the recommendation of the American consultants, was not enough to make them see the point in informing each other). Three subsidiary leaders had to go. Everybody had to realize that this was a bigger issue than the individual subsidiaries' autonomy. It was about SKF being competitive in an enlarged European market.

The implementation of GFSS was successful. It was a matter of stabilizing volumes at a higher level (per plant), adapting technology to those levels, and reducing the work force by a third. LJ is rather pleased that this could be achieved "without a revolution". The international unions then appeared on the scene. They could have been dismissed as having no real power (real power rested with the national or company unions). But the SKF management team put extra efforts into arguing the case for looking at the GFSS as a necessary adaption to competition in the Common Market, even to make the Common Market itself more competitive (against, for example, US Timken) – and the unions agreed.

This was an important step that required a lot of attention. So, when the GFSS had been implemented and the next step in automation was being planned, LJ decided that its implementation was a job for the next generation, and it was time for him to retire from the position of CEO. He was somewhat surprised to be offered the chair of the board of the Gothenburg subsidiary (but not as a working chairman, LJ said when he accepted). "You have earned it," the main shareholder said. LJ was chairman until he was 70 (the age of compulsory retirement in the group) after which he focused on machine improvements and patents – continued automation – together with retired co-workers who encouraged younger engineers to present their ideas for improvement.

"But there is a logistics component in all this GFSS coordination," I said. "Oh, yes," LJ said, "thanks for reminding me. That was the main argument against the GFSS. We solved that by engaging one of the big trucking companies in a tour of five sites in Europe, loading and unloading at each one." The cost increase for those transports was about 2%, while the saving through automation was 30%. Added to this (after LJ's retirement) has been the establishment of a central warehouse in Brussels for supplying distributors and the aftermarket. The cost problem that SKF has now (which is smaller than that of their competitors) stems from the steel.

After all, ball bearings are a commodity, and customers do not care about brands; standard quality and low cost through automation is the name of the game.

When I asked whether there was a consultancy business through which SKF can offer ball bearing solutions to its customers, LJ responded that there wasn't, because SKF has issued an extended catalogue with all kinds of information about that. It is used as a textbook in universities.

I also brought up the fact that LJ had been chairman of the main industrial association (SAF). Wasn't this a political job? Yes, there was the debate on energy in the mid-80s, then there was also the liquidation of the wage-earner funds (whereby large companies were taxed and the proceeds used to buy shares, by which means unions gained seats on the board) after negotiations with the Prime Ministers at the time (Olof Palme and Ingvar Carlsson). LJ points out that he can be stubborn in discussions, but he has never sought media exposure.

LJ gave a lengthy account of the role of lawyers in the US, what he saw as the arrogance of the engineering elite (although they are better engineers than the Brits)… all by way of providing context to the statement that the strength of Swedish industry (largely in the mechanical business-to-business industry, you know) is to accept context as it is and work from there. He notes an increasing emphasis on selling ideas rather than selling products, by having salespeople that sit down with customer firms to discuss new solutions to their problems and, consequently, build long-term relations with customers.

Comments

A striking thing about Lennart Johansson's account of the learning experiences of his career is how carefully he lays the foundation by talking about his origins, his mentor relationship with his father, how he was given ever more complicated tasks in automation and the organization of production in different countries. The climax of his career was the design and implementation of the Global Forecasting and Supply System for the emerging European industrial environment. Management, he said, is the selling of ideas. And negotiating, one might add. These are aspects of his **Practical Identity**, discussed above and later. He is careful to name the co-workers in his team – he couldn't have done it without them.

He was not too keen to speak about his post-career work as chairman of the Industrial Association and the lobbying work against the wage-earner funds, which included negotiations with two consecutive prime ministers. Lobbying in Sweden seemed to differ greatly from the processes in the US, where the trick seemed to be to find a new lawyer.

Lennart Johansson did not seek public attention, but worked in smaller groups based on trust. His deliberations (or explanations) seemed to start from concrete production issues. He is an old-school efficiency person, but also well aware of the implications of the new context supplied by the integrated European market. Structural change and adapted technology catered for his intensive problem-solving work.

Jan Carlzon (JC), the customer in the "driver's seat", communication (1990 interview)

Jan Carlzon described leadership as serving as a kind of travel guide pointing out the sights for others to engage in and enjoy. His book *Riv pyramiderna* (Tear down the pyramids) that argued for extreme decentralization was a huge success internationally. JC told me that it had been translated into 17 languages and sold well everywhere – except France ("where management is more authoritarian").

JC starts his account of learning experiences by talking about the evolution of management thinking over time. In the post-war era up to the 1970s, the producers were in the driver's seat. Customers had to adapt to that. You started with the production factors and ended in the market. Income was a given because you produced and marketed locally. The focus was on cost and productivity. The leadership style was "to be but not to be visible". Machines were at the centre. "We (SAS) were the first to buy the Caravelle because it had the lowest CASK (cost per available seat kilometre). We were the first to fly across the North Pole. That had nothing to do with customer value – it was cost value.

Then came the oil crises in the 1970s. This is of special interest to JC because each time the market stagnates it generates re-evaluations and new directions. There was such a severe crisis in the mid-70s, and what happened then was that the thinking in terms of production factors continued to increase; there is a lead time for new ideas. SAS had ordered new planes; Volvo was building a new plant – these things cannot be stopped – and consequently the customer climbs into the driver's seat. Output exceeds demand – producers need to search for new markets. Competition now influences the income side. You need to control from the income side – from the market into the company. The "to be but not to be visible" style is no longer valid. The "do the job yourself" approach (being in command of production issues) must be replaced by "see to it that the job gets done". That is a great difference – and to achieve this you must be visible. The job has to be done hands-on, so you have to transfer the strategy and mission to people, so they know in which direction you are aiming, and you have to delegate responsibility for getting things done. Because now the energy comes from the outside. Simple as that!

In that situation, SAS introduced The Businessman's Airline. JC illustrates this with a scene from his first year at SAS. He met with the technical director who said, "Nice to meet you! Now you can help us 'sell' the Airbus planes we have bought." And JC did just that: sold the Airbus planes. That was not what the technical director meant. He wanted the seats sold on mass markets because Airbus made them at the lowest cost. But that market was not of any interest now, since the planes were large and required full planes and several stopovers. The product was not the right one. "Globalization" acquired a different meaning. Now it meant that when McDonnell-Douglas made plans to build a new plane, the M95, they said that it would be manufactured in China, but components would be produced in 30 different places and flown into China for assembly; did that make it a Chinese plane? It does not matter so long as it is a good plane! Leadership now means creating conditions whereby you can get things done; you do not run the business yourself (by command) anymore.

The Japanese had understood this. Their production included both quality and efficiency. The CEO of Honda told JC that they had the best quality and the lowest cost, but any car company could achieve that: "We are in the business of 'repeat purchase" (that the customer will come back for his 2nd, 3rd and 4th car). You can no longer sit on your 'centralized' chair in Paris and believe that you can sell cars in the USA if you focus on the individual customer! You have to be close to them."

JC believes that the foundation for this focus on the individual customer had in reality been established in the 1930s and was built on the political ambition to promote as equal a society as possible. That platform – respect the individual – is what is required for the extreme market-oriented company, focused on the individual customer. Such a company can muster a lot of energy. What is required is communication – strategic leadership instead of authoritarian. You must be a visible leader. JC states with emotion that if you want to build an equal society through education and respect for the individual, you also must make use of the competence you have built into organizations. When you have made huge investments in people, you can't control them by instructions that limit them. The leader's task is to create confidence in people – "management by love". A high tolerance for mistakes (made in good faith) stimulates people to perform to their full capacity. The most important thing is not to always do the right thing but to learn from mistakes.

After these statements of management principles that JC represents, and has written a best seller about, he is (gently) reminded of my longing for learning experiences. He starts by describing a loving home environment, that he was the editor of the school magazine and active in the resistance to a Swedish nuclear bomb… on the far left of the political spectrum. At the Stockholm School of Economics, his main interest was in the students' association, parties, carnivals. In the summers he worked as a travel guide. After graduation, his first job was with a travel agency, in which he advanced to the position of CEO in six years (at 32 years old). After four years he was recruited to a (mainly) domestic charter airline (Linjeflyg), where he stayed for a couple of years. Then in 1980 he was recruited by SAS to become Group CEO in 1981. He summarizes by claiming that "I have always been a social [deleted]". He often says (and he is often ridiculed for this) that he is "the eternal travel guide" – always ahead of the crowd, pointing to the sights. He believes that his career hinges on his being socially accepted; he likes to "perform", not in the middle of the group but in front, "on stage".

When he was promoted to CEO at the travel agency he fumbled and started to behave according to what he thought was the CEO script. A colleague admonished him: "Who do you think you are? Did you think that you were hired to perform as somebody else? Be who you are!" That was an eye opener. Contact and communication were re-established. When he took up the position as CEO of Linjeflyg (as the world's youngest airline director) he gathered all the personnel in one of the hangars, climbed a service ladder and told everybody: "I don't know anything about airlines! If this is to succeed you must take responsibility for your activities and tell me what is required of me." He learned a lot from the response. They had expected an upstart who thought he knew it all, but this call for help and a pledge to work together surprised them. It generated a lot of energy. But to live up to that trust you must live up to your own role by gathering knowledge and learning. People don't ask for a leader that knows it all, but they ask for a willingness to learn.

JC had a host of new ideas and a growing self-esteem, but there was the eternal problem of Linjeflyg's big brother, SAS. JC told them, "Forget about SAS!" and they made Linjeflyg into a "people's airline" within a year (almost). It was a matter of liberation – of giving them courage.

When JC was recruited to the SAS organization, there wasn't that much new to learn – "I knew about airlines!" It was a matter of going out among people and talking about strategy – where we are heading – and letting them realize the vision.

But what about the situation with three principals (the three Scandinavian governments as co-owners)? "Yes," he says, "there was a little of that, but not much, really. You know, in this production-oriented world one tends to build all kinds of fences. Whatever I said, the answer would be 'fair enough, but we are not allowed to do that by the authorities, the board, the Unions'. There was a lot of 'we would like to, but…'". (JC tells an entertaining anecdote about an admiring foreign journalist who returned frustrated by the frequent "buts" she had met when touring Sweden.)

The emphasis at the time of the interview (1990) was on extending the platform for the service concept applied. That required very effective communication – like when you check in at the airport and information appears on the receptionist's screen about earlier flights that helps to make the event personal. Then the customer will come back again and again. Individual customer orientation is coupled with a culture that judges it unethical to carry any cost that does not help the customer.

What about people (employees) that give up when facing all those varied demands that individual customers may display? "Well, why do they give up?" JC asked. Expectations may be part of it. Another aspect may be that you fail to live up to your own ambitions. But the most important from a motivational perspective is lack of recognition. Bureaucratic organizations tend not to recognize a job well done. JC summarizes by pointing out that he may seem fanatical about communication, but for him the core of the job is to instil in people that they must assume responsibility for their own life: I won't force my support on you, but I am available. (It is a balancing act.)

Comment

Jan Carlzon is, in some ways, the opposite of Lennart Johansson, in the sense that he talks very little about operational issues (capacities, timetables, volumes, costs). He is totally focussed on the individual customer and the provision of value to the business traveller. (He did admit, though, that it was a mistake to invest so heavily in hotels – tying up capital.) He was extremely visible in the media as the champion of decentralization and communication. When he talked about being visible as a leader, it included being exposed in the celebrity pages of the evening press (at opening nights at the opera, for example; he pointed out that this was part of the "visibility" effort). This is his nature, and he was promoted (very rapidly) to do what he was good at. Communicating.

Hasse Johansson (Scania) - the technical problems of getting closer to the customers' value creation process (2020 interview)

Hasse Johansson (HJ) has been selected as representing a merger between LJ's orientation toward automation, the right technology for the right volume, cost effectiveness, and JC's individual customer orientation with extreme decentralization and trust in local decisions made by well-informed employees. In the final analysis, it is digitalization that has made this merger possible, but there are complexity problems where solutions require intuition (Larson, 2021) and responsibility (something AI machines do not possess).

HJ starts his life story in his father's bicycle workshop in the basement, where he used to help him with all kinds of chores. As technology developed, they had an increasing number of two-stroke engines (mopeds, lawn mowers) to service. There were two kinds of problems with these engines: either there was dirt in the carburettor, or the spark plug didn't "spark". Later, he had an old Saab that would not start on cold mornings. There had to be a smarter solution using a power distributor, cables, etc. HJ talks with enthusiasm about his early trouble shooting experiences concerning electricity in engines.

He took this topic up in his master thesis at the technical university and designed a solution. His tutor took him to meet the chief electricity engineer at Volvo to present his solution (there were no electronics in cars at the time). He was told that it was a pretty good solution, ".... but, you see, we buy our ignition systems from Bosch". This was HJ's first experience of how difficult it is to "attack" large companies with new ideas.

He put his ignition system on the back burner and got his first job with the Swedish branch of Philips, using light emission spectrometry to detect impurities in metals. But then an opportunity emerged to work with a smaller company (SEM) in western Sweden that produced ignition systems for chain saws; that industry was being restructured at the time and volumes were growing rapidly. HJ's proposal to offer such systems to the automotive industry was rejected as being too risky, so the project was moved back to the back burner. Instead, he became involved in developing the ignition system for the Swedish army's new motorcycle, which could not have a battery but needed strong light. (Leif Johansson talked about this project as part of his turn-around efforts as the newly appointed CEO for Husqvarna.)

Next, HJ moved to a division of Atlas Copco that produced combustion engine-driven rock drills in Kalmar. While there, he came, in a roundabout way, into contact with Saab. They had launched their turbo-engine at the time (about 1980) and were having problems with the ignition system (HJ described the details). Saab was too small a customer for Bosch to bother about the necessary development work to find the solution. The designer of the turbo system heard about HJ's solution and asked him to come to Saab to work on the problem. HJ was hesitant about the bureaucracy and rigor in large companies, so he proposed starting a consultancy firm instead and doing the work on contract. The deal was strict: no payment for the idea, all patents free of charge to the principal, the project divided into four phases with strict performance requirements, payment on delivery, and the principal could terminate at any time without payment if results were not delivered as specified. It was really a kind of slave contract, but HJ was quite confident he could do it. He had calculated how many hours each phase would require and set a cost per hour. He and his partner (from the old days at SEM) had both started families and built houses and were heavily in debt. So they went to the regional Development Foundation to ask for help with the share capital. But the representative of the Foundation did not believe in the idea and caused all kinds of problems. In the end, the Foundation's bank stepped in to help, saying: "If you don't do this, we will lend them the money." Then the Foundation were willing to share the risk, etc. In the end, HJ and his partner did not need to use borrowed capital. They had a decent cash flow from the start. They bought used equipment (HJ reminisces about buying a large lathe in Poland) and they scraped by. The company grew to something like 200 people at the end of the 90s. Then the people from Saab came to HJ and said they wanted to buy the company because they had decided to go into production with the system they had developed. HJ said, "You can buy part of it," to which they replied, "What are you talking about? We'll buy 100% or nothing." HJ: "Well, I suppose it is nothing then." Soon they came back and settled (in 1985) for 60%, with the head of development at Saab as chairman of the board.

The formal buyer was a group of spin-off companies called Saab-Scania Combitech, an interesting combination of all kinds of electronic applications (including space, marine electronics, missiles, training system simulators). At the time, HJ's company had five employees, and suddenly they had access to 1,000 engineers in this technology matrix, which was quite advanced; every part of the matrix was responsible for one technology/discipline, which they could allocate to different projects. You could discuss and get advice from a lot of qualified people.

This was in 1985, but then, in 1990, GM went in and bought 50% of Saab's automobile division. The CEO phoned and told HJ that he had included HJ's company in the deal ("You don't mind, do you?").[1] After the complications noted below, HJ's company ended up being split, with Saab owning 60% and GM 40%. Centralized decision making on the board became complicated and HJ laid down an ultimatum, which resulted in GM buying 100% and placing "his" company in DELPHI Automotive Systems, which was listed on the New York stock exchange in 1998 (in the largest IPO at the time; with 220,000 employees it was larger than Bosch). HJ oversaw Advanced Engineering, with 10 development centres, in a dedicated effort to establish links to Europe. He stayed in Sweden with his family and commuted to the European centres.

---

[1] For group accounting reasons Saab's share in HJ's company had been increased to 91%. HJ did not mind being 91% owned by GM. But GM had sold it to Delco Electronics (later Delphi Electronics); Delco later sold 51% back to GM and kept 39% for themselves. Then came a policy decision from GM that they could not accept minority ownership in their subsidiaries (they pointed to bad experiences with the super-entrepreneur Ross Perot).

At the same time, there were intensive contacts with Scania, because Håkan Samuelsson, its technical director, was adamant that Scania needed to become better at using software in its trucks. It seemed impossible to recruit the right people to come to the relatively small town of Södertälje, where Scania was based (Ericsson and Nokia drew everybody into their Kista centres, north of Stockholm). HJ asked around for help to find people. Was there anyone who would be interested in moving to Södertälje? No luck. The solution was to set up business in Kista: Scania Infotronics. But then the deal between Volvo and Scania fell through and Samuelsson left for MAN. Leif Östling, (LÖ) who was very angry with Leif Johansson of Volvo (Östling, 2020) asked HJ to take his (Samuelsson's) place. HJ accepted and started in early 2001. He is very positive about his work with Östling, who was reputed to be grumpy after the merger deal failed. There were several critical/difficult decisions to be made, but they never had any serious disagreements. He explains in detail a number of such decisions that demonstrate how regulations and legislation (IFSR, the length of trucks (cab-over-engine), etc.) limit what can and cannot be done. He explains the effectiveness of the co-operation with LÖ by stressing his capacity to delegate responsibility to subordinates. He was competent technically as well as managerially (he held two university degrees) and very interested in the products. Scania had six executive meetings a year to discuss technical issues and 90% of the time, the topic was "nuts and bolts". Östling stressed quality as measured by what the customer wanted (the ability to carry a heavy load, no break downs, low fuel consumption).

The strategic situation after the proposed merger between Volvo and Scania failed was that Scania felt itself to be in a defensive position vis-à-vis Volvo. A market study initiated by Samuelsson had shown that the typical product properties that customers appreciated when it came to Scania were fuel consumption, availability (no unplanned stops), price and service. This boiled down to HJ preaching a focus on qualities such as fuel consumption and up-time. HJ illustrates this by telling the story of the Scania "transport lab":

Used to benchmarking from his time at GM, HJ asked how Scania was doing on these quality aspects in comparison to the competition. The answer was that as Scania was ahead of the rest of the field, comparisons were unnecessary. So the first thing was to make a start on systematic benchmarking. Soon they arrived at the conclusion that they knew too little about their customers and their business. HJ proposed to LÖ that Scania should start its own haulage firm to learn what was important for their customers. LÖ's first reaction was the traditional "one should not compete with one's customers". But, after persistent persuasion, he agreed to start a ten-truck Scania haulage company. Resistance came not only from LÖ – the whole marketing department was upset. HJ was about to back down, but he had an ally in the purchasing department who was quite pleased about the project. Part of their pleasure came from the fact that this would give Scania the chance to understand their exact transport costs. Scania was a big buyer of transport services and now they could negotiate with the big operators from a position of strength. Go! Next, they put an ad in a local newspaper inviting applications for drivers for the Scania Transport Lab, stating the requirements and contractual pay. The next day, the CEOs of all the haulage companies in the region were on the phone: "What are you doing? How the hell are you going to break even with contractual pay? You can't run a company in this business on contractual pay! We have competition from drivers from Eastern Europe today! You will ruin us all! If you do this, we won't ever buy a Scania truck again!"

After deliberation, and some tips from the head of the purchasing department, it was decided that the best thing would be to invite these people in and show them what they were trying to do. So, half a dozen CEOs from the major haulage firms in the region were invited to Scania. They were taken through a detailed demonstration of all kinds of tests of components and then at full speed on the test course ("Sorry, you are not allowed to drive on the course yourselves. Let me show you."). The message was: "We are still not satisfied! We want to learn more from how you use the trucks out there!" "That's why we need the transport lab!" They bought the argument, and work started.

The manager of the transport lab was told that he would not receive anything for nothing. He had to go out there, on the market, and buy trucks, service deals, etc... the whole package. The requirement was that the trucks must be serviced 24/7 (the service must be available if there was a breakdown between 4 and 6 on a Saturday afternoon), which was too demanding for the local garages. So they made a deal with a garage in Zwolle (where Scania has a large assembly plant). The run between Södertälje and Zwolle was a nice stretch to test things like fuel consumption; monitoring the effects of driver behaviour was useful since it was the same run for all trucks. Observation: the difference between drivers could amount to 15% in fuel consumption. HJ pointed out that this amounts to 30 years of engine development! Furthermore, the best driver (by far) in this respect was a 22-year-old woman. The computer information from the trucks showed that her mastery was in "rollout", i.e., the truck rolling without the accelerator being used. (I asked: Downhill all the way?) It is simple, really: approaching a crossing or a red light, you don't break and then accelerate again, but adapt to circumstances. You really don't lose much time by taking your foot off the accelerator! She had the second fastest time between Södertälje and Zwolle. HJ described how they constructed a scorecard for four of the essential variables that appear on screen. Drivers competed against themselves. He himself drove to test and found that it is only possible to concentrate on holding these variables at 90-95 % of the maximum. This led to the insight that they needed to design an auto-pilot to assist the driver and help them to adapt to other variables like topography, or reports of a *stau* (traffic jam) on the motorway ahead, in order to arrive in a specific time, etc. All this can be programmed to optimize driving efficiency. The haulage companies, who were not interested at the start, gradually realized the value of this extra information. Scania itself was more interested in checking up on the status of the truck, for preventive maintenance purposes, among other things. Here this meant the use of sensor fusion to collect big data on the trucks and use AI to look ahead for whatever might soon be needed in terms of service. Things are moving fast in the truck business now. There is more business to be found closer to the customers' value creation process.

Our conversation shifts to talent management and HJ tells a rather detailed story about coaching talent to prepare them for greater things. The main character in the story was discovered early, but he was about to accept a top job at another company, and that triggered action. "We can't do without him." So they found him a top managerial job in a European subsidiary and on his return, he was promised, the engine development job in a couple of years. When he came back, he was told that while he was waiting for his predecessor to reach retirement age (in about 18 months) it would be a good idea to work on the market side (where, incidentally, he was promoted to director for the truck market quite quickly). Thereby he learned how to penetrate and present market issues (this was not foreseen by HJ & co.), which, in turn, led to him making presentations to the board, where he excelled; his presentations were followed by lively discussions. It felt only natural that he should take over as CEO when LÖ moved to the Volkswagen organization.[2]

When talking about his experiences with production technologies, HJ points to the American tradition of underinvestment (too old

[2] I have interviewed that candidate manager (as well as LÖ) and his life story corroborates what HJ told me.

machinery) due to the management by objectives applied there. "This is your target ROI, do whatever you need to achieve it!" In Germany, it is more like management by fear (you do as you are told), but in Sweden it is management by consensus. To achieve that, you cannot overload the board with complexity and details. You need to present your proposal in digestable portions to avoid overload that might trigger a rejection. Given this conception of how the board and top management tend to interact in problem solving, HJ quotes, with approval, the three basic duties of the board according to the legendary Marcus Wallenberg (Sr.):

1. Appoint the CEO
2. Dismiss the CEO
3. Indicate the desired development direction.

Simplistic perhaps, but when arguing the case for a proposal there are always several principles, rooted in earlier examples/ experiences, that you need to relate your arguments to. Use those earlier examples (pointing out variations of them), let board members make associations, and you will see from their questions where they are going and what corrections are needed. You reach consensus when they feel confident that this is right. (Philosophers like Scanlon (2014), Rawls (1971), as well as psychologist Kahneman (2011), call this "reflective equilibrium".)

The trick, when it comes to the company meeting varying individual customer needs, is to modularize and standardize components. If you take care to also standardize interfaces, you can build solutions that fit the customer while keeping most of the economies of scale. Some companies approach this problem with multi-brand strategies (one brand for each customer?) but they find that guarantee costs soon swallow any benefits from the multiple brands. So what you need is serious thinking about base platforms and modules, so you have well-reasoned performance steps (it is like using Lego bricks, really), by way of value analysis (rather than cost analysis). Here is the fundamental principle that HJ argues for in his current positions on company boards: you must have an operational basis in tune with financial strategies (see also Sjöstrand, 2016).

Comment

Hasse Johansson does not have a background in elite business circles (just like Lennart Johansson and Jan Carlzon), but he has an intensive passion for invention and improvement. That passion was also the basis for his leadership throughout his career. He did not like being constrained in bureaucratic straitjackets. When he found (or was found by) a boss who trusted him and delegated authority to solve problems to him, he became a kind of a developmental engine for the company. Some people (if not all) are at their best when they feel trust and respect while they engage in a mission. Johansson seems to argue from operational problem statements most of the time and is not suspected by his colleagues of playing power games.

Dan Sten Olsson (Stena) – developing the family business

Dan Sten Olsson (DSO) is an important person in Gothenburg. We talk about him now and then at the Business School. He donates to and cooperates with the technical university (Chalmers) and with us. We worry about how he can manage the much-expanded family business seemingly on his own (at the top). He took over after his father, but his own children have chosen other life paths. What is to become of this multi-business empire (ferries, shipping, oil rigs, recycling, real estate)?

DSO starts by characterizing Swedish management and says, "We are rather good at consensus building"; he himself works towards a "forgiving" culture. People must dare to make mistakes. From this entry point he describes his company's strategy as being to make good use of opportunities. We don't have a strategic plan, he says, it is more like we make use of other companies' plans. When an opportunity appears, we should go for it. (I point out that this presupposes a good liquidity ratio. He responds with an account of how having a good liquidity ratio means that you can focus on the quality of the acquisition (or deal) first and worry about financing later.) But it is difficult to spot opportunities; he claims that he is not very good at this himself, he tends to get stuck in the old ways of thinking, so he discusses things with his team members and, when he is convinced, he sanctions propositions.[3] When I ask him where the opportunities are now, he says he really doesn't know. He is frustrated by the problems in oil drilling now and the difficulties of solving them without other the businesses suffering. It is quite demanding; he discusses the form of ownership and public participation. One of DSO's basic principles is to "manage your pound" and he discusses the appropriate indicators to help you keep on the safe side.

Starting with the firm's beginnings as a scrap yard, he soon comes to the joy of the re-cycling business. Stena has contracts with the vast majority of industrial firms in Sweden. This includes managing certification processes and guaranteeing clients that they will stay within sustainability limits. The recycling plant in Halmstad recovers more than 95% of a car and is approaching 97% today. That requires a lot of knowledge about every fraction and element.

His principle concerning real estate is relations-based management, which means that tenants in the block should flourish and feel safe. Secure tenants mean less turnover and lower maintenance costs. "We have invested in youth recreation centres and clubs," DSO says. Cooperation with the municipalities has become more difficult with

---

[3] Some of this mentality is captured in Bergenek & Sahlsten (2020): *Stenability – The Story of Stena RoRo*

the increased immigration flows (and New Public Management – my comment). Integration is not made easier by the system of "free" schools; private schools tend to increase exclusions rather than mitigate integration. He is contemplating investing in schools, not to make money (note) but to improve the chances of better community integration, which will reduce costs for housing. The welfare state ideology (reducing segregation in society) is useful, but difficult to manage. He describes a joint venture with the municipal council in one of our cities to cater for youth recreation, which worked very well. But when it proved to be successful, the municipality "jumped ship". They find more heart-warming causes all the time. This points back to the basic task of municipalities: to reallocate resources from the healthy, strong and young to the sick, weak and old. Their mission is to invest in misery. This makes them unreliable; they are ready to abandon the project once it works satisfactorily.

From this topic, the conversation moved to Eastern Europe, where large parts of the public sector activities have been privatized. Poland is doing all right and Stena has moved a large part of the ferry business to that part of Europe. It is a problem, though, that the corruption that thrived under the socialist regime seems to have survived in many of these countries. By and large, the Polish venture has been quite successful.

Shipping is a commodity business. DSO is preoccupied, constantly, with the issues of how to generate surplus value there. If you can be just a little more cost efficient than your competitors, you scrape by, but it is very dependent on the general economy. We talked about what the Northeast passage (north of Siberia) between Europe and China means. This is to be used to transport nickel and liquid gas, but the ships must be reinforced in different ways, which means that you lose flexibility.

We talked about the financial sector being in control, and how trade in financial instruments expands the economy (but is fragile) and the fact that DSO is not satisfied with the IFRS regulation of accounting reports.

Although DSO has bonus systems in operation for some types of business (trading), he prefers to work with "the object", giving people a concrete task (objective) and providing them with the resources to carry it out. That generates commitment (not conflicts, as bonuses sometimes do).

Comment

One cannot help admiring Dan Sten Olsson's ability to keep such a diverse business portfolio together. He seems to be at the centre of everything, but he admits freely that he is not very good at spotting opportunities. Such skills come with specialization, while DSO deals with recycling, oil rigs, housing projects and shipping (there is also a business in plants and gardening supplies) at the same time. So, he encourages business unit managers to take initiatives, listens to their arguments, and lets himself be persuaded. He is an entrepreneur in a classic sense, built on community concerns rather than on some operational invention.

Summary: four selected representatives of good Swedish management.

A striking fact about these representatives of Swedish management traditions is that they were promoted on some specific skill, rather than family or academic achievements. (The exception is Dan Sten Olsson, who grew up in an entrepreneurial family and was put to the test by his father, but he has developed the business considerably over the years.) They were spotted by mentors and promoted by way of new challenges. It's possible that the structure of the interviews – tell me the life story of your career – tends to favour stories about one-off learning events, and the focus is thus on the particularity of specific situations. I am sure it is possible to design research to test this conjecture.

The life stories approach tends to place the individual at the centre. Looking at how the stories unfold, one can see a pattern of "practical identity" (Korsgaard, 1996) – "a person like me in a situation like this". It is not so much that they want to exhibit themselves as somebody they really are not (image performance); it is more like a justification of action:

- Lennart Johansson emphasized, again and again, that he did not like working in the office, designing solutions on the drawing board. He preferred going out close to the process and watching it carefully, discerning steps (parts of the process) that could be improved – a practical man.
- Jan Carlzon described himself as a "social son of a bitch". He used the metaphor of the travel guide several times. He justified his arguments for the delegation of decision authority to front line managers with the argument that having built the welfare state (once referred to in Swedish as *folkhemmet*, the people's home) with its emphasis on equality and respect for the individual, you have to live up to your own policy and trust people to be competent at their own work – their practical identity.
- Hasse Johansson is a different character. He is passionate about invention and appears to value his independence and being in control of his own work. Still, when he finds himself in interaction with Leif Östling (2021) (CEO of Scania) and is entrusted with embarking on a new drive towards quality (from the customer's view) as technical director, he is stimulated to live up to this broader responsibility. He is at his best leading a team by example and communication rather than pulling rank.

- Dan Sten Olsson cannot escape his role as owner (principal) of the conglomerate but tries to build a culture of "forgiveness". Subordinates are expected to take initiatives; you are allowed to make mistakes if you learn from them. He sees his role as that of a mentor, with the specific task of financing new initiatives when opportunities emerge.

Looked at together, they seem to represent different stages in managerial discourse over recent decades. First, there is Lennart Johansson, with his preoccupation with problem solving in an ongoing process of automation in production against a background of institutional change (not least towards an inner market in Europe), and his skill in negotiation with government as well as unions.

Then Jan Carlzon with his vision of "the customer in the driver's seat" rather than aeroplane technology, routing and maintenance routines. His argument for moving a large part of the everyday management decisions to the frontline facing the customer (treating the customer as individual) is rooted in his conviction that the ideology of the welfare state implies trust in the employee. He represents a shift in attention from the cost effectiveness of large technical systems to enhancing the customer's value creation.

Hasse Johansson is the dedicated inventor, who found a platform for his drive towards using technology (and digitalization) to generate information from the customers' value creation process. This could stimulate improvement in designs and awareness of the context in which products are used.

Dan Sten Olsson, at the centre of a family-owned conglomerate that has grown by acting on emerging opportunities, needs to be alerted to changes in an extended context. In the competitive environment in which he finds himself, it is imperative to know what drives costs and to keep them below those of his competitors – "commodity business" is how he describes shipping. He is watching context and mentoring internal problem solving.

The life stories I have been told tend to give meaning to managerial principles by reference to situations where they emerged. Those events often serve as the background for respondents' descriptions of who they are, i.e., their practical identity. This practical identity is built around principles they live by and what can be expected of them. It makes them predictable, in a sense, which, in turn, provides a basis for delegation of authority – provided that you can communicate this practical identity to colleagues and subordinates. I have seen several examples of productive interaction (mentorship) over time between CEOs and principals, but also more group teamwork. The system has selected these leaders because their practical identity fits the context. (Not a very original conclusion, I know, but wait for my account of what kind of deliberations underpin this kind of management.)

Chapter 4
My own experience in researching complexity and time

In writing this text about the meaning of management in complexity and lack of time I have often paused to reflect upon why the reader should believe that I know what I am talking about. It is not a matter of my publication list, my position as department head for 30 years, or my chairing of the Scandinavian Academy of Management during its first seven years. No, it is about seeing, close up, with my own eyes, management in action, real life, real time, and seeking a plausible explanation. Admittedly, leading a university department with all its policies, rules and sub-committees can seem unreal at times, but universities are large organizations too. But when you go out into the "real world" of project management and see the complexities of deliberating in a large team about a relatively obvious improvement in design, as in the case I am about to use as an illustration, you realize how complex managerial work is. Trying to understand, from the outside, how managers deal with these complexities in action – here and now – is a challenge. As academics, we tend to simplify matters for ourselves by using theory. This is a matter of utility maximization, we say… next data item, please! If I were asked to characterize myself as an academic, I would choose to describe my work as a constant effort to understand how the practitioners – our study objects – go about solving the problems they face, in their context, on their terms. I have not been very interested in judging how well they live up to the gospel of our textbooks. So, here it is, a snippet of my research history that I believe illustrates how I think the study of managerial deliberation should approach its subject. I will focus on the minutes taken from two project meetings in one of two car development projects that we followed, over a period of more than two years, video-filming meetings and conducting extensive interviews about what was going on.

Background

In the late 1990s we were given permission to videotape meetings in the project management group (PMG) for the development of a new year model in the product portfolio of a car manufacturer. Being given access to the very centre of the practical work with a strategy to establish the model more firmly in the premium segment of the market was, in itself, a unique accomplishment. It was a sign of trust that had to be reciprocated by discretion. I have reported on the project in Jönsson (2004), possibly too discreetly. (It was an extremely exciting experience, once we started to understand how the different specialists argued their case.)

The study was built around our videotaping of several PMG meetings for two projects over a period of close to 2.5 years in the late 1990s, interviews with all members of the PMG at least once, interviews with the leadership of the production plant for this model, and participant observation of one cost review meeting. The project was disciplined by a stage-gate planning system that divided the project into periods according to when a certain stage was to have been reached for each system (a component part of the new model determined in a pilot study). Each stage was "opened" and the budget for that stage released when the project had passed an intense review process (the gate). Part of that review was the cost review, where the current cost estimate for each component was compared to the target cost set by the pilot study.

The cost reviewers (tough guys) came from the cost engineering department and were not part of the project. An incident that stuck in my memory may illustrate this: Bill, who oversaw Interior Design (the 'system') was feeling confident he had done a good job until the cost reviewers – who had come to the meeting with printouts of target costs and current cost estimates for each component – came to the gear lever knob. Johan had chosen a more elegant knob and the cost was above target. There was a pregnant silence; you could see that Bill was searching for a valid argument for keeping that component. Then he said: "It is 8 grams lighter than the knob in the pilot study." Focused on cost accounting issues as I am, I must admit I was baffled; later, I learned that top management had recently prioritized a reduction in weight in all models to save fuel. The argument about the 8 grams was relevant in the new policy context, but that information did not seem to have reached Cost Engineering. Johan got away with a metaphorical slap on the wrist and a promise to save on other components.

The PMG oversaw the project between the end of the pilot study and the start of production. The group consisted of about 20 people, most of them system engineers responsible for a particular system (like engine or chassis), and some project administrators, including Testing, Controller, Quality Control. They met a couple of times every month to report on progress and problems. Each system engineer had a group of subordinates working on specific modules, like brakes. A standing item on the agenda was a five-minute report from each system engineer on the state of their part. The project leader chaired the meeting, assisted by the deputy project leader. A senior engineer recorded each decision, e.g., to go above budget (pending acceptance from the department in charge of that model.) Although there was a tight time schedule, usually two hours, we did not experience any meeting that lasted less than four hours. ("This is not supposed to be a seminar!" was a frequent complaint.)

The most significant result of this study was that people constantly misunderstood each other. We took excerpts (one-two minutes) from the videotape of meetings and played them back to the participants with the question: "What is going on here?" You must remember that most participants had good reasons to pay attention throughout the meeting because propositions from other members might impinge on their own area of responsibility. This was especially important to the Project Controller, who saw it as his mission to stop budget overdrafts at an early stage. The Production Control representative told us that this project was notorious for its late design changes, which might ruin all the plans for the production process, as well as logistics for components. His mission was to nip all these late design changes in the bud. Electricity seemed to be affected by everything in terms of changes of processors or cabling. Such issues might, of course, explain why the presenter's intention was misunderstood, but there seemed to be more to it than technical consequences across disciplines. Further, there were many other meetings surrounding the PGMs. We asked one of the project leaders to draw a map of all the meetings he had to attend (or send someone else to). That map (Jönsson, 2004, Figure 5, p. 84) contained 28 boxes (with potential suppliers represented by only one box). A Belgian engineer from Product Planning complained:

Meetings! Meetings! I spend 75% of my time in meetings! I don't get any real work done!
Question: What do you do during the other 25%?
Answer: Prepare for meetings!

In the projects we followed, there was a new resource of particular interest, a Human Resource manager. In addition to his initial assistance to the project leader in selecting members of the project, he organized off-site team-building conferences a couple times a year; he had also acquired the right to interrupt the discussion if it was threatening to de-rail the meeting. His intention, when this happened, was to help members reflect on what was going on. We did not see any such intervention during our time with the project team, but he told us it had happened a couple of times during the first of the projects. Our impression was that he was a well-liked member of the team. The project leader chaired all meetings.

The data – case 1

As mentioned, getting access to the project included negotiations all the way up to the top of the corporation, with the project's HRM manager mentioned above being a guide to the right people (including the CEO). We appreciated the trust shown to us; we know of no other outside researchers who have had such access. The projects concerned a periodic update of an existing model – at that time cars appeared in year models – and a project lasted up to three years from approved pilot study to production start. We videotaped two-three PMG meetings per year and interviewed all team members at least once. A development project of this kind is an important event in all the members' careers. All seemed to dream about becoming a project leader, and they all seemed to enjoy pointing to a detail they contributed in the final design.

The main data capture technique was to videotape whole sessions of the PMG (usually about four hours), pick five incidents of interest to us that lasted for one-two minutes, transfer those to a separate disc, and play them back in individual interviews one-two months after the meeting, with the question "What is going on here?" We taped and transcribed those "self-confrontation" interviews. About half of the members of the PMG were available for these interviews each time. Further details are available in Jönsson (2004).

I will use two such incidents to illustrate the theoretical approach presented earlier. The first example is divided into two parts, with the first capturing the aftermath of the debate that took place in the meeting before.

Background: The project was about halfway through when a subordinate to Bill heard about a project that the Quality Department was working on. The Spanish authorities had issued regulations that favoured cars with diesel engines. This was important, since a large proportion of the sales in Spain were in the form of leasing contracts with corporations and public sector units for fleets of company cars. The solution Quality had worked out was to lay a thicker coat of insulation on the firewall (the wall between the engine bay and the passenger compartment). The subordinate's idea was simple: Why not do that for all cars! It was a good idea, since the project was aimed at premium value. A low noise level was a definite premium value. The problem was that this was not included in the project and its budget. The money would have to come from the Product Department as an addition to the budget. The formal decision in late October was straightforward, but the meeting before that was less successful:

PMG meeting 1997-10-29, excerpt 9:58-9:59
Legend:
Adam, Project Leader
Bill, Lead Engineer Interior

Adam (reading from the agenda): Firewall insulation!
Bill: Yes, we would like to have a decision..... You already know about the content ... it is about X million SEK approx....
Adam: Yes?
Bill: ...... and we would like to go on with the study for firewall.... insulation
Adam: Designing it?
Bill: Designing it! Only the CATIA work! And we would like to have acceptance to start up the supplier....
Adam: You have it.... You have it!

It was a simple decision to grant Interior permission to place an order with a supplier to produce the necessary CAD design for the added firewall insulation. The project leader was fully informed, and it was he who had negotiated with Quality to pick up the bill. This was a formality, for the minutes. No big deal! An obvious improvement at an acceptable cost. Note how Adam, the project leader, leads the presenting engineer towards a formally correct decision for the minutes. It was a very different story two weeks earlier.

PMG meeting 1997-10-15 13:09 – 13:12
Legend:
Bill: Lead Engineer Interior
Caesar: Project Coordinator (minutes)
Dick: Project Controller
Erik: Product Planning
Fred: Production Control
Greg: Deputy Project Leader (leading the meeting in Adam's absence)
(F9QT is the code word for the diesel engine version; 903 means 1999, week 3, consequently 820 means 1998, week 20)

Bill: .... And we have decided to fit the F9QT (insulation?)... in all cars. So it can improve all cars. And the cost.....for mainly.....
Caesar <breaking in>: This is a first request?
Bill. A first request, yes ..... and the costs here ....<pointing at the overhead projection> are related to the CATIA work – to make the design of it. So we need this information to carry on..... eh..... we need the yes for this money to carry on.
Dick: This is not the final cost of the solution?
Bill: This is just to start up the supplier ..... <name of supplier>
Dick: Who is going to pay for it?

Bill: Eh … I asked John (his subordinate in charge of this task) about this, and I think it is Erik <turning to Erik> Are you requesting this from Product Planning?

<In the meantime, Fred has stood up and moved closer to the whiteboard, trying to read the text, squinting. This movement is duly noted by everyone. Fred is a tough customer when it comes to changes in the project, because they also affect logistics, tooling and supplier contracting, making extra work for Production Control>

Erik: No..... But personally, I think we need to do a lot regarding noise on the F9QT!
Greg: <talking in a low voice to Erik, who sits two seats away from him>*… of course …. financing it…* <pointing to the overhead picture>
<4 seconds general silence>
Fred: <pointing toward the overhead picture> *….. I think we get a lot of these study requests!* (inaudible) *should be very careful!* <he talks in a low voice, standing behind Erik and Greg. Everybody shifts their attention to him>

<several people start to talk to each other in pairs, some turning away from the head of the table – silence, general mumbling for 6 sec.>

Bill: <in a slightly raised voice> *If we get an early answer we might meet the project ….. eh recommendation. If we wait with the decision, there's a risk that we won't get it in time for 903. As it looks now, if we get a decision this week, the first shot sample can be delivered somewhere 820-830 <a hand gesture to mark uncertainty>*
Somebody: Who is paying for F9QT?
Fred <breaking in – stressed by the time pressure?>, *That is the situation now, huh?*
Bill: Yeah!
Fred: If we are forced with our backs to the wall – to say yes now – I don't accept anything! <expressive body language>
Bill: Okay <subdued>

Fred: <starting to walk back towards his seat, hand in pocket, then turning and pointing towards Bill <finger moving downwards> *First you have a proper study of this and then you come in…* <turning toward his seat again>

<4 seconds silence. Several people smiling awkwardly, looking at each other for a cue on how to react?>
Bill: This is the ….. to accept this money… who owns the budget …. Who can finance this?
<4 seconds silence>
Dick: Who is the customer? …………. Who wants it? …… Who asked for it?
<3 seconds silence>
Greg: Quality asked for it! …. <body language!> *… Bill thought you asked for it, Erik! … as the Market!*
Somebody: This is part of F9QT!
Dick: No! It is ….(inaudible*) total sum forcasted (sic!)*
Somebody: This is for the F9QT …. But it is necessary to get (unfinished sentence … get the noise level down for all cars?
*<Greg stands up to take away the overhead slide from the projector. The meeting breaks down into several conversations (*23 seconds*). After this moment of confusion Caesar stands up and walks over to Greg, whispering something in his ear (*You have to cut this item short!(?))>
Greg: Bill, I don't think we can….
Bill: You are not ready for a decision <bends over to pick up his papers and leave the head of the table>
Greg: I hope you understand…

Recap.
Bill, who had worked in the project since the start, but had been promoted to system engineer (Interior) a couple of months before, was presenting the state of his part of the project. It was late in the session, past lunch time, and everybody was a bit tired after concentrating on diverse issues for more than two hours. Bill had been briefed by his subordinate (John) about the firewall insulation improvement issue just before the meeting and told that Adam

(project leader) had approved it. It was just a matter of taking it to the minutes – a formality. John had also provided him with an overhead slide with all the necessary information. However, the project leader was at another meeting and Greg, the deputy project leader, was in the chair. Fred, representing Production Control, and a sworn enemy of late changes to the design of the model, was present. Most of the time he had other priorities.

Caesar (project coordinator – keeper of the minutes) broke in early in Bill's presentation wanting clarification as to whether this was the first time this matter was on the table (new item in the project). Bill was visibly disturbed but found his way again. When Dick (Project Controller) asked what kind of cost this was and who was paying, Bill was properly thrown off track. (He was under the impression that the item was just a formality and was not prepared for any questions.)

While everybody was preoccupied with the issue of financing, Fred (Production Control) sneaked up behind Eric's back to read all the fine print on the overhead picture. Then he took his chance to educate the project on the devastating effects of changing project content. What was the use of planning production and the sequencing of components for the assembly line if they kept changing all the time? When would they learn to keep to the specification? After all, their job was to design the car according to specification!

Bill tried to save the situation by pointing out that time was short. Fred responded by refusing to make decisions with his back against the wall. Bill asked for help, but received vague suggestions in return. Caesar told Greg to bring matters to an end, and Greg, who was recently appointed deputy project leader, realised that he must adjourn the issue. The formal decision was taken two weeks later (post factum) as shown above.

A closer look

This small part of a three-hour meeting illustrates how much complexity is dealt with in situations like this:

- Bill had framed this item as a pure formality – getting a decision by the project leader to spend the money on the supplier's CAD work for the insulation on the firewall into the minutes. But he is surprised that information he does not have is asked for. He fields the first two questions about formalities. But when the Controller asks who is going to pay, he realizes that he does not have proper information for a presenter – and he has only been a system engineer for a couple of months! His practical identity is in jeopardy. He asks for help.
- Bill's first thought (Kahneman, 2011) is to assume that the Product department in charge of this model will pay. He turns to Eric and asks if Product Planning has accepted the cost. The answer from Eric is No! But he agrees that it is a good idea to also reduce noise for the petrol engine models.
- The meeting seems to disintegrate into smaller groups trying to make sense of what is happening.
- Bill, even more frustrated, raises the issue of time, a frame that always provides good arguments in projects; if the money is not granted now there will be delay.
- Fred (Production Control) redefines that argument into being a form of blackmail ("back-to-the-wall") and thereby refuses it. He acts on a frame that this is an opportunity to teach the project proper project management (no late changes).
- Bill asks the meeting in general for help …. "Who owns the budget?" – and is asked helpful questions that might serve as keys to a solution.

- Greg is reminded by Caesar that he is responsible for an orderly meeting. Greg realizes that it is his duty (practical identity) to adjourn the matter.
  (Two weeks later the decision to go ahead is taken in a matter of seconds.)

The discussion consisted of quite short statements, except in the moments when the meeting seemed to pause for private discussions between persons sitting close to each other. There really was no time for Bill to recover from the shock of realizing that this was not a pure formality.

What is going on here?

We played back this sequence to most of the participants individually with the question "What is going on here?" and audio-recorded the answers. (Fred declined to participate – lack of time).

Bill's first comment was that this was an awkward situation, but he had learnt a lot. He was not briefed well enough beforehand, but knowing who is financing an addition to the project is basic. He knew that the project leader supported it (but he could not use that as an argument when the deputy was in the chair). The trouble was that the key people (Quality and project leader) were absent. He knew that he could have cleared this with Quality beforehand with a phone call. He did feel some uncertainty before the meeting, but since it was a mere formality, he did not expect any problems and went ahead so it would be recorded in the minutes.

After those comments on his own role, Bill turned his attention to Fred. This was a golden opportunity for him! When he sees a weak spot, he goes for it! "I felt like a piece of meat dangling in front of a shark!"

When the Controller asked about the costs, Bill knew that it must be either Erik (Product Planning) who could answer – it wasn't – or Quality – who wasn't there. But "OK, I learnt something from this!" namely, always to prepare a decision point by talking to the key people in advance (Bill had learnt a principle of project management, and he would never forget it), and that nothing is a mere formality. "But you know," Bill said, "if I bring it up now and get a decision, there will be more time to work out the solution." (In this case it was a matter of starting work early on the tools, because this would bring the firewall solution up to be included in Phase I of the project, while it would otherwise have stayed with the F9QT, i.e., it would have remained in Phase II). The lead time for tools would have been shortened by 13 weeks. There were good reasons to try to force a decision. When Bill, together with John, checked with the engineer who was responsible for Interior before Bill was promoted, it turned out that Quality had already agreed to pay for all extra costs related to improving the fire wall.

I asked Bill whether Fred came across so aggressively because he was surprised, or if he was always like that. Bill answered that Fred shouldn't have been surprised, because a design concept sheet (a drawing specifying the design change) for this change had been sent to him in advance. It was on his desk! Maybe he received so many changes that he couldn't keep track of them all.

But one can understand Fred's worries. Since this project was a joint venture in a temporary alliance with another producer, who was developing another model on the same technical platform to be produced at the same assembly line, Production Control automatically had a bigger say on these matters. It was different back home where the projects took the lead and Production Control had to adapt. Bill seemed to be in a better mood after talking through the incident and explaining his behaviour, even if it had been embarrassing standing up there in front of everybody without good answers.

Comments from participants that spoke

Greg, the deputy project leader, was relatively new in this role and this was the first time he had chaired a PMG meeting. He started his comments by stating that he had not been informed beforehand. There was not much he could have done, in his opinion, given the way things developed. The problem was that the discussion got stuck on who was paying. Erik (Product Planning) was surprised when a request for such a large sum of money came up without him being briefed beforehand.

Greg pointed out that an issue like this would normally have been brought up first in the TMG (technical management group, a sub-committee of the PMG) meeting, but this particular week most of that group was away at a strategic meeting about the new technical platform (context setting the stage for this meeting). Concerning Fred's interference, he argued that this issue was none of his business until a study had been presented to the production company through the proper channels.

Greg regretted that he had been unable to help Bill. Perhaps he should have been more prepared to put an end to the discussion at an earlier stage, but the group had all been feeling tired due to the meeting having gone on past lunchtime. He repeated that he had not been informed beforehand by either Bill or the project leader.

Dick, the Controller, started his comments by describing this presentation as ill-prepared. When asked about whether this item really belonged in the TMG meeting, he claimed that it belonged in the PMG and should be recorded there. The proper thing for Bill to have done would have been to talk to Erik beforehand, but it turned out that it was Quality who paid in the end. Dick put the incident down to Bill's inexperience and joked that sometimes it is good to "learn the hard way".

Erik, from Product Planning, started his comments by stating that this was a new item with a rather high cost. It was new to most participants. It was not entirely clear what kind of improvement in noise levels (in terms of decibels) could be achieved and how it would contribute to the whole solution. The meeting was not prepared for this. Bill's second mistake was that he was not clear over who would pay. Everybody had jumped to the conclusion that it was Product Planning that wanted this – and of course the customers wanted less noise, but that was not the way to bring up an issue like this. Bill must have felt he was well-enough prepared since he had all the figures on the overhead slides, delivery times, cost, etc. and he knew that the properties of the car would improve. He had thought he had a good proposition, and he was treated like this! All of this could have been avoided if he had talked to the right people and brought it up via the TMG. The cause of the incident was Bill's inexperience.

Comments by other participants who did not speak in the meeting

Adam, the project leader, who was not present at the meeting, started his comments on the video clip by explaining that it was Quality that had ordered the job, and he gave good reasons for why it should be taken over by the project (early implementation). He also expressed a certain understanding for Fred's premature intervention, describing the difficulties of working with the logistics of change in product content. He did not say much about Bill being in a difficult situation.

The Testing engineer explained that Bill's predecessor at Interior had already hired the supplier to do the job. So, Bill had stumbled into a package deal that was already in place (more or less). There was little choice but to go ahead with the firewall insulation deal in this case. He remembered saying "Fred is back!" to his neighbour when Fred intervened. (Fred had been absent from the last couple of meetings, but now he was back on his hobbyhorse – to warn against new studies and late changes.) In a sense it was good that he did this, because these studies tended to disturb projects by generating undue optimism about time schedules for the changes. Changes simply came in too late!

A senior project engineer started by saying: "I feel really bad about his! We should have helped him!" Had Greg been informed, he could have helped Bill by asking the right questions.

He also stressed the problem of late changes, which was even more serious now that they had two producers developing cars for the same assembly plant. The power balance was different here compared to projects back home, where Production Control could make a more constructive contribution in the meetings. The fact that the two producers did not communicate well enough created a space for local managers to play one against the other. That was the kind of game Fred was playing here.

Quality Assurance, who were not present at the meeting, described the situation as arising from the fact that the rules of the game were not clear enough. Bill had not been trained well enough and Fred had understood the situation as the project forcing Production into a position with its "back to the wall". Bill's frustration was partly due to the recent change in the project's time schedule.

Three other commentators explained the situation as a breach of the procedural rules (proper channels, Bill's subordinate not informing him properly). A new manual for the work in development projects in an alliance was under way. In a historical perspective, one commentator said, a "fix-it" mentality had developed in this alliance because of the Job I adventure (the original project to develop a new, small model on the partner's technical platform in a hurry). To manage this (keep to the time schedule) in Job I, they had to cut corners, and now, when all kinds of improvements to the original design were required, the "fix-it" mentality remained.

Analysis

A striking feature of this situation, and of our entire stay in the field in this study (Jönsson, 2004) is the complexity and polyphony of the meetings we recorded. The multidimensionality of the smallest incident makes one think of Boltanski's (2011) efforts to combine confirmation and criticism in a sociology of emancipation. However, on the level of observation used in this case, it seems obvious that participants made sense of what was going on by way of narratives, much in line with the Propp/Greimas/Cooren (2000) tradition. They used narratives to explain why Bill stumbled into this kind of trouble, and they used narratives to justify their own action/inaction. Some narratives are more memorable than others and stick in memory ("memes") as new principles of conduct, as in Bill's case – Always talk to the people concerned before the meeting! – which he certainly knew before, but which assumed new significance through this experience.

The situation in the meetings was complex and erratic, as each member was focused on his own contribution while also paying attention to any indication that suggestions from other members might interfere with their own task. This generated uncertainty for everyone. But uncertainties exist in different dimensions due to the different framing (Goffman, 1974) applied by participants and related to their own area of competence. While this contributes to complexity, it also opens paths for associations across areas. There is, for this reason, much to be gained from communication. To demonstrate how this can be achieved we need to look closer at the use of the template (I will come back to the canonical form of narrative) discussed by Cooren (2000). This can be understood as an interpretive tool in conversation, for sense making across areas of competence, as it were. But the complexity goes one step further:

All members were aware of the fact that they were working inside an alliance between two companies sharing the same technical platform; also, a primary ambition of the project was to place the new model more firmly in the premium segment of the market; and top management had stressed the need to reduce fuel consumption through engine design as well as weight reduction. These are not restrictions in some optimizing model, but goals to always be pursued at the same time – one may muster them as good arguments.

I have chosen this incident from a study some 20 years ago because it illustrates how one member, far down the hierarchy, is impacted by, and must deal with, a changing context. It was smart of Bill's subordinate to bring up what he had heard about the initiative to reduce the noise level in the diesel engine versions of the car, see the value of extending the solution to all versions, and the value of bringing it into this model now, rather than waiting till the following year. It was worth the trouble for Bill, even if his loss of standing among the project team members (due to his inexperience) was painful. Management as deliberation touches all members, and the value of paying attention to changes in context can bring early benefits in competition.

(Again: I bring up this incident from one of our field studies to illustrate the kind of research I have been involved in, and the complexity of management on every level of organization. Certainly, there are routine ingredients in a cost review meeting, but the responsible members being reviewed must be ready to respond to “surprising” accusations of misconduct – like missing a target cost – or of not knowing who has agreed to pay.)

Part II

Reflections on the role of moments of truth in managerial deliberation

Chapter 5
Two main dimensions – complexity and lack of time

An overview of the two sets of interviews leads to a conclusion that it is reasonable to assume that the difference between the managerial problems faced by top managers can be described in two main dimensions – lack of time and complexity.

1) The issue of lack of time has to do with IT and various information systems that tend to invade deliberation on solutions. After all, the core of management is to change some part of the world into a better place. The ideal model that the world is supposed to adapt to is increasingly, for small as well as large problems, lodged in a computer. The thinking that Kahneman (2011, Ch. 4) calls fast thinking he describes as an "associative machine" and posts numerous questions concerning the risks of error. (One might object that nobody knows the right answer at the moment – now! – when fast thinking takes place.) One might assume that the role of fast thinking in deliberation is to direct attention towards promising paths.
2) It is not easy to describe increased complexity in so many words. It has to do with the presence of more dimensions to be considered at the same time as there are more value criteria to be applied. The dominating models of thought have varied over time, from structural change (centralization/planned economy vs. decentralization/the invisible hand of the unknowable market), retreat to financial measures, finding "the right people" (and incentives), short-termism, cooperation (supply chains,

conglomerates, multilevel regulation), neocolonialism (Nkrumah, 1965) and more. For the individual corporation this may take the form of shifts from being an exporting firm, to internationalization by acquisitions, to 'multidomestic structures', supply chains, and efforts to respond (compliance) to increased efforts in supranational regulation; all under the energetic input of the latest solutions offered by growing international consulting firms (Bogdanich & Forsythe, 2022). To illustrate this, consider the fact that a frequent topic of discussion in 1990 was internationalization, while the corresponding concept in 2020 is consolidation. What does that mean in terms of required deliberation?

My approach to these vast topics is not to try to cover all possible dimensions but to be alert to the extent and way they appear in the accounts of important learning experiences given by interviewees. I do this by reflecting on some interesting moments of truth in the life stories using literature that seems to be relevant for understanding the "meaning" of the account.

The first step, in Chapter 5, is to give an account of my own somewhat rebellious understanding of managerial rationality. In my many years as a field researcher in the management and regulation area I have come across few economically rational individuals. In management, we need another kind of rationality (Searle, 2001), one which can handle multiple values, multiple areas of knowledge and multiple-level regulation, as in sustainability (Bebbington, 2001) and communication about these dimensions in efforts to get things done. That is not an easy task, as Sjöstrand (2016) has shown.

I will then choose a few illustrative moments of truth and do my own deliberation on those cases to work out what meaning they convey. My hope is that together these cases will provide glimpses of what managerial deliberation is like in conditions of complexity, and what lack of time implies (for research as well as for policies and practices).

Finally, I will try to paint a picture of the bits and pieces that have emerged from the reflective exercises on the meaning of moments of truth in life stories.

Chapter 6
Management as deliberation – when context matters

Apologia

I write this in defence of a different philosophy about social sciences because we need to give management a meaning beyond the barren, desire-driven "rational choice" version pushed/ taught by economists. We know a lot about what actual managers do, and rational choice is a tiny, largely insignificant, part of their activity. They build organizations, adapt them to changing contexts, and also care about sustainability. They cannot afford rational choice – not in the long run!

No! Of course, I cannot prove that this is the case, since the framework surrounding rational choice – like the "protective belt" of hypotheses mentioned by Lakatos (1965) – prevents any other data than those describing management as (more or less) rational choice from being used in testing hypotheses – at least if you want your article to be published. This unfortunate situation is the result of social sciences adopting a conception of scientific research that was developed over the centuries for natural sciences, with their laws of nature and calibrated measurement instruments (cf. Pentland (2015), *Social Physics* or Skinner (1971), *Beyond Freedom & Dignity*).

In practical life we meet phenomena like the enormous computer centres in the north of Sweden (and elsewhere) that store Big Data about our every move and conversation at taxpayers' expense under very profitable contracts with local (and central?) authorities (and using a lot of scarce electricity). Zuboff (2019) calls it surveillance capitalism, Piketty (2014) argues that wealth does not "trickle down" to us from the very rich – if anything, it "trickles up". Larson (2021) claims that machines cannot think like humans; Artificial Intelligence cannot save us. We tend to compartmentalize our discussions about social, economic and environmental matters without regard for how the compartments interact. Part of the blame for this state of affairs is the refusal of academic disciplines to accept that other disciplines may have something useful to contribute. I come from a discipline, Business Administration – reluctantly admitted to academia in my country some 100 years ago – which I have myself, as the first chairman of the then newly formed Scandinavian Academy of Management, described as a theoretical donut – no core theory. Maybe that – growing by borrowing from other disciplines – is an advantage. But now it might be necessary to re-label management to being about getting things done. Such a view may move us closer to pragmatist philosophy (Misak, 2016) and the problems of acting – here and now – on insufficient scientific, or other, evidence in a complex and changing world.

Good social science is not like physics. Why? For the simple reason that our study objects read our reports, reflect on them, and are sometimes – we don't know exactly how or when – influenced by them (at least indirectly). Since people change due to such reports, they also make them invalid. We don't think about that specific difference between physics and the social very much – even if we should – but tend to resort to numerous "tricks" to avoid the facts. Let's take a tiny problem of logic, "reversing the direction of causality": we all know from secondary school that it is wrong to reverse the causal logic. (It may be true that if the lamp is broken then the room will be dark, but we cannot reverse the logic and say that if the room is dark then the lamp must be broken, because there are many other possible explanations.) Yet we say that people make a certain decision because of their preferences – and then we conclude that a certain choice has revealed a preference (reversed logic!).

Since we have a theory about preferences, the fact that there has been a choice is said to prove that the revealed preferences are operative. And on it goes. The logical mistakes in forcing natural science onto social science are indeed numerous. When Deirdre N. McCloskey showed, in her impressive three-volume study (2006, 2010, 2016) that the rapid economic growth in the second half of the 19th century was not caused by Capital or Institutions, but by a new rhetoric that granted the bourgeoisie dignity and equality, the clerisy (those who know the proper theory) did not budge. Traditional economics, and all its illegitimate children, have been made fireproof against empirical counterevidence. What happened?

I believe that management as a human activity, often carried out in very large organizations (of the 100 largest economies in the world 60 are corporations (Fleurbaey et al., 2018)), needs better theoretical support. As Searle (2001, p. 167 ff.) argues, we need a theoretical basis for the "remarkable" capacity of human rationality to create new solutions and to act on desire-independent reasons for action. Such reasons are always a matter of the agent committing himself in various ways to the truth of a statement, which requires a kind of passion (Cooren, 2011). When I claim that my statement is true, other members of the organization accept that and act on it, making it important to me to stay true to my practical identity (Korsgaard, 1996). My statements bind me to my role and their reliability saves a lot of time (and my standing in the group). The Classical model of economics cannot account for such binding reasons (a contract is a legal concept that presupposes laws, courts, jurisprudence and other social structures), but they are necessary in the management of organized action.

In this essay I will try to show what happened, what is wrong, and what can be done about it. A tall order! Deirdre McCloskey has tried for a long time; it did not even help to ask, "If you are so smart, how come you ain't rich?" (1990). She is still a firm believer in market solutions. Fair enough! Markets seem to function by other means than just prices and volumes. But this is not about the functioning of markets, but about management of organizations. Yes, I know it is a hopeless task, so I will focus on the way we draw conclusions in science and hope to find a "key" (Goffman, 1974) there, and I will refer to the stories about learning events that top managers in our largest corporations told me in interviews in 1990 and 2020. When we tried to code these events for the logics in use (more than 1,600 instances) we ran into trouble. All the events seemed to be different! How do you learn from single, unique events? By discussing them with mentors and in teams? It seemed these top managers were always in the hypothesis generation stage, to use an academic phrase. Testing was a matter of action in complexity and with lack of time. Testing by one "shot"? What kind of rationality is that? I try to reflect on this unique interview material in context, fully aware that I will not be able to prove anything. I will use "I" a lot to mark these reflections as personal. If what I say makes sense, I will be satisfied. Testing all the hypotheses that follow will be for the next generation.

So, what is the problem? The problem is that those who have been promoting "scientific rationality" (Wasserman, 2019) since the 1920s believe that all disciplines that want to call themselves scientific must adhere to the cannons of classical rationality. This means that you should strive to reduce complexity by naming one measure (goal dimension) that serves as the criterion of choice at all problem-solving junctions and analyse all the alternatives that come up for action on that criterion. But as Bertrand Russel said, there is no rational way to choose the goal dimension – it is based in value arguments (or, as the early philosophers/economists believed, bestowed on us by God, in terms of desires or preferences which we cannot control). The purpose of this reduction of complexity is to make the problem calculable, so you can prove that your argument is right by logic. And those leaders of our most successful corporations must have made many right decisions over a long time (one of the respondents was the CEO of Stora, a company that was founded in the 13th century).

Darwin (1859), for his part, was way off the proper scientific path to knowledge when he claimed that natural selection would explain the origin and evolution of species. He applied, it seems, "Inference to the Best Explanation" (I will come back to that). He did not have enough biological evidence to make that conclusion, but if natural selection was true, then the evolution of species would follow. He presented good reasons to believe that variety, selection, retention was the right explanation. (He did not know how retention worked either; now we know that it is a matter of genes.)

Problem 1. The evolution of world views – travelling ideas

The problem is, I believe, that in the name of science and rational, civilized conversation about how we should live our lives (all the time ever more congested by chores), we transplanted templates from natural sciences to social sciences, which are fundamentally different as to their study objects. While the objects of natural sciences obey laws of nature, the social sciences study objects that learn from social science and other sources. They also have a "free will" and "responsibility". And they are "civilized" (most of the time). We judge each other as to performance, and prestige, and we care about our practical identity. Surely a philosophy of science concerning social practices – social science studies being one – must be different from that of natural sciences!

A further problem with philosophies of science is that they discipline their practitioners. That is good in one sense, since they provide vocabularies and criteria of quality that help the community to communicate and eliminate error. But they also introduce intolerance to innovation, due to their longing for calculation, which, if we apply its rules correctly, guarantees that our conclusions are true (premises + proper application of the rules of logic = truth). For example, under a discipline of economic rationality the problem of living a good life is solved by reducing complexity to individual rationality under a simple rule: utility maximization. No-one knows what "utility" is, besides "pleasure" and "pain". It is assumed to be there to guide our actions; it must be, since we posit it as a premise. One part of the simplification is to claim that whatever we do, it is aimed at satisfying our preferences. Then we observe action and take those actions as proof – we have revealed our preferences by acting in a certain way. A second part of the simplification is to assume that action consists of packages of acts (taken in a context that is "frozen" by way of assumptions) the consequences of which can be summarized into flows of cash that are made comparable by way of calculation (Ramsey discussed a "social rate of return" in the 1920s. We do not seem to have advanced much since then (Misak, 2020).) To make calculation easier, and to cover up some of the glaring simplifications, we assume that nature comes ready-made with probability distributions – that these distributions are part of nature and can be measured! (They discussed this in the 1920s as well, but then in terms of "degree of belief" that agents held in their assumptions about the future world. One of the participants in that debate was John M. Keynes (1921) in Cambridge.)

But an alternative view of the world of humans also grew from the discussions in Cambridge and Vienna. In the end, it came to use "strange" concepts like "forms of life" and "language games" (Misak, 2016). Given its energy by American pragmatism (Peirce,

James) it started from the question of to what extent a person has reason to believe that a statement about the world is true. The confidence with which a person can act (to achieve change) in the world on such beliefs could be called "degree of belief" and later translated to "subjective probabilities" by Ramsey, and then to Bayesian statistics. The interesting key word here is reason, which introduced the small matter of other people to be persuaded by that reason. We are, after all, social beings with a need to confirm our identity as reliable members and earn the respect of others. (I guess one could call that "utility" as well!) We do that by communicating our "reasons" and listening for reactions. This is the problem! Deliberation and action (even if it is only talk) must bring the contemplated action (mental representation) into context and consider its reactions under this world view.

When reading these old texts, one gets the impression that the conception of truth is moving from being a property of propositions towards finding its roots in the consequences in the world. What kind of philosophy will support social sciences if they give up their striving to become "natural" science? If they place individuals in contexts inhabited by other individuals and care about how others will judge their action? It will certainly bring in new complexities and an extended conception of time. As we all know, the only time one can act is "now" – not in the past and not in the future. An extension of the "now" can be thought of as deliberation on the sequence of acts that constitute action. It seems to be a good idea to deliberate on action <u>before</u> one acts. Once one acts in an organization, other members will start ascribing intentions and evaluations of competence. One's standing as a member depends on their judgement. One needs to act competently for good reasons in organizations. Hence, a shift from thinking to acting is problematic.

Problem 2. Ideas about the nature of the world of humans have usually travelled a long way when they reach us

I will deal with this problem in two steps: first, I will remind the reader of some philosophical precedents that seem relevant for the discussion of the life stories of my respondents, then I will focus on how what has been called neoliberalism emerged from the ruins of the First World War and how it bifurcated into one branch focused on international regulation of the world economy (trade and capital movements) and another focused on free competition, property rights and individualism – a winner-loser conception.

"Free will" and its consequences

For as long as I can remember I have been fascinated by philosophic reasoning, but I never had the stamina to read up properly on the area in focus at the time. All the different literatures seem to have started with a Greek school. It was interesting to read Aristotle's reasoning around free will in the Nichomachean Ethics (Thomson, (1955). I noticed in particular his method of illustrating the limits of the free will by the narrative of the captain who saved his ship in a storm by dumping the cargo overboard. Was that his free will? Obviously not, but the storm is a natural power that created a crisis, and to resolve the crisis he chose to dump the cargo. So you might call that a mixed free will. A bit further on there is a scene where the cargo floats ashore somewhere. The cargo is still the property of the captain (or his principal). Anybody who takes the cargo is a thief. There we are! Property rights survive all crises! ("Mixed feelings" anyone?). Property rights are required for contracts to hold in all circumstances. So the free will must be embedded in a legal framework.

There was not much free will in Plato's *The Republic*. Imagine what would happen if the mob on the agora in Athens were to be let loose to make decisions! Better stick with the Spartan way! The Philosopher Kings (the Principals, we say today) had their power base in heritage and education. They – of course – saw to the good of the people. There was not much estate circulation in Plato's republic (except for the occasional war hero who was admitted among the privileged). Plato argued against the emerging idea of democracy, which could only lead to chaos and misery in Athens. The people on the agora are too easily manipulated.

In time, the Church took over part of the responsibility for keeping the people in line. "In the beginning was the Word" (John 1:1). Thomas Aquinas preached humility and mutual help. It was said that if the rich were to give their alms to the priest, instead of distributing them on the steps of the temple themselves, he would see to it that they ended up in the right hands, and not in the hands of sinners.

The issue of how to secure a safe passage to heaven in the afterlife (Brown, 2015) brought the free will back into focus. It was needed to define sin. After death, the immortal soul found itself in a kind of limbo (including purgatory), whereupon the path to heaven was entered. On the road, the soul could be attacked by demons. To defend it there were angels and saints. They could tackle the evil to the side. That would be easier if you were without sin. A sin is only a sin if you do it out of free will. You are responsible for your sins.

Sinners ended up in hell; usurers – those who lent money against interest – were destined for one of the very lowest levels – on smouldering sand (Dante, 1320). Usury is a sin because it is a good deed to lend money to your neighbour in need, but if you do it against interest you are exploiting his misfortune (Langholm (1979). Langholm pointed out that in the old days a contract was valid if it had been entered into without **force, fraud or ignorance**. One needs courts to judge this).

But there were things you could do to secure safe conduct to heaven, beyond giving of your surplus to the poor, namely arrange to have a grave close to the church building (or even close to the altar), close to the angels and saints. That would require a large donation to the Church.

The Church had a large positive cash flow into the Vatican. It could not all be invested in art, so the house of Medici assisted (discreetly, since the Church could not strive for profit or interest income) with investments that could give a return for the future (Roover, 1963; Jönsson, 2019). One family member even became pope: Leo X, a spendthrift. The power of the Church over people's souls increased with the fall of the Roman Empire and was personified by Charlemagne, who built a second Franco-Roman empire over the latter part of the 8th century (Nelson, 2019). He used monasteries as key points in expansion, but also promoted the spread of learning and education from the monasteries. He justified his conquests toward the northeast by the need to expand Christianity. Business, Church and State powers were intertwined.

Protests against the excesses of the Church came partly from inside the Church (Luther, Calvin and others). Luther preached that entry to heaven is a matter of God's grace. There is not much you can do about it, other than live by the rules laid down in the Bible. Calvin's disciples, on the other hand, taught that success in business is a sign that you already enjoy God's grace in this life on earth (Weber, 1930).

The birth of Modernism

The showdown came with The Thirty Years' War. (This was devastating! It reduced the population in the German area by a third.) The need to sustain such prolonged warfare required (besides acts of plunder) an enlarged cadre of civil servants and administrators with professional training in different skills. The state apparatus grew to cover larger territories. This cleared the way for Modernism, in the form of new scientific achievements and the establishment and exploitation of colonies. New justifications for treating people unequally were needed. Colonization of foreign lands was often carried out by companies sanctioned by the state, in addition to the soldiers. Several countries established East India Companies. The Dutch East India Company was the first to be listed on a stock exchange. That model was copied by the British. A particular case in point is the South Sea Company established in 1711 as a public/private company. It got off to a good start, since the peace treaty after the War of the Spanish Succession included a virtual monopoly for the company in the slave trade between Africa and South America (Utrecht, 1713: *Asiento de Negros*). Soon there was not enough trade between the two continents and the company's adventure ended in the South Sea Bubble in 1720, with losses for the shareholders. The Spanish did not fare much better, notwithstanding all the gold and silver in El Dorado. Even collecting tax for the state (the king) as an extra income did not save the banks of Seville (Jönsson, 2019). Only about 10% of the taxes reached the frustrated king.

The activities related to colonialism transferred wealth to those who could organize the whole supply chain, i.e., slaves from Africa, land in the West Indies, growing cotton and sugar cane, transports across the seas to Spinning Jennies not too far from Liverpool, and onwards to the markets in cities.

The state, increasingly inhabited by bureaucrats with administrative competence, saw these companies as a problem, since wealth bypassed the state coffers in different ways (Pistor, 2019). The bureaucracy started to think more in terms of flows of goods and saw possibilities in the state's control of that flow (it was no longer only a question of in and out of market towns, with collection at the gate). Regulating the flow also offered opportunities to tax it. This was not a new idea, but systematic regulation was something that required the state to organize accordingly (mercantilism) (Magnusson, 1999). When you have statistics describing the flows, it is easier to tax it (going in as well as out). All, of course, in the name of economizing scarce resources. Free trade became a political issue. Adam Smith (1776) argued for free trade with the core argument that markets are unknowable. Therefore, they cannot be analysed, and thus could not be regulated to perform well. The solution, to promote the wealth of nations, is to let individuals freely "truck and barter" and seek the worth of their assets through many individual deals between sellers and buyers. Then the market, like an invisible hand, will arrange everything for the best. This argument – the market being unknowable – returned during the Second World War in Hayek's pamphlet (1943) against the planned economy of the east.

But the battery of available arguments was also added to by the Industrial Revolution, which brought people from the countryside to the places where entrepreneurs with investments in new machines to turn raw materials into saleable wares provided work with wages. The misery of the emerging proletariat generated arguments for reforms and revolutions in 1798 and 1848, but little changed. Socialists and communists realized that they had to become more "professional" (Hobsbawm, 2002) and organize, admittedly as an elite, but still representing the working people. The aristocracy found no reason to loosen their grip since they were best suited to care for all members of society. The growing bourgeoisie (McCloskey, 2006, 2010, 2016) provided the most powerful challenge to the aristocrats. It demanded dignity and equality. A new kind of rhetoric emerged. The struggle between socialists and capitalists at the end of the 19th century took place against the backdrop of economic growth. Then came the World Wars, and the success of rational calculations concerning convoys, bomb patterns and logistics opened the gates to "scientific management" and the regulation of free trade and capital movements by economists and jurists.

"Boundary work" (Gieryn, 1983) concerning the area of influence of the professional ideologies of social scientists

Somehow all the new currents in economics seemed to converge on Vienna and Munich (Janik & Toulmin, 1996, Wassermann, 2019). There was a new economic ideology combined with the criticism of the old ways of life as well as traditional methods in science.

The new view on economics, the Austrian School (Menger, 1871) argued that subjective utility should be the basis for value (since the market is unknowable). But there was at the same time this new debate about what is scientific and what is not.

We have come to call the new ideology of science "logical empiricism". It stresses that the road to knowledge goes via critical testing of hypotheses against observational data, and discards those that do not meet established criteria ("falsificationism"). All you need is facts and logic. The generation of hypotheses was not discussed much. Popper (1963) later called them conjectures. In this process, economics had become "political economy" (Slobodian, 2018), aimed at giving good advice to governments.

The problem with this is that data become information when they are given meaning. Value can only exist when a phenomenon/thing has been given meaning. Now the meaning-giving mechanism was theory about how the world should be (the focus of economics is, after all, on future cash flows). Criticism of the Austrian School came from Berlin. The Berlin group is called the Historical School, because they maintained that subjective aspects should not be brought into a scientific treatment of the economy. Being engaged in nation building (after Bismarck united Germany in the mid-1800s), they focused on the flow of raw material through a national value adding process. It was not the individual but the whole nation that would benefit from having a visible hand (the state) in charge of the economy. Menger's (1871) line of argument was the opposite, that the individual (with free will) should do this by choosing whatever he or she preferred. In that way the invisible hand was able to do its job. A precondition, of course, was that property rights were upheld and that contracts were respected. So the state should provide laws to regulate transactions and courts to uphold the law but stay out of managing the economy.

The socialists (and communists) argued from the perspective of the people, or rather the proletariat. By definition, that category of people had virtually no opportunity to cater for their own lives. A first precondition for prosperity for all is thus to have equality between individuals. This could be achieved if an elite, chosen by the people and representing the people, regulated the economy. When equality is reached there is no longer any need for a state, the socialists said, because then individuals, in the spirit of Aristotle, will enter into contracts of their free will – without force, fraud or ignorance. Contracts that do not live up to these conditions are invalid. Therefore, those who exploit the weakness of others must be eliminated.

The difficulties of the emerging liberal/social state were formidable. A revolution in itself is not enough, as 1789 demonstrated. There were counter-revolutions as cliques of true believers in competing ideologies tried to take over. Those cliques had one thing in common: the need to get organized! The Bolsheviks thought the elite must become more professional and disciplined. "Democratic centralism" is well-described by Hobsbawm (2002, esp. Ch. 9). Both sides can be deemed to have mustered their forces just after the turn of the century, in 1900. The end could be said to be the same in both camps – the greatest happiness to the largest number of people – but the means differed. The market saw free competition as the solution. Those who know what a market should look like should also be responsible for its regulation.

Socialism saw central control of the use of resources, including labour, as the tool for them to come to the best use. They argued that the construction of a new society takes time, so you need a five-year plan. The market argued that the state will never know all the preferences of all the people, so it cannot make that plan. The planners pointed to the injustice to the poor and the weak. Both reduced the complexity of the problem to prove their point to a degree that prevented any communication. There have been efforts towards a neutral analysis, e.g., Schumpeter (1954), but for some reason such books never become bestsellers.

And so it goes on! Why this amateurish history lesson to introduce the problem of the philosophical/scientific basis for management as a human activity? Because I want to show how world views change over the centuries and, with them, the basis for what constitutes a good argument for how we should regulate our life together. I believe that it boils down to three basic types of regulation of conduct, the concrete manifestation of which is determined by context and charismatic leadership (Weber, 1930).

Those three basic modes are

- **Market**, where problems are solved by free competition. This mode must be accompanied by a rhetoric that justifies that the winner takes (almost) all. The winners must be protected against loss of their gains, which is accomplished by legal protection of private property (Pistor, 2019; Greenfield, 2001), and keeping taxes low.
- **State**, where centrally forged rules that apply equally to all citizens, and hierarchical control (Streeck & Schmitter, 1985)

guarantee equal treatment. Inside the hierarchy, holders of positions are appointed based on merit.

- **Community**, where problems are solved by dialogue. The best argument carries the day. Expertise brings prestige, but so does care for the welfare of the other. (Habermas, 1981, vol. I and II).

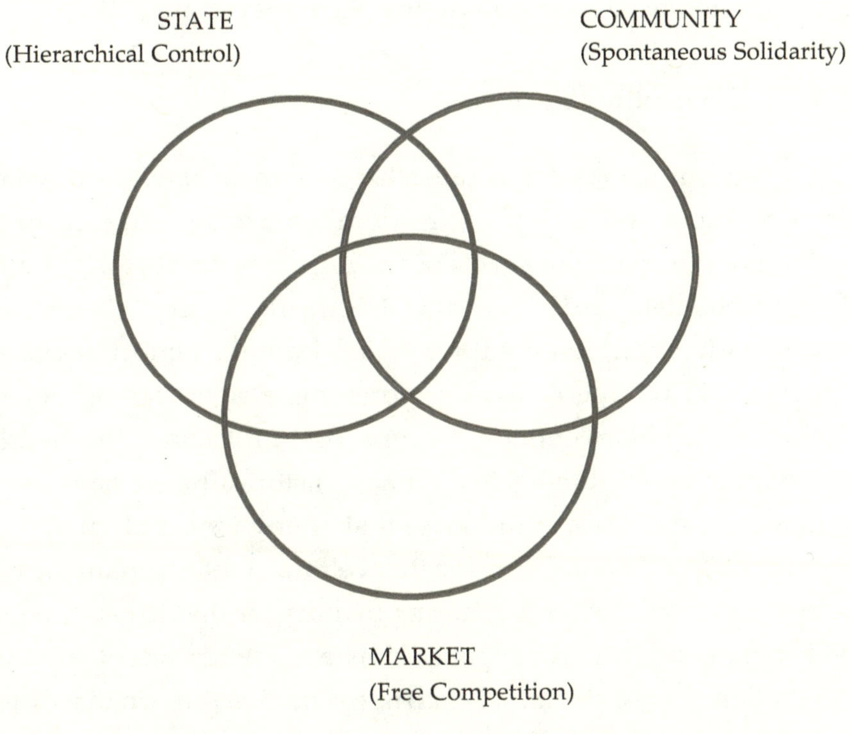

Figure 2. *The three modes of regulation of society (Streeck & Schmitter, (1985)*

All these modes are always present, but the balance between them is influenced by changes in context and the available interpretations by way of world views (ontology, as it were). This means that communication patterns and the validity of arguments will shift. We can study that balance by studying debates on policy and narratives about experiences and expectations for the future (and lobbying).

At present we have one dominating world view when it comes to what is considered good and bad in economic matters – the neoliberal view of the market economy (never mind the current commotion in Ukraine and state capitalism in China). I will now try to recapitulate how this situation emerged. It is an important background to our current understanding of management in large organizations. (Remember that out of the 100 largest economies in the world today 60 are corporations (Fleurbaey et al., 2018).)

The road to neoliberalism

Neoliberalism stands for a radicalized form of liberalism, where property rights and individual freedom come before our care for the welfare of our neighbour (MacLean, 2017; Rosenblatt, 2018; Lewis, 2018; Slobodian, 2018). In the USA, the term "liberal" has traditionally been reserved for a left-leaning, almost socialistic opponent. In Europe it usually represents a right-leaning defence against state interventions (except for protecting the market economy in crises, and against crime). Historically, we have seen a shift in liberal politics in the sense that after winning elections on a rhetoric of equality and care for the welfare of fellow man, the core of politics shifted towards granting favours for the rich and mighty (Rosenblatt, 2018). This happened only a few years after the French Revolution, whose slogan was *liberté, égalité, fraternité* (in that order). It seems that liberal ideas gain currency some time after a nation has recovered some of its energy after a crisis. But soon the good liberal ideas are given new meanings by way of lobbying and other methods. There is reason to look a little closer at such developments, if nothing else to get a feeling for how the meanings of lead ideas change over time.

There seem to have been two (related) starting points for the new neoliberal world view that dominates today in the USA, one in Vienna and one in Cambridge. (But one should not forget Geneva.)

Vienna

At the turn of the century, France and Britain could embrace modernism and welcome science, technology, and entrepreneurship, while landlocked and agricultural Austria had to look to the south-east (real estate) for imperial expansion (as did Russia). This had a conservative effect on society. The landowning aristocracy (the oligarchs of those days) was in firm control. However, Serbia was not the only nationalist movement that bothered Kaiser Franz Joseph. Newly formed Germany/Prussia, also a strong state, but with more elaborated hierarchical/military control, embraced science and technology, and also had thoughts of expansion. Russia, with its vast tsarist empire, cared less about planning than about honour and keeping the new socialists at bay. The world was preparing for the First World War.

There was an intellectual rebellion brewing in Vienna as well as in St. Petersburg. This stemmed partly from a dissatisfaction with the superficiality of social life in the capital, but chiefly it concerned what was to count as proper science. The nature of a good society was also a topic. Were the teachings of Freud scientific? A lively activity in seminars, often in private homes, much like the custom in Cambridge, developed into a manifesto in 1929 – the basis for logical empiricism, which is still taught on PhD courses today. Karl Popper (1963) was a young boy on the fringes of the intellectual debate, as was Ludwig Wittgenstein. They lived in a time of battles in the streets between "Red Vienna" and "Black Vienna" (Janik & Toulmin, 1996).

Karl Popper (born 1902) found his first job after graduation in New Zealand, where he started to write his book in defence of liberalism, *The Open Society and Its Enemies*, which was published in London in 1945. This book was a by-product of Popper's earlier work *The Poverty of Historicism*, a critique of the social sciences with a base in induction from historical data which made it impossible to make scientific predictions to be tested in this area. Given that historicism is untenable, we should **not** place our hopes in the ability of a central authority to coordinate, predict and plan the development of a good society. In the meantime, Popper had been recruited to the London School of Economics, where he developed his arguments for falsification as the core activity of scientific research. In scientific research there are no limitations as to where hypotheses (conjectures) could come from, so long as they were subjected to our most severe tests.

Ludwig Wittgenstein was born in 1889 into an immensely wealthy Viennese family. His grandfather was an authoritarian who refused to allow his son Karl (Ludwig's father) to study engineering (it was not deemed suitable for someone in his position). Karl rebelled, went to the USA, where he worked in menial jobs, but was later reconciled with his father and allowed to study. Karl became a leading industrialist through industrial rationalization and the leading patron of art in the town. His attitude toward his children was authoritarian too, however, and Ludwig was taught at home until he was 14. When he went to university, he had high hopes of learning from Ludwig Boltzman, his scientific idol, but those hopes were frustrated by Boltzman's suicide in 1906. Wittgenstein also experienced the suicide of three of his brothers, two in destructive opposition to their father, the third when he faced capture on the Italian front during the war. Ludwig himself was also a prisoner of war in Italy, where he wrote his *Tractatus Logico-Philosophicus* (1921/22).

From 1911 and up until the war, Wittgenstein studied at Cambridge, where he formed friendships with Russell, Keynes and Moore. His *Tractatus,* which among other things tries to show that logic has no content (understood as meaning), had considerable influence on many logical empiricists. A young doctoral student in Cambridge,

Frank Ramsey, was charged with translating *Tractatus* into English, and had several objections, which led to intense discussions between the two. Ramsey's argument that there is no such thing as a completely transparent language – language always gets in the way – seems to have influenced Wittgenstein's (1953) later repudiation of his own *Tractatus* and turn towards forms of life and language games as central to understanding in human communication.

Wittgenstein continued to spend much of his time in Austria working variously as an elementary school teacher, a gardener and the architect of a house for his sister in Vienna. While there he held influential discussions with Schlick, Waismann and others. From 1930 he held teaching posts at Cambridge and increasingly distanced himself from the logical empiricists. His later work focused on ordinary language and inspired many other philosophers.

The family disasters mentioned added to his controversies in the academic world. Wittgenstein published *Tractatus Logico-Philosophicus* in 1921 after having failed to persuade several publishers of its merits. It was a determined effort to reconcile the language problems between ethical and scientific discourse in Vienna circles. Janik & Toulman (1973) argue that *Tractatus* is an exercise in ethics and draw our attention to the last part, which Wittgenstein intended to be the climax of that book, but which was looked upon as an insignificant addendum by contemporaries such as Bertrand Russel. Wittgenstein's main work by current standards is *Philosophical Investigations* (1953), which has had a fundamental effect on social sciences in terms of the linguistic turn that many of them (but not economics) have adopted. However, even if Wittgenstein was present at the time in Vienna, his exotic behaviour distanced him from the core of the new "modern" grouping of scholars there.

The Austrian Schools

Even before the war, Austrian intellectuals had been pushed into action by the obvious lack of tenability of the Austrian-Hungarian imperial lifestyle. The Vienna Circle, a gathering of scientists, philosophers, humanists, artists and journalists (Janik & Toulmin, 1996), found reasons to question most of the fundamental principles of social life and articulate new world views. Economists debated the foundations of the market economy in opposition to the failed state coordination of people's lives. Kaiser Franz Joseph had ruled according to the principles of *Ruhe und Ordnung* (Quiet and Order). He had come to power in 1848 at a very young age amidst the revolutionary movements at the time, and allowed no change. A proper railroad system could not be built because it might promote revolution. The royal palace was lit by kerosene lamps until his death. The military also had to be kept on a tight rein, and was allocated its (meagre) resources, so as not to become too powerful, by royal decision (*Hausmacht*). Austrian administration had degenerated into formalism that was only a façade – Franz Joseph did build some notable buildings in Vienna, however, with impressive façades – to cover up the chaos and contradiction inside.

Vienna was known as the City of Dreams, and for its Strauss waltzes, chic cafés and pastry. You could sit all day with a cup of coffee and read newspapers from all over the world – and discuss matters. Vienna was a very bourgeois city in a crumbling multinational empire. To escape dark thoughts about revolutionary developments, the bourgeoisie attended to the upkeep of appearances.

The intellectuals found it necessary to get rid of a language use that tended to obscure realities and prevent a more realistic building of a good society. One line of reasoning in this *Sprachkritik*, before the war, had landed in the conclusion that "the meaning of life" is not a matter of rational debate, it cannot be given an "intellectual foundation" (a position held in common by such giants as Schopenhauer, Kirkegaard and Tolstoy). Tolstoy had shown in his stories (*Twenty-three Tales*) that it is mystical in a sense and can only be "shown". The alternative line of reasoning was that of Mach, further developed by Hertz and Boltzmann, where the analysis is based in general principles that are external to the subject, i.e., keep the rigorous language of a particular science and depict a phenomenon in mathematical models (instead of metaphors), which, applied in the proper way, can yield true knowledge; this could be extended to all sciences, and to society.

The problem that remained, given these two positions, was: "Is there any method of doing for language in general what Hertz and Boltzmann have already done for the language of theoretical physics?" (Janik & Toulmon,1996, p. 166) This is where Wittgenstein's *Tractatus* comes in. It uses a language of logical propositions (or, rather, aphorisms) to argue that ethics cannot be dealt with in the same way as the sciences. There is no "rational" basis for ethical statements. They can only "show" their meaning. By separating reason from fantasy – the mathematical representations of the physicist from the metaphors of the poet, and descriptive language from "indirect communication" – Wittgenstein thought that he had solved the problem of philosophy (Janik & Toulmin, 1996, p. 198). He was recognized as a genius by G.E. Moore (Wittgenstein became his successor at Cambridge) and Russel, who were on the same kind of crusade against the abuse of language of the Victorian age in Britain, but they used the term "analytical philosophy" (propositional logic). Wittgenstein felt misunderstood by Russel but failed early on, and kept failing, to articulate how Russel had misunderstood. He also failed to participate constructively in a discussion with the Vienna Circle representatives on a propositional philosophy that would support their work on a "unified science". He insisted on reading poetry to them. It seems that he could not articulate the meaning of ethics "showing" itself via indirect communication, which the last aphorism of the *Tractatus* (6.54) seems to encapsulate:

> My propositions serve as elucidations in the following way: anyone who understands me eventually recognizes them as nonsensical, when he has used them – as steps – to climb up beyond them. (He must, so to speak, throw away the ladder after he has climbed it.) He must transcend these propositions and then he will see the world aright.

Again, ethical statements (goals and values) must show their meaning. They cannot be understood by deductive reasoning. (Neither can they be "calculated" into "utility" measures in the spirit of Bentham, which Moore and Russel had already found inadequate and vulgar.)

Popper, on the other hand, fitted nicely into the positivist thoughts about what constituted science.

In sum: In Vienna, as in Cambridge, there was a tradition of holding private seminars. Out of these two groupings of significance for the development of a social science theory emerged the Vienna Circle and the Austrian School in economics.

The Vienna Circle (*Der Wiener Kreis*), in which a group of scientists among whom Otto Neurath, Rudolf Carnap and Hans Hahn were the leading names, went public with a manifesto in 1929. The scientific world view promoted in the manifesto is mainly known as *Logical Empiricism* (or positivism). It is the dominating view in social sciences (including financial theory) today. Its name describes its main tenets; there is a world, separate from us, that we can obtain sense data from (by observation or experiment). Further, only propositions that can be analysed by the tools of logic into elementary propositions (that are either tautological or empirically verifiable) can be said to be meaningful. Logical empiricism therefore rejects metaphysics, theology and, sometimes, ethics as meaningless. The boundary between scientific and non-scientific approaches was also an area of contention between members of the Vienna Circle. It should be noted that a left-wing faction of the Vienna Circle, led by Neurath, argued that society itself could also be improved by applying scientific methods to its problems. State (imperial) or Market as the principles of coordination of social and economic life was already on the agenda before the First World War.

The other school (Wittgenstein), if one could call it that, went to Cambridge to discuss the role of language in modern society.

Cambridge

In Cambridge, the discussion about truth and probability was intense in the early 1920s (Misak, 2016). Moore, the professor of ethics, believed the value statement "good" is undefinable; it always refers to circumstances. A version of analytical philosophy, where all you need is facts and logic, was being established in Cambridge. Names such as Bertrand Russel, Ludwig Wittgenstein, Frank Ramsey and John Maynard Keynes participated.

If probability is a justified belief about future events, and induction is forecasting future events based on historical ones, what, then, is truth? Russel and Wittgenstein both worked from elementary propositions which are obviously true. Analysis is then a matter of segmenting every proposition into such elementary propositions by, you could say, getting to the roots of the statement and deriving truth by logic. Ramsey, still in his teens, had early objections, but they came to the fore with his translation of *Tractatus,* which was about this "perfect" language. (Several of his colleagues had been asked to do the job, but Ramsey found it interesting and inspiring.) He got stuck, however, on the matter of how we can understand these elementary propositions. Wittgenstein claimed that the main task of philosophy is to make our propositions "clear" (it should not concern itself with the foundations of physics). One "sees" that they are true – since they are elementary propositions one cannot "analyse" them by breaking them down further.[1] Wittgenstein had a final message: "Whereof one cannot speak, thereof one must be silent." Ramsey was not satisfied with this claim that an object "shows" its features. What do we "see" when something shows itself? Wittgenstein had escaped this trap by claiming that we recognize a "logical form" which becomes reality. Ramsey was not satisfied with this treatment of "mental representations". He also criticized Wittgenstein's coupling of elementary propositions with "operators". But Wittgenstein read the translation carefully and finally approved it[2] and came back to Cambridge in 1925.

Another authority challenged by Ramsey was John Maynard Keynes, who had published *A Treatise on Probability* in 1921. It was considered a breakthrough in the logical treatment of probability by people like Russell and Moore. A central principle was that of "indifference", which said that if there are no known reasons to hold one outcome more probable than another they should be treated as equally probable. The fact that Keynes required a "logical" reason to relate statements about outcomes upset Ramsey. He claimed that there are "reliable habits of mind" that support our following of rules. Ramsey did not like the argument for having "logical" reasons to put values on probabilities. He focused his efforts on devising a method to measure subjective probabilities. This work constituted a turn towards pragmatism for him, which can be explained by the

---

[1] My comment: One should look upon elementary propositions as dependent upon the purpose of the conversation. If I sit with my girlfriend in a meadow and say something about how beautifully green it is, it serves no purpose to break the statement down into the wavelength of light and the refractive index of a prism (romance kind of disappears).
[2] The abrupt language of the original has to do with the fact that it was written while Wittgenstein was a prisoner of war in Italy, with little writing material at his disposal.

fact that he was now acquainted with Peirce's writings on pragmatism, and that he had travelled to Puchberg (Austria) for two weeks of intense discussions with Wittgenstein on the problems of translating *Tractatus* in 1923.

Peirce argued that "clarity of thought" should be achieved by considering the "practical consequences" of different alternatives. He primarily intended that hypotheses should be formulated with testability in mind, something Popper (1963) posited as the criterion of scientific inquiry. Weber's (2020) lecture on the scholar's work, in 1917, stressed that the task of scientific inquiry was "disenchantment", i.e., elimination of unsubstantiated beliefs.

With Peirce's pragmatism on board, Ramsey (1926) was ready to attack the problem of "justified belief" in propositions about the world (the same problem as Keynes (1921) had dealt with). His starting point, I believe, was the statement about "reliable habits of the mind" that give us reason to follow rules. (If one bumps into facts that contradict these reliable habits one should, of course, change those habits. That is called learning!) Peirce reasons from the same point of departure as Ramsey's thesis advisor: that probability (as well as truth) is about whether we have good reasons to trust that a proposition is true. But he also holds to the maxim that one should consider what consequences (in the world) trust in the proposition would imply. He starts from the "confidence" with which a proposition (about the world) is held, proceeds to "degree of belief", and lands in a method to estimate "subjective probabilities" (later developed into Bayesian probabilities). What he needed to get ahead was an idea of "mental representations" (Wittgenstein had claimed that they "show" themselves, but you cannot "talk" about them). Ramsey's solution was that one sees a picture and that picture is what one deliberates about. What trust is the picture and its properties worth? He used the expression "degree of belief" and commented:

> The degree of a belief is a causal property of it, which we can express vaguely as the extent to which we are prepared to act on it. (Ramsey, 1926/1931 p. 169)

I prefer to understand this idea of a "causal" property as that which pragmatism (Peirce) meant by "doubt" driving further inquiry until one is satisfied with the whole of the understanding that deliberation has produced and is ready to act on that understanding. Rawls (1971, 2001) and Scanlon (2014) call this "reflective equilibrium" and Kahneman (2011) calls it "associative coherence". This is where the reference to reality/practice becomes central. Continuous inquiry gives reason to "correct" errors as you go on with your deliberations.[3]

How Austrian economics travelled from Vienna to Chicago (via Geneva)

Ludwig von Mises was senior to Hayek, and his mentor. Both came to be neoliberal inspirators in the USA.

Von Mises was born in 1881 in the city of Lemberg (at that time part of Austria, then the Soviet Union, then Poland and now (Lviv) in western Ukraine). Entering the University of Vienna at the turn of the century, as a leftist interventionist, he converted to the Austrian School as he discovered Carl Menger's (1871) *Grundsätze der Volkwirtschaft* (Principles of Economics) with its emphasis on individual action as the unit of economic analysis, and to the importance of a free-market economy. As a post-doctoral student, he was also inspired by von Böhm-Bawerk, who had disproved the Marxian labour theory of value. During this period, Mises was

[3] One scene that was used to discuss the principle of indifference was the hiker arriving at a crossroads without any signpost and nobody to ask for directions. Then it makes no difference whether you choose left or right. Ramsey's solution was to turn, say, right and to be on the lookout for somebody to ask.

recognized for his *The Theory of Money and Credit* (1912) in which he integrated the theory of money into the general theory of marginal utility and price, i.e., micro and macroeconomics. However, the Austrian School did not accept this integration, so he chose to take an opposing stance, arguing for a neo-Austrian approach. His theory claimed that an increase in money supply was not beneficial for society since that increase would generate bank credit expansion and therefore inflation and business cycles in the form of overinvestment in "higher-order capital goods" rather than consumer goods. Such a credit-based and inflationary boom requires a painful recession while the market liquidates unsound investments to re-establish a connection with "real" consumer demands.

The business cycle theory Mises, and his mentee Hayek, developed led them to warn that the prediction of a New Era of permanent prosperity was a sham. Instead, bank panic and depression were to be expected. In 1931, Hayek was invited to teach at the London School of Economics by Lionel Robbins, a former student at Mises' private seminars. There he was able to convert most of the younger economists (Coase, Friedman, Gailbraith, Kaldor, Lange and others) to this perspective. On a collision course with John Maynard Keynes and his disciples at Cambridge, Hayek was quite critical of Keynes's *General Theory* in a review. But he could not stem the tidal wave of the Keynesian Revolution that swept the economic world after its publication in 1936. From now on Mises was strictly in opposition to this new global fashion in macroeconomic policy by governments. Mises was the leading laissez-faire free marketer, and Hayek was his disciple. However, the tide of Keynesianism after the Second World War put them on opposite sides.

Friedrich von Hayek (born 1899) was awarded doctorates in Law and in Political Science at the University of Vienna in the early 1920s. He was hired (by Mises) to work with the legal aspects of the Treaty of Saint Germain (including the Covenants of the League of Nations). He started (with Mises' support) the Austrian Institute of Business Cycle Research, which he directed until he was invited to the LSE in 1931. During the war he published the anti-collectivist *Road to Serfdom* (1944), which brought him public fame.

When he left the LSE for Chicago in 1950, it was to be employed not by the economics department, but by the Committee on Social Thought (he was critical of the positivist approach that dominated the economics department). He focused on the constitution of a liberal society and published *The Constitution of Liberty* in 1960,[4] although he was somewhat disappointed that it did not receive the same attention as *Road to Serfdom* (1944). Again and again, he comes back to the argument that a powerful state organization is likely to be damaging since the myth of coordination for the common good is a real myth. The state tends to serve special interests.

It might be useful, these days, to note Hayek's arguments for why collectivist societies tend to promote their worst members to leading positions:

1. People with higher levels of education and intelligence tend to have more differentiated opinions. Therefore, mobilization must turn to "lower" sections of society, which have lower moral scruples. A "strong" man talks to them with a simple recipe and converts them to this simpler view.
2. The dictator can appeal to people with vague and unfinished ideas.

[4] Berlinski (2011) reports that at a Conservative Party conference, Margaret Thatcher, then in opposition, interrupted a speaker who argued for a middle road approach, took a copy of *The Constitution of Liberty* from her briefcase and slammed it on the table saying: "This is what we believe!"

3. It is easier to gather around negative slogans (against capitalism, injustice, etc.) thereby dividing people into "them" and "us".

Once in control, the central planners "kill the truth". Only the market, which is unknowable, can sort out the multitude of values and goals people hold. Money has the capacity to translate between the different ends people strive for.

As far back as the 1920s, Mises and Hayek, from their position in Vienna's Chamber of Commerce, had been involved in the difficult task of devising a plan on how the new, small, German-speaking, post-war Austria could develop a sustainable economy. Mises believed that Austrian workers would have to take a considerable reduction in wages, unions should be banned and foreign investment invited.

Looking at the situation after the Second World War, when economies were to be re-started, the arguments about what design would generate "the good society" tended to come back.

But there was an extra emphasis on modernist ideas about the benefits of science. The war effort had mobilized different kinds of academic expertise into specific tasks, not least using statistics and mathematical models in analyses of risk and coordinated activities. That would provide the state with better tools for planning (?).

To appreciate the bifurcation that happened in the development of neoliberal ideas about how to manage economic development nationally, we need to look back at the intense conference activity – mostly in Geneva – in the 1930s.

One of the first conveners of such a conference in Geneva was the Swedish economist Bertil Ohlin (1933), who had gained attention with his book on how comparative advantages improve economies engaged in trade. A central person in Geneva was, however, William Rappard, director of the Graduate Institute of International Studies, who invited Mises and Röpke[5] to professorships, and Hayek and Robbins to a notable series of lectures. The debate among economists in the early 1930s was, in a sense, self-contradictory. On the one hand, there was a growing agreement that supra-national regulation of trade, finances, credits, money and law was necessary to protect trade and the free movement of capital from the whims of elected governments. On the other hand, they longed for the good old days (of the Habsburg empire) when the free economic territory seemingly managed to balance the differing demands in multiple nationalities (Slobodian, 2018, Ch. 3). The matter was in need of study. In 1936 the League of Nations charged Haberler, a Mises protégé, to carry out a comprehensive study. As well as an extensive review of literature, Haberler used a method that came to be called the Haberler method, which allowed groups to do local/regional studies and report to a joint seminar to draw conclusions. He formulated his own "synthetic" explanation of the nature and causes of economic cycles.

However, the experiences of the Depression in the early 1930s convinced a growing number of economists that standardized statistics (measures of GDP or inflation) and conferences were not enough. One must consider cultural and social bonds in populations, and, not least, the rule of law. Economists started to think in terms of "orders" to safeguard markets. The Geneva School brought legal aspects into the debate on how markets could be stabilized (Slobodian, 2018, Ch. 2).

So, with the Austrian School of microeconomics (subjective values, marginal costs and benefits, and an invisible hand that balances

---

[5] Rappard and Röpke argued for a more "social" liberalism ("ordoliberalism") that would give the state and the central bank a larger (interventionist) role in the economy; this inspired the post-war leaders in Germany (Konrad Adenauer and Ludwig Erhard).

markets to everybody's benefit), and the Geneva School's proposal to regulate markets from a supranational level, the stage was set for the Mont Pèlerin meeting at which Hayek would form the Mont Pèlerin Society in 1947.

The Mont Pèlerin Society – arguing the case for market solutions

So much for the ideas of what are good reasons to act, or hold a belief, as they emerged 100 years ago. The evaluation of risks and probabilities came to good use in planning war efforts during the Second World War. The enthusiasm for planning reached business schools in the form of Operational Research, the use of mathematical models to solve management problems; I was one of the enthusiasts in the early 1960s. But there was also a keen interest in central planning. After all, the Soviet Union had survived the Nazi onslaught and come out victorious after so much suffering. But several authors had written pamphlets during the war (Hayek in 1944, Popper in 1945). Central planning was impossible because nobody could know all the preferences of all the people – the market is unknowable – leave it to a myriad of free choices and the invisible hand will sort things out for the best. Conscious of the chaos that emerged after the First War, the neoliberals focused on the importance of taking the initiative to create an order that could secure free markets. Friedrich Hayek invited 36 colleagues to Mont Pèlerin to discuss the matter.

Repairing an economy after disruptions such as war and other crises is clearly a major project. The experiences after the First World War had taught economists that there were two dimensions to the problem. One was that it seemed necessary to have supranational regulation to stabilize economies and allow competitive advantages to do their job. The problem was that some governments, influenced by special interests, tended to favour domestic activities like industrialization; there was a lack of discipline. The other dimension was the age-old belief that free competition between individuals (and the related property rights) will safe-guard the appropriate balance between demand (desires) and supply. The problem with this world view is that it tends to generate a rhetoric cast in winners and losers. This brings with it an overwhelming temptation to cheat to become a winner. In both cases, the cure is ethics backed up by legislation and other forms of regulation, which is a tall order.

Then there is the discursive problem of justifying inequality that follows from competition. Darwin could be called upon to show that the winner is fit and should be left to pursue further gains. Those who used (liberal) equality as a political argument for re-distribution of wealth to gain a parliamentary majority for their ideas were playing by the rules of democracy. The complexity of the world we are dealing with caters for only a temporary validity of arguments. Loyalties come and go. The good arguments must be constantly repeated and reformulated.

There were many prominent economists, and some others, at the meeting in Mont Pèlerin. Friedrich von Hayek was backed by Ludwig von Mises. Karl Popper was there. Milton Friedman was an enthusiastic participant. It was a lively meeting. Friedman has described Mises being dissatisfied with the acceptance of self-determination of nations and slamming doors to underscore his arguments for free markets. An MPS (Mont Pèlerin Society) was formed to constantly review and reformulate the arguments for a market economy. Membership would be by invitation only. Meetings would be held annually. (Homepage: Montpelerin.org).

Later, Edwin J. Feulner (1999, p. 2) of the Heritage Foundation and a prominent US neoconservative explained what the purpose of the MPS was:

> to uphold the principles of what Europeans call 'liberalism' (as opposed to 'statism') and what we Americans call 'conservatism' (as opposed to 'liberalism'): free markets, limited governments, and personal liberty under the rule of law.

It seems the very word liberalism may cause definitional problems. But on the other hand, the ambiguity would allow some leeway in forging compromises within the emerging epistemic community itself.

Haas (1992) defines an *epistemic community* as a network of professionals with recognized expertise and competence in a particular domain and an authoritative claim to policy-relevant knowledge within that domain or area of issue. Although an epistemic community may consist of professionals from a variety of disciplines and backgrounds, they share a set of normative and principled beliefs that provide a value-based rationale for social action. They also share causal beliefs and validity criteria for knowledge in their area of expertise, which obliges them to enter into policy initiatives "presumably out of the conviction that human welfare will be enhanced as a consequence" (Haas, 1992, p. 3). DeMartino (2022) argues that economists have not solved the problem of justifying that their policy proposals cause harm for some and benefits for others. They argue that compensation to those suffering harm is possible – but often such potential compensation remains potential – and it is calculated in money (which makes everything comparable!). The argument that the benefits "trickle down" to the poor was debunked by Piketty (2014) – if anything, they "trickle up". As to the current situation at the time of the first MPS meeting, there was already a Keynesian revolution in full swing after his *General Theory* (1936) which focused attention on government deficits as a tool to achieve economic growth by way of the multiplier effect. Government investment will generate increased employment and investment in private firms to match the increased need for capacity; the government spending will multiply in other actors' spending.

The MPS moves to Chicago

The main actors at the first MPS meeting, Hayek and Mises, had got used to thinking and arguing in terms of "orders" that would protect the freedom of markets from state interventions. They proceeded with their policy-oriented work inside the network of Chambers of Commerce and in Geneva. Mises had toyed with the idea of designing a supranational regulating entity modelled on the Austria-Hungarian Empire before the First War. That empire had, notwithstanding its other deficiencies, managed to keep the multiple nations separated politically but integrated economically (Slobodian, 2018, Ch. 3).

Milton Friedman (born 1912)

The major link between the MPS/Vienna and Chicago seems to have been Milton Friedman, who was a (junior) founding member of MPS and had studied in London (LSE, Robbins, Hayek). He was also instrumental in tipping the scales in the balance between (supranational) regulation and reduced state intervention towards the latter option. He was a gifted agitator for market solutions. I will focus on that part of his skills (and pay less attention to the achievements that brought him the Nobel Prize in Economics). Two aspects stick out: his relentless efforts to debunk Keynes, and his firebrand preaching on the blessings of freedom and individualism.

Friedman grew up in New Jersey, was an excellent student intent on majoring in mathematics, but was persuaded by Arthur Burns (later economic advisor to President Eisenhower) to switch to (Marshallian) economics. His PhD thesis in 1945, written together with Simon Kuznets, was on professional practice and the effects of the limitations on the number of entrants to professions set by the state. He worked, with George Stigler, for a while on rent control for the Foundation of Economic Education (a lobby organization). When Stigler turned down a job offer from the University of Chicago in 1947, it went to Friedman who accepted. His brother-in-law, Aaron Director, taught trust law there. Friedman, who was acquainted with Hayek (through his studies in London), helped him persuade the university to start a new study programme, on which Director taught, called Free Market Study. When Hayek was offered a position at the university it was on the Committee on Social Thought, not in the Economics department. Madrick (2011, p. 36) thinks this was because his radicalism would have threatened the established order in that department.

As mentioned, Friedman directed his energies in research towards showing that Keynes was wrong in recommending deficit spending by the state in times of recession. His line of attack was to update a theory on the effect of the money supply that had been taken up, again, and refined by Irving Fisher. (Note that this was a topic that the "Doctors of Salamanca"[6] had discussed some 500 years earlier (Jönsson, 2019).) The theory held that the amount of goods and services produced was dependent upon the size of the money supply, and upon the velocity (rate of turnover) of money. Keynes was wrong, because if a government were to finance its increased spending by borrowing it would crowd out valuable private borrowing and growth would stay the same (or be reduced).

To prove his point, Friedman embarked on a very large project, together with Anna Schwartz, to reconstruct the money supply data since the Civil War in the USA and relate them to the ups and downs of the GDP. The results (Friedman & Schwartz, 1963) showed that there was, indeed, a link between money supply and GDP changes,

---

[6] Monks discussing money, credit and trade, see Jönsson, 2019)

but it was too broad to make any policy conclusions (the critics thought), and one could not be sure about its direction.

Friedman & Schwartz also gathered data to show that people do not spend as much as Keynes had assumed; they managed to show that the multiplier effect is smaller. The explanation was that spending decisions are based on *expected future income* rather than the one-off effect of current government spending. But, in the process, they exaggerated the ability of people to foresee their future income (so the critics claimed).

The project established a new interest in monetary policies, which now became the main tool for combatting inflation. However, the instability of money velocity undid monetarism in the 1980s, even if the simple act of flushing the economy with money is still popular (and maintains, as in Sweden, the interest rate below zero, causing the currency to depreciate, which promotes export (and jobs), which is good in election times).

Arguably, Friedman's most important theoretical contribution was his claim that there is a normal (later called "natural") rate of unemployment, below which inflation is stimulated. The argument is that as unemployment falls below the natural level, wages go up and firms have to compensate by raising prices. As the government will try to stimulate the economy (Keynesianism) to push the unemployment level down again, prices will increase again, eliminating the purchasing power of the wage increases, and unemployment will return to its natural level. Nowadays, economists argue that the natural level shifts from time to time (and therefore has lost its explanatory value – my claim).

Friedman, the activist, was a gifted speaker and clear writer. In 1962 he published *Capitalism and Freedom* which gained little attention. In 1964 he joined Barry Goldwater's presidential campaign as economic advisor. In 1966 *Newsweek* offered him the opportunity to write his own column. He made television appearances. Almost all his proposals in *Capitalism and Freedom* were taken up in policy debates by his proponents. The Federal Reserve adopted his monetary policy in 1979 but abandoned it a few years later. The 1980 book he wrote with Rose Friedman (his wife, a devoted libertarian) will now be reviewed briefly.

Free to Choose – A Personal Statement (Milton and Rose Friedman, 1980) is based on *Capitalism and Freedom* and a TV series of 10 programmes. It is decidedly "populist" in its presentation of arguments against an interventionist state and for increased freedom of choice for individuals as the solution to most social and economic problems. Having been alerted to Plato's rhetorical methods by Popper we can see similar patterns in the Friedman approach.

There is frequent reference to "origins", i.e., going back to old historical sources to "prove" a point about current problems. Adam Smith is frequently held up as an authority on free trade and competition, as are the founding fathers' formulations on democracy (See also Lui, 2022). Nothing wrong with that, except that the facts were different then. The phrases were convincing, though. Another (pre-modern) rhetorical device that the Friedmans used was to categorize assumptions they needed for their argument as normal or "natural". They used introspection as a source of knowledge concerning human behaviour (as Adam Smith did – even if he recommended the "impartial spectator procedure" in moral reasoning[7]). They use single cases to show the meaning of general statements.

---

[7] The impartial spectator procedure was discussed by Adam Smith (1759) who argued that the decision maker should consider how an "impartial spectator" would judge the contemplated act before acting (ethics).

The book starts out by praising the strength of the market, where cooperation through voluntary exchange, makes everybody better off. The invisible hand metaphor is extended to cover all progress where people cooperate, such as language or science – spontaneous interaction leads to progress!

Then "the state" is brought in. Adam Smith defined its duties as (1) to protect citizens, (2) to carry out careful justice and (3) to promote voluntary exchange by introducing generally applicable rules. The third duty is the difficult one since we cannot allow unlimited expansion of state intervention. A third chapter describes the emergence of the federal reserve system, the crisis of 1929 and the failure of the FED to combat the crisis by increasing the volume of money in the economy, and, finally (December 1930) the closure of the Bank of United States (its name was thought to constitute unfair competition for immigrant deposits). A plan to save it by setting up a guarantee fund failed because the New York Clearing House backed out at the last minute. The consequences were dire. In that same month (December), 352 banks went bankrupt. Since banks had to call in repayment of loans to pay their own debt, the economy stalled, and the Depression was a fact.

The crisis generated space for a discourse on safety and welfare; the New Deal was established. The idea of the welfare state, with extensive obligations for the state, gained adherents, but the results were frightening. In Britain, unemployment grew, and Margaret Thatcher came in as the saviour; Sweden has fared better than Britain, but the people were fed up and replaced the social democratic government in 1976 (although the Friedmans claim we have still not seen any real change of direction). The most dramatic example in the USA is the failure of New York City. The city had invested, unwisely, in a large hospital, a university and in education free from tuition fees. Federal money saved it. The welfare state does not work because it transfers money to the middle class (notably the bureaucrats), at the expense of the rich and the very poor. This chapter concludes with recipes for what to do to put a stop to the waste.

Now the Friedmans have set the stage to discuss the reform requirements in different sectors of society in more detail. First schools; the problem there is that public schools have been bureaucratized and the solution is free choice based on a voucher system. This will improve teaching! The same is true for higher education. Consumer protection should be achieved by information rather than regulation. (Prohibition did not stop the consumption of alcohol, did it?) If the government has information about the benefits of using safety belts in cars or avoiding cyclamates or DDT it should let us know. But we should decide for ourselves what risks we are willing to take with our own lives.

Who protects labour? Labour unions, one would assume. The Friedmans claim that unions, which do not have many members anyway, simply redistribute resources to those who have jobs from those who have not. Their power comes not so much from threats to damage the employers' equipment as from their ability to elicit help from the state, for example concerning minimum wages, or to limit the number of workers, as in the medical profession, where the authorities set the criteria for legitimation to practise medicine.

The argument in this final descriptive chapter is full of illustrative anecdotes from many countries. The important conclusion is that inflation is a monetary problem. Nowadays it is the government/ state that decides about the money supply.

This final chapter indicates that the tide is turning, the collectivist solutions are giving way to individualism and freedom of choice. Margret Thatcher is one good sign, Proposition 13 in California another. (However, being a Swede myself, having experienced the

Swedish tax revolt, I cannot help wondering why the change of government in the 1970s is not described as an election victory for liberal ideas rather than a revolt (being against something).)

Consolidation of finance as the main actor against collectivist solutions

The final step in the transfer of Austrian microeconomics to Chicago was to shift the focus from the entrepreneur/owner maximizing profit in the spirit of the Austrian School, to the investor in equity seeking shareholder value by holding gains (Jensen & Meckling, 1976). There remained, of course, the age-old problem of the separation of ownership and control of large corporations, which Berle & Means (1932) had so eloquently illustrated.

By assuming that members of the organization were on a contract (rules of the game written down) the agency problem (how do owners control the professional managers running the company to avoid cheating?) could be translated into promoting an ever-increasing value of the shares of the company. This could be done by monitoring financial results (rather than the operations themselves) and by designing incentives to be tied to shareholder value. The owners who do not like what they see can just leave – the market will determine fair share prices. We call this shift of focus from the management of the firm to the investment and control (sometimes disloyal to a firm in trouble) "financialization". Financial instruments (promises to pay a certain amount if certain conditions are fulfilled) were now at the centre of attention, and the expected value changes of these instruments in financial markets had become the object of modelling and calculation. In this way, the manager's operational concerns had been disconnected from the owner/principal's wealth seeking. The political and academic discourse had directed attention toward efficient markets as the solution. They are admittedly unknowable but there was now a strong belief in the invisible hand – all that was needed was individualism (utility maximization) and free markets. Since markets are unknowable it makes sense to deregulate them (backed up by Thatcher's rallying cry "This is what we believe!" on *The Constitution of Liberty* (Hayek, 1960)) at a party meeting). The Big Bang signalled an effort to re-establish London as the leading centre of finance. The study of financialization and its effects on society was a growing and interesting field that engaged economists as well as legal scholars (Ireland, 2009).

The problem with de-regulation is that it tends to generate creative ways of using the letter of the law to one's advantage and avoiding that which is detrimental to the individual pursuit of utility. The gap between the efforts of managers to design an efficient organization and the financial sector's search for market inefficiencies widened. As creative solutions to the problem of "compliance" became too conspicuous, and when the financial crisis of 2007/08 had struck, a process of re-regulation set in. This generated more work for lawyers and an activism, especially in the USA, from some business circles to influence the rule of law and by way of the political system promote the "right" people to the higher courts and review precedent rulings.

A more radical development that focused almost entirely on limiting the influence of the state – libertarianism –inspired partly by people like Ludwig von Mises and Ayn Rand (Duggan, 2019), and supported by lobby organizations such as the Cato Institute, need not concern us here since I am only trying to illustrate how the background in terms of thinking about what constitutes a good society changed. My claim is that there have been fundamental changes in our view of large corporations over the last few decades, which, in turn, increases the complexity managers of such organizations must cope with.

What does this mean for the traditional work of managers in large organizations? Let me try to illustrate this by showing how the task of management control has changed.

The effects on the work of professional managers

"Managers work with words!" I exclaimed in an article arguing for keeping management control research close to the work real managers do rather than what finance theory thinks they should do. The foundation for this drift away from the work of managers (supposedly supported by research) to information provision to actors in financial markets had already been laid by the debate in Geneva in the 1930s on how such markets (and markets in general) could be isolated from the vacillations of elected governments in search of re-election. One such shift to generate facts was the emphasis on planning and standardized, comparable statistics to support business cycle management towards the creation of an international barometer that could predict economic developments in the same way as weather forecasts. Part of the basis for this was the accounts of companies.

In the olden days of Eugen Schmahlenabch (1919) there was a firm belief that the use of a standard chart of accounts and proper accounting would generate the truth, and since all firms in the same industry would use the same standard, the resulting figures would be comparable (and the market could function well). The German standard of accounting systems (closely related to German DIN) was imported to Sweden; my predecessor's predecessor in the accounting chair in Gothenburg (from 1926), Albert ter Vehn, was a driving force (Engwall, 1985) in standardization here. He wrote an instruction to the chart of accounts for the mechanical industries that was generally accepted rather quickly. The problem during the war was, obviously, price regulation that focused on full cost. With a standard chart of accounts designed to produce full cost, one could refer to "generally accepted practices" in dealing with authorities.

But then came the news from England (Hayek) about marginal costing. The engineers who dominated the debate (at the time) dismissed this idea as "academic" (Jönsson, 1995). But in 1950/51 the debate took off again as two prominent CFOs, representing steel and forestry, argued that a common problem in their industries was whether or not to accept an order. When a customer was not willing to pay more than a certain price, they had to calculate whether that order would cover variable costs (the fixed cost would be there with or without the order). They had a point! Soon committee work on making charts of accounts more flexible to meet the information needs in different contexts started, and then the computerization of systems and, finally the integrated information systems finished the job of making accounting more flexible. The world view among the management control profession had to adapt to context, from a belief that standard practices will produce the truth to an understanding that accounts may be manipulated to fit different purposes – it is no longer the fountain of truth.

For non-accountant managers, the meaning of management control started to change in the 1950s with the arrival of the ideas of cybernetics. In academia we were fascinated by Ashby's ultra-stable system:

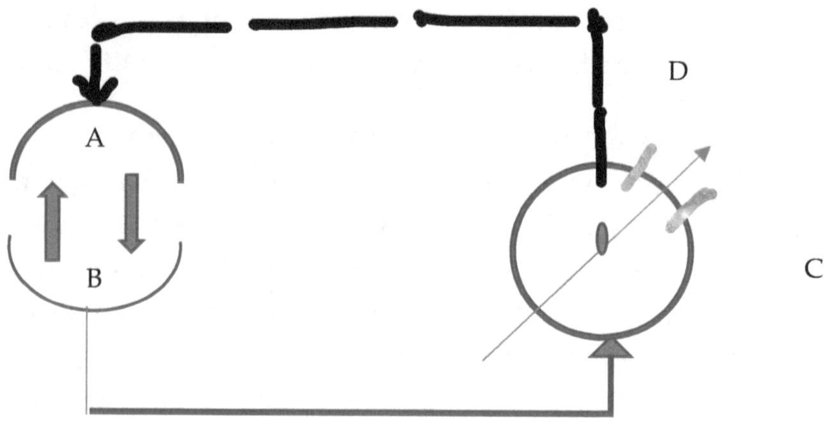

Figure 3. *Ashby's ultra-stable system*

Legend:
The "controlling system" (A) controls the "controlled system" (B) by frequent interaction. An instrument (C) measures the values of a few "critical variables". Should a value fall outside given limits of tolerance a step function (D) is activated. This adjusts the repertoire of control options for A until stability is reached. A necessary precondition for ultrastability is that the interaction between A and B has a much higher frequency than the interventions from the step function. This is how a thermostat works.

But my 2020 interviews revealed a complication: top managers were sceptical of the usefulness of integrated information systems in the job they do. Analysing the many learning events that the respondents included in their life stories, I have found that most learning events start with a surprising observation – a relevant fact that required an explanation. (As when Ronnie Leten discovered that the dealers were making more money than Atlas Copco, the producer of the compressors, and initiated a project to set up a service division.) The increased complexity and lack of time had made it necessary to pay greater attention to developments in context (technical, economic, political, environmental, social…), judge the significance of observations and initiate action when necessary to stay competitive. Agility is a catchword some use to characterize this being on the lookout for signs of change/opportunities and adapting before competitors. I chose to depict this phenomenon in Figure 4:

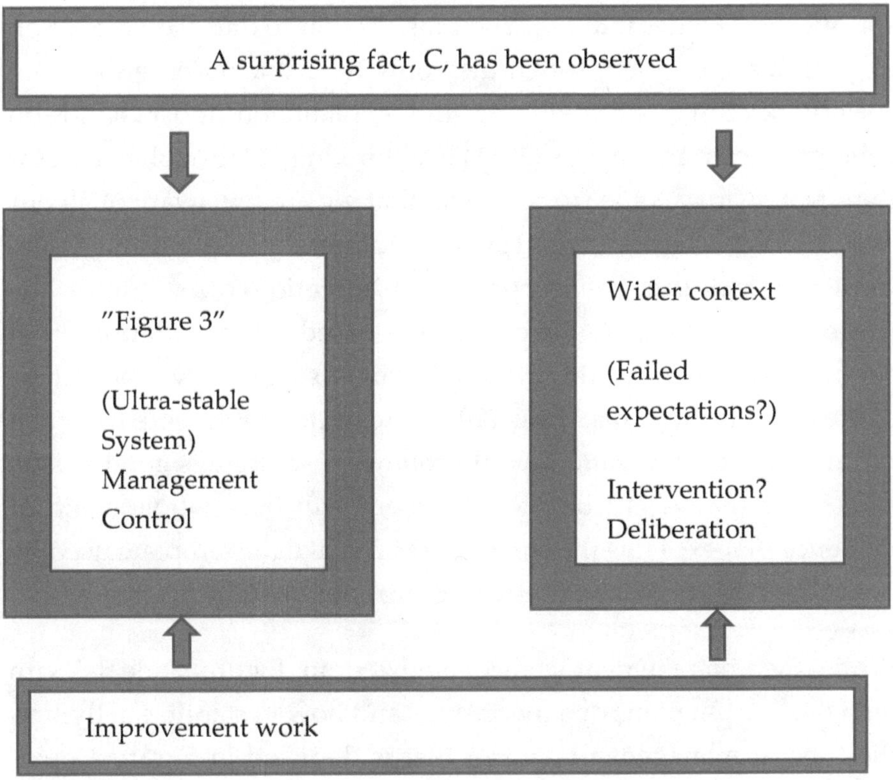

Figure 4. *A surprising fact, C, has been observed.*

Legend:
The control mechanism pictured in figure 3 is now complemented with a different control mechanism that attends to changes in context that might be relevant. When a surprising fact, C, has been observed the manager needs a trusted ally to ask, "Do you see what I see?" If the surprising observation indicates that some assumption, on which the current management practice is based, is no longer

valid, deliberation toward an "Inference to the Best Explanation" is initiated.

When top management on the look-out for changes in the environment that might be significant for the conduct of management in their organization make a surprising observation, a specific logic comes into use. Their task now is to find an explanation for it, and the problem is that they only have one observation – not a very scientific situation. So the explanation must build on coherence (cf. Kahneman's (2011) fast thinking). One explanation for the surprise may come from the fact that we are not aware of all our expectations – hence the surprise. Another explanation may stem from the fact that the surprising observation does not fit the assumptions on which our business is based. The configuration of circumstances that would explain the surprising observation will be of the type "if-then" (as Misak (2016) illustrates, "if A were true then the surprising observation would follow" – so there is good reason to assume that A is true). Maybe there will be a whole chain of evidence that explains the surprise. (Much like the template used by police and courts of law: motive, means, opportunity.)

While the management control stylized in Figure 3 deals with deviations from plans or expectations and how to stabilize activities, the type of management control that is depicted in Figure 4 deals with the re-configuration of activities (large or small) that are judged necessary due to "Inference to the Best Explanation" of a "surprising observation, C" (a fact). These two types of management control operate under different logics: the change/improvement control type of figure 4 includes creativity, while the stabilizing control type in Figure 3 manipulates variables inside a given set. Making those two logics compatible (for a moment of change) requires **human intelligence, trust, and hope** – properties not held by machines (Larsson, 2021). My current belief is that machines cannot do this job because they would have to be programmed to do it and then there would be no creativity. Believers in the ability of machines to do all human tasks see the solution in increasing (indefinitely) the repertoire of configurations of activities the machine can do (AI - and the immense set of data to back it up –Big Data). What has emerged so far (Zuboff, 2019) is surveillance capitalism, which uses the reverse strategy – to make machines out of humans. The big IT companies are doing alright (from their perspective) so far, but they are (collectively) no doubt increasing their contempt for the people that are willing to comply.

It is this human achievement of bridging the gap between routine control according to plan and bringing about creative solutions when facing surprising observations (facts), that will be the topic of the next chapter. Looking upon management as the art of getting things done – sorry, it seems I am getting into philosophy again – seems necessary.

The following chapters will discuss issues that have emerged in the interviews (1990 as well as 2020) by giving an illustrative example as an introduction and then discuss how the organizational consequences of a surprising observation can live on.

Chapter 7
Inside the corporation looking out

Introduction

My first choice is the experience of Jan Wallander (whom I much admire), the CEO and later chairman of SHB (Handelsbanken), when he discovered that most of the credit losses in the bank he was recruited to manage (in the 1960s) were due to central decisions. This observation was significant enough for Wallander to put it at the beginning of his account of his banking career:

When **Jan Wallander** (1990 interview), a qualified economist, took the job as CEO of a bank (in trouble) in northern Sweden (against the advice of his, then, mentor) he soon discovered that most credit losses in that bank were on loans granted by means of central decisions. So he implemented a policy of relying more on local credit assessment and personal responsibility for branch managers. All credit decisions, including those taken centrally, had to be endorsed by branch managers close to the sources of complex, local information. When he was recruited to head Handelsbanken in the early 1970s he took that insight with him, and all credits had to be endorsed and monitored by the branch office in charge of that customer. Well versed in the system of national financial regulations, Wallander argued that when Handelsbanken outperformed the three other big banks it was due to the performance of local branches (central management was the same for all banks, partly due to regulations). Therefore, the bank should set up a foundation (*Oktogonen*) which would be financed by donations from the bank by virtue of a rule for how to split the surplus return for Handelsbanken in comparison with the average return of the other three big banks. The foundation would then pay a handsome pension to its employees on their retirement.[1] The foundation invested heavily in Handelsbanken shares and the employee unions held two seats on the board. (I was given positive assessments of their contribution by other board members in the interviews.)

When in another study (Jönsson, 2019) I interviewed a second-tier manager (regional HQ) about his early experiences as a branch manager, he told me that one of his duties was to place some of his most promising co-workers[2] in positions that would give them valuable experience. When I questioned the idea of getting rid of one's most competent co-workers, the answer was "I get a good network, in return."

Bo Damberg, Wallander's right-hand assistant and "grey eminence" since his time in the bank in the north, would organize regular conferences with branch managers where different performance indicators would be compared. He told me that the primary function of these conferences was to allow branches to find other branches in the country to compare with. It is notoriously difficult to assess whether a branch is doing well since contexts and conditions are very different (residential area, small business area, dominating corporation, downtown, rural area, competitors present, etc.).

When I interviewed the chief credit manager (and co-workers) for my book about bank failures (Jönsson, 2019) and asked why Handelsbanken had done so much better on credit losses through the financial crisis of 2007/8, the answer was "We have better

---

[1] At a meeting with staff that I attended 35 years after the start of *Oktagonen*, the then CEO of Handelsbanken reported that *Oktogonen* had received donations in 34 of the past 35 years.

[2] This is an awkward term for foreigners. We had occasion to experience this awkwardness at close hand when Ford acquired Volvo Cars in the 1990s. US managers did not seem to "get" the point of the concept (that you listen to and respect other members of the organization).

customers!" (obviously). It is easy to realize that it is too late to start selecting "good customers" in the midst of a crisis! Alert branch managers had done that long before.

This example illustrates how Wallander cultivated a mentorship atmosphere in several ways, over a long time, and over several levels of the organization. As a result, most branch managers would have a network of mentors (or speaking partners) that could transfer information and creative solutions across the organization quite quickly. Managerial action, based in that first observation of credit losses caused by central decisions taken far away from the actual sources of detailed information, confirmed again and again that local responsibility is the key to success for the organization.

Reflections on the consequences for the nature of deliberation with an inside-out perspective

Now consider the top management team of a large corporation trying to cope with the increasing concern with sustainability, severed supply chains, war in Ukraine, lack of components for electrification of vehicles, soaring electricity prices .... There are a host of developments in the world, the consequences of which must be judged, and action prioritized and initiated. Increased complexity and faster changes in the relevant context are differences that stand out when I compare the accounts given in the 1990 and 2020 interviews. What does that mean for the job of managers? For the task of "getting things done"?

Well, when things are complex and changing one must act on what one believes is the right thing to do, and one is obliged to able to provide good reasons for these acts. Responsibility grows more significantly than under "normal" circumstances. I will first try to describe this predicament and the thinking it might imply.

The theory – inside-out

I mentioned above that one should try to do what one believes is the right thing. What does "believe" imply? Belief has three properties: First, it is something that we are aware of; second, it appeases the irritation of doubt; third, it involves the establishment, in our practical identity, of a rule or of action proficiency. How do we form a belief that we are willing to risk our reputation as competent managers by acting on it – to expose ourselves as agents?

"In the absence of a belief or a habit (and in the presence of caring about the matter) we are motivated to inquire." (Misak, 2016, p. 20f.)

1. An agent is (by definition) an agent because s/he has reason to act.
2. A reason is, according to Scanlon (2014), a relation R(**p**,**x**,**c**,**a**) – **p** is a reason for agent **x** to do **a** under condition **c.**
3. **p** is multi-dimensional in the sense that it "binds" an actor (**x**) and his/her act (**a**) to certain circumstances (**c**). Each part of the relation must be judged in relation to the others (*mutatis mutandis* ('things being changed that have to be changed') – not *ceteris paribus* (other things being equal)). Furthermore, there is a "direction of fit" (Searle, 2001) component. From speech act theory, we learn that a promise is a commitment to change the world to fit the words (world-to-word fit) while a statement (of fact: "It's raining!") can be checked directly against the world (word-to-world fit).
4. Deliberation about whether there is a reason for **x** to do **a** takes place in the (mental) presence of others (except in the case of Robinson Crusoe before he had met Friday) while conscious of the fact that others will judge things in a similar manner (or differently).
5. There are practical reasons for carrying out such deliberations in a particular order.
   a. Judging what situation this is comes first because that generates a "framing" (Goffman, 1974) for the other parts of the deliberation process. One should note that Goffman

illustrates how a "key" serves framing with the following scene from the zoo: A child says: "Mum! Look, the otters are fighting!" Mum says: "That's all right! They are playing!" "Playing" serves as a key to the child's understanding (framing) of what she sees in a different way. If one is applying the logic of appropriateness (March & Olsen, 2008) the proper question to ask is "What (kind of) situation is this?" (And then: "What should a person like me do in a situation like this?").

b. When the situation (c) is judged to be ("reasonably" well) understood, it is time to construct action (a conglomerate of individual acts). In that construction, operational as well as value-rational aspects are considered at the same time. Resources at hand, operational skills available, timing (project plan with budget as well as review schedule – like the stage-gate system used in product development project mentioned above). The reasons for choosing one path ahead instead of an alternative one will generate a vocabulary of arguments that are valid in the project. (This is the operational aspect of action – and the reference is to experiences of "means" effectiveness.)

c. The agent (x) who does the planning/deliberation, conscious of the fact that his action will be judged by others, will do the deliberating in the light of their identity in the eyes of others – and with the possible intention of changing that identity in their eyes. March & Olsen (2008) (and Luther) use the expression "here I stand and can do no other". Korsgaard (1996) calls this "practical identity".

d. When the agent is confident that he has an understanding of the situation and a solution to the need for action, there follows a two-step process: 1) the agent needs "internal" reasons (Williams, 2012/1979) to secure that the contemplated action is compatible with their conception of their own identity, and 2) the agent needs to muster the arguments expected to persuade significant others that this is the right thing to do ("external" reasons). This amounts to framing the situation and its solution of internal and external validity. This is a communicative task of some difficulty, since the internal reasons refer to the agent's conception of their own identity, while the external reasons will refer to the identity of the organization (or, possibly, to the identity of individual recipients of the message). An engineer would require different arguments to a salesperson. There is a risk of contradictions, which could initiate interpretive work by recipients that might expose the agent as having a hidden agenda. One possible solution to the communicative problem is for the agent to package the arguments into a narrative form. It is likely that the recipients of the arguments will use a narrative template (canonical form of the narrative) to understand the message (Cooren, 2000, 2006). The appeal of this narrative template is that it provides space for operational as well as ideological "keys".

Moment	Description	Possible sub-narrative
Manipulation	Want to /have to	What drives the action
Competence	Resources/skills	How they were acquired
Performance	Doing	Operational details
Sanction	Reward/Punishment	Justification for commendation

Table 1. *The canonical form of the narratives*

When the narrative of the suggested plan of action is ready to be presented to the other members of the management team, the next stage may be entered: putting the situation and related action on the agenda. In a trusted team, the message may have a fair share of "hunches and half-baked ideas". A complication (and hope) under such circumstances is that to reach an understanding of the message, recipients are likely to "fill in" assumptions to eliminate gaps in the received account. Cooren (2000), and modern linguistics in general, posit that it is the receiver that determines the meaning of what is said. Consequently, it is a good thing to know your recipients. Still better to have their trust.

There will be questions, which it is hoped will be based in the other's specific area of knowledge. The answers will extend or rectify the narrative in different directions. If doubt remains, further inquiry is required.

When significant parts of the surrounding organization have a coherent understanding of the proposed action and its benefits, they are willing to endorse it, and the project enters the initiation phase. This is at the core of management as deliberation: to prepare for taking the plunge into the cold water, to take the risk under uncertainty. It is, by definition, a matter of action under uncertainty, since the contemplated action is initiated by a "surprising observation", i.e., not part of what routine operations (inductively justified expectations) would justify. The initiation of action may represent a kind of "thrown-ness" for some of the members. This sense of being thrown into a new assignment appears in many learning events that respondents told me about. That sense is easier to deal with if you have a variety of earlier experiences to refer to in deliberation. One respondent said that, in his corporation, experience from three continents had earlier been a requirement for reaching the top, but now (with "internationalization" being replaced by "consolidation") that requirement is fulfilled almost automatically, as you work closer to many customers' value generation processes. This attention to how the customer uses the product to generate value yields a higher frequency of surprising observations.

To return to the introduction: For Jan Wallander, the realization that most of the credit losses in the bank in the north were due to central decisions provided a powerful "key" to many different organizational issues. The insight that central decision makers often do not have the detailed information to be able to judge properly under uncertainty is a strong argument for decentralization and emphasizes personal responsibility for all employees. Trusting subordinates to "do the right thing" conveys a message that commits them to responsible action, but it also generates a demand for information and cross-hierarchy communication. This, I believe, is the essence of Jan Wallander's approach to managerial deliberation (and communication).

Chapter 8
Coherence and inference to the best explanation

Introduction

My next choice of illustration of the role of learning events is taken from the interview with Lennart Johansson (1990), who personifies SKF (ball bearings) for many Swedes. Again and again, he came back to his preference for studying the "real process" to solve problems. He was a practical man. He started his life story by talking about how, as a child, he enjoyed working on different mechanical projects with his father. His first managerial job – rationalizing a machine workshop – was clearly an important experience. At that time, during the War, there were many women working in production and the set up included heavy or monotonous lifting. He liked to "see" the process in operation, and the opportunities for improvement emerged in his mind as he watched – for that movement we could adapt the mechanism we have installed on the X machine – from the details to a systemic solution. He never (much) liked working at the drawing board. As his skills were recognized, his tasks grew more complex. He was regularly sent to analyze ("see") production systems in acquisition targets in different countries. As part of the re-design/automation of production processes, he developed an expertise in negotiations with unions. Similarly, his great achievement of adapting the mainly national production systems in the SKF group to an integrated inner market-orientated system of specialized plants was a matter of moving from "seeing" details and whole systems. That took a lot of exhaustive negotiating from EU level to many shop floors. In retirement, he continued to work with people at a former machine supplier to invent better designs.

Reflections on seeing the whole in the details of a complex situation

My respondents (1990 as well as 2020) talked about "making sense" of complex situations with many value and operational dimensions to be integrated into a communicable understanding. It was a task of reducing complexity without losing too much information and there were almost always time constraints. This was a prominent concern, especially when preparing to present a proposal to the board of directors. If you overwhelm the board with a very complex proposal, it is likely to be thrown back at you, and you will have generated a kind of scepticism that is harder to overcome the second time you try. Better to present the proposal in well-formed portions, so it will have a chance to "grow" on them. This also requires the proposer to deliberate on how portions of information should come in the right order and be coherent to fit together.

That is the final part of deliberation – how to present the proposal to the board. But there is also a problem on the "input" side: how to observe and take notice of the "surprising observation" in the tumble and noise of everyday activities. Some people seem to be good at seeing opportunities, deviations or threats and making sense of them, while to most of us it is just "noise" (Kahneman et al., 2021).

To make sense of a surprising observation one must construct a coherent narrative that accounts for available facts and adds plausible assumptions to fill in the blanks.

I have shown Cooren's (2000) template for a narrative above. It is worth remembering its structure – Manipulation, Competence, Performance, Sanction – and comparing it with the format police forces all over the world use when investigating crimes and building the case against the most likely culprit that will stand up in court: Motive, Means, Opportunity. Both are tools for arriving at "Inference to the Best Explanation". Under rule of law conditions, the final link – Sanction – is in the courts. The police have the Public Prosecutor as the final check on whether the case will hold. That official will take the case to court only when there is enough evidence covering Motive, Means, Opportunity to argue the case.

Under the rule of law, the courts use a procedure called jurisprudence where first, the prosecutor presents the evidence that speaks in favour of conviction, then the defence presents the arguments in favour of acquittal (or leniency), and finally, the judge pronounces the sentence (in some countries sharing this duty with a jury). This pronouncement weighs the pros and cons of the case and thereby justifies the sentence; that is, it articulates, by its procedure, the "Inference to the Best Explanation" of the case. The arguments justifying the sentence may be used as support (precedents) in later cases. Praxis develops over time in step with social developments.

Still, Kahneman et al. (2021, p. 13ff.) argue that there is a flaw in the procedure since the same crime is subject to widely different sanctions in different states and with different judges. A study has shown, they say, that in juvenile courts, judges are more severe on days after the local football team lost. (One wonders how the researchers generated such a hypothesis to test. And one comes to think of the fact that the crimes themselves might be widely different, even if they are sentenced under the same paragraph.)

Sometimes we resort to "professionalism" as the remedy against bias and "noise" in judgement. Professionalism can be thought of as judging while disciplined by a set of **standards** that allow some discretion when applying general rules to individual cases. For standards to work as intended, there is a presumption that those who apply them have a professional training. The standards then need to appear in justifications (Boltanski & Thèvenot, 2006) for action in specific circumstances. There needs to be an alignment between the standards and the particularities of the situation. Professionalism provides the link in justified judgement. Standards drawn from a certain field of knowledge are usually backed up – or even dominated – by scientific research.

The problem here is that in these days of super modernity, several scientific areas of knowledge are usually relevant in all kinds of judgment. Situations become more complex the more types of scientific knowledge are relevant. One way of reducing complexity in such situations is to use **rules** as regulators (Kahneman et al., 2021, p. 350ff.). Rules reduce the need for judgement. Instead of the law saying that a car should be driven "prudently" at all times (a **standard**), it will say "inside city limits the maximum speed is 50 km/h" (a **rule**). It should be noted that this use of rules directs the police attention to fact-finding (measurement, use of speed cameras) at the same time as it significantly eliminates the need for judgement. Standards, on the other hand, direct the attention of the driver towards soul-searching – what is "prudent" in a situation like this? Rules point towards measurement; standards point towards deliberation.

The difficulty with judgement hinges on its generation of uncertainty. There is an important difference between uncertainty and risk that we tend to forget. Uncertainty has to do with degree of belief, while risk is a measurable property of a natural system. (We are not concerned with the everyday use of the word "risk" here). We live our lives by action based on degree of belief. Judgement includes asking oneself, "Do I have good reasons to act in this way? Can I justify this action?" Or, according to the logic of appropriateness (March & Olsen, 2008): "What should a person like me do in a situation like this?" The judgement is against that standard.

It is here that language always gets in the way, because several areas of knowledge are involved in complexity, each with its specific language. Wittgenstein (1953) called those areas "forms of life" and the argumentation within each one of them "language-games". To be a "member" of a certain "form of life" you must be an acceptable player of the appropriate language-game.

This was at the centre of attention in Cambridge's learned circles in the early 1900s when pragmatism entered the scene. Misak (2016, 2020) gives an account of how it happened.

Analytical philosophy, with Bertrand Russel as the dominant figure, sought a transparent language that did not distort facts that go into logical analysis. Wittgenstein, who came to Cambridge to study under Russel's tutorship and then served in the Austrian army during the First World War, wrote his *Tractatus* (1922) in an attempt to solve Russel's problem. He did this while he was a prisoner of war in Italy. Frank Ramsey (Misak, 2020), who was involved in the translation of the *Tractatus* into English, raised objections against Wittgenstein's central claim that things/facts "show themselves" to people, i.e., that the observations of things go directly, undistorted, into the mind of the thinker. He claimed that every "fact" is an interpretation. Language and vocabularies get in the way. It took a while, and Ramsey died very young in 1930, but in 1953 Wittgenstein published *Philosophical Investigations* where he repudiated the *Tractatus* (and thanked Frank Ramsey for convincing him) and introduced "forms of life" and "language-games" as a solution.

The main topic in Cambridge at that time was probability and degree of belief. Keynes (1922) wrote *A Treatise on Probability* in which he discussed aspects of probability. To what extent am I justified in believing that this "fact" is true? What is my degree of belief? Russel and the analytical philosophers preferred to start from the assumption that probability is an objective property of Nature that can (in principle) be measured.

Pragmatism, with its claim that inquiry starts with a surprising observation in need of explanation, then entered the scene. It persuaded Ramsey (Misak, 2020) that this was a promising way ahead for scientific inquiry. Russel was moved (a little) to argue that our beliefs are not available to our mind most of the time; they are embedded in habits. But since our beliefs give rise to expectations, those beliefs become visible when expectations fail in some way. Then our attention is oriented towards the problem of explaining the failed expectation. Inquiry starts. Yes! Frank Ramsey seemed to have taken that argument (about beliefs, expectations and inquiry due to failed expectations) to heart.

But then logical empiricism emerged out of the Vienna circle, a conglomeration of several circles (Janik & Toulmin, 1996) that criticized the old lifestyle of the "double monarchy" and wanted to demarcate scientific research from non-scientific by designing "logical empiricism" as "proper" science. Since then, social sciences have tried to live with their "physics envy" – a longing to make social sciences "proper" sciences by measurement of factors that are assumed to be causal (beyond the free will of deliberating humans).

But management is a matter of changing/improving the world through joint efforts in single projects. There are no laws of nature here, just people who read the news every morning and change their minds. That is a different human activity compared to scientific research to falsify a hypothesis (Popper, 1963), although scientific research can be useful when it finds its proper place in relation to the complexities of management.

So, we have a group of humans deliberating on whether to do something and if so what – here and now – under these specific circumstances and with these specific resources at hand. It is the group's duty to consider all available evidence and embark on a justifiable course of action. They are not doing it for themselves but for the organization. How can they know that now is the time to act (and expose themselves to the risk of being blamed for a failure)? James (1907), the most well-known proponent of pragmatism, argues that the criterion of pragmatic truth is that one is willing to act on this information. That sounds reasonable, but what is the basis for that willingness to go into action? I come to think of the "moments of truth" in my respondents' life stories.

Kahneman (2011) argues that it is a matter of coherence. Fast thinking is a "coherence machine". The pieces of evidence need to be aligned with the values that characterize the acting person's practical identity to form a complete narrative that constitutes an "inference to the best explanation" of the solution to the problem. A team will have a collective practical identity to serve as a compass in conversations. Korsgaard (2008) argues that this is a form of neo-Kantian constitution of agency. So be it. You need the arguments to justify action (Scanlon, 2014) that concerns other people.

Obviously, a best explanation/solution for the single situation at hand must consist of operational parts describing how the project can be carried out, integrated with the skills and competences constituting the practical identity of the agent(s) to form a project worth doing. Coherence will be a property of the narrative (Manipulation, Competence, Performance, Sanction) that describes the intended action. It is a narrative since it relates to the future, and it is intentional since it commits (Searle, 2001) the speaker/agent to action. Predictions can be used as arguments, but there is no room for measurement of consequences/facts in the future – unless the "world" (which this action intends to change) behaves law-like, which is a rather strange thought now that we are discussing how to change it.

It seems to me that "the best explanation" will have to use standards as well as rules – at the same time – to reach coherence. Williams (2012, orig. 1979)[1] discusses the difference between internal and external reasons. Here the difference is between the fact-finding (operational experience) and soul-searching (normative experience) orientations of deliberation. The (surprising) gap between the observed fact **c** (operational) and our expectations (at least partly normative – we were, perhaps, too optimistic) must be bridged. To deal with (explain) this gap we need to return to Boltanski's (2011, p. 103ff.) hierarchy of tests, to justify a critique of the current situation that explains the failed expectations:

- First we distinguish between "**reality**", which is the part of the world that we can understand and analyze with our current knowledge, vocabulary, and methods, and the "**world**", still outside reality, vast, unknown and not analyzable due to its lacking conceptualization.
- Then we note that rational arguments are only valid in "reality".
- Now the first test in our deliberation is a "**truth test**". Is the surprising observation, **c**, factual – a reliable fact? If the answer is yes, the observation has been rendered visible because it does not conform to expectations – it is worth a second look.
- Next there is the "**reality test**". Is this (surprising) observation relevant? Does it concern operations? To what extent does the outcome deviate from the expected one? Is

[1] Williams defines these two kinds of reasons by reference to the sentence "A has a reason to do X". If first (internal), A has a motive that will be furthered by doing X and it turns out not to be the case, the sentence is falsified. But second (external), if A does not have a personal motive to do X then the reason sentence will not be falsified.

the difference between the "is" and the "ought to" caused by our own efforts? Can it be analyzed within our current conception of operations?

- Finally, there is the "**existential test**", which tries to find an explanation to the (surprising) observation of **c** outside our current "reality". To deal with such an "unrealistic" observation we must transfer the factor in question from "the world" across the border to "reality" (for analysis). The problem with this is that rational arguments are only valid inside "reality". Therefore, to bring a new and/or different argument to bear on the situation[2] and make it subject to rational analysis, we must use "non-rational" arguments (ideology) to cross the border into "reality". Such normative arguments are value or existential ones. They dwell in the normative part of our deliberations.

In an organizational setting....

In an organizational setting the strongest instrument in the normative realm (beside raw power) is commitment – the kind of commitment Searle (2001) discusses (above) – the kind of commitment that comes with my vouching for the truth of my own statement. If my statement turns out to be false, I will lose face. My identity will be tarnished among my colleagues. They will conclude that extra truth tests are required when I make statements.

The concept of practical identity has been a topic of philosophical discussion over centuries. Brown (2018) argues that both neo-Aristotelians and Kantian constructivists fail to show how practical

---

[2] Boltanski & Thévenot (2006) argue that their book *On Justification – Economies of Worth* is about the relation between "person-states" and "thing-states" (Preface). They want to escape from the notion of "men without qualities" used by economists and introduce men qualified as persons. I read this as having the same aim as Searle (2001)

identities provide us with obliging reasons for action. Nonetheless, I will use Korsgaard's (1996, p. 101) definition of practical identity:

> a description under which you value yourself, a description under which you find your life to be worth living and your actions to be worth undertaking[3]

Nagel (1996) questions the role of the "self-reflective" individual in relation to universality, i.e., principles that are valid for everyone. If the individual is (overly) self-reflective where does the universality of the "free will" come into play? Philosophers cannot do without the free will of the individual; without it, no (universal) morality is possible. When the "situation" starts to assert causal influence on reasons, the purity of normativity is lost (the same happens to economists when they give up "desire" and "perceptions" as causes of action). The "gap" between "internal" and "external" reasons remains. I claim that this gap must be filled by the commitment of the individual as a member of an organization. This commitment to the selectivity of reasons for action equips the individual, *qua* member, with responsibility and accountability for actions taken. Responsibility and accountability can both only exist in context. Self-reflection is deliberation on the self in context. The free will is disciplined in some of its aspects but expanded in others.

Self-reflection is likely to be framed in narrative form. This is where meaning and commitment come in as intellectual tools – to the narrator as well as the receiver of the account. The account for action is likely to be shaped into narrative form, and the understanding (for the receiver) of an account will emerge from an interpretation cast in a "canonical form" that serves as a tool of interpretation and as a source for questions of clarification.

---

[3] It is true that this definition points to an isolated individualist (albeit with ethics) rather than to a member of an organization with responsibilities.

It is close at hand to accept Cooren's (2000) claim that we use the canonical form of a narrative in sensemaking by filling in reasonable assumptions (from our experience) in those parts of the template that lack current information. The criterion for acceptance of an account as "reasonable" will be **coherence**. Doubt will initiate further inquiry (questions) as pragmatism prescribes (Misak, 2016). I will argue that this canonical form of the narrative is useful in dealing with judgement and deliberation in complexity, a point being that the narrative will contain multiple "keys" (Goffman, 1974) to various competence areas that may be implicated in a complex, organizational problem. It will help the collective of members involved to withstand the temptation to reduce complexity by transforming everything into one dimension, e.g., cash flow.

The narrative (account) describing an accomplishment, or the planned project, should cover all four moments (Table 1 above), otherwise the account cannot meet the account giver's intended coherence: What sets the action in motion (manipulation), how the actor gets hold of the necessary resources, and help from friends (competence), the sequence of operational activities involved (performance), and why this is commendable action that will be rewarded with an improved standing in the organization (sanction).

Again, if not provided properly by the narrator, members will "fill in the blanks" with reasonable assumptions (based on their experience, possibly from another area of competence) to achieve coherence.

Coherence may be understood as a state of mind – reflective equilibrium – of the individual, who is now ready to act based on this information (as James (1907) argued). More recent discussions on the concept can be found in texts by Rawls (e.g., 1971) and Scanlon (2014, esp. p. 78 ff.). It means that the agent has arrived at the conclusion that he or she has good reasons to consider the set of information pieces (and their links) sufficient to justify action. One is reminded of the extra dimension implicit in Korsgaard's definition of practical identity (above) that relates, also, but not explicitly in her wording, to being a trustworthy and respected member. (Being trusted and respected makes life "worth living" for members.)

As to sanction, the final moment of a narrative, one must remember that the words of commendation – this is an exemplary act! – may be produced by a team member as part of deliberation, or by anybody ex post. Usually, it implies that rewards and punishments are awarded by some principal (as in agency theory) with legitimate authority. But in modern organizations such authority is distributed – due to the complexity of missions – among knowledge areas, business ventures, departments, teams, etc. The formal principal (highest in rank) needs to consult many others to pronounce sanctions that have improvement effects on the organization by setting standards for further deliberation.

Bridging the gap to other people's deliberations

A narrative is probably the best instrument to establish "contact" with other people's deliberations, on facts as well as values. This is so because a narrative is rich in "keys" (Goffman, 1974). A key provides links to frames, like the scene I have mentioned about the child who saw a small otter attacking a bigger one at the zoo. But she understood the scene differently when the mother told her that "they are playing". Those words (the key) set the stage for a different understanding of the same scene, i.e., for a frame change. This is the way dialogue changes the world.

This theoretical framing of how managers deliberate (with others) to form an understanding of the surprising observation in context seems to fit many of the accounts of learning events I recorded in the interviews with business leaders in 1990 as well as 2020.

At this stage, I feel that it is time to make a preliminary statement concerning what seems to be going on in the management of complex situations under time pressure that I have been told about. The phenomenon to focus on seems to be a continuous balancing of management based in standards and rules. Let me develop that.

Kahneman et al. (2021) discuss (in Chapter 28) two ways of regulating behaviour. Their aim is to find ways of reducing "noise" (= differences in judgement between individuals and between similar situations). They claim that it is useful to distinguish between rules and standards. A rule says, for example, that a driver is not allowed to exceed a certain speed limit (say 50 km/h) on a stretch of road. The actions of the police in such a case are directed toward **measuring** speed. A standard may say that people must drive "prudently" at all times. The police will look at **judging** whether a certain way of driving (including speed) is **prudent** or not in a particular situation. Rules are meant to eliminate discretion, while standards are meant to grant such discretion (judgement). Rules will produce facts; standards will produce good practices.

Now relate this to Figures 3 and 4 above. Traditional management control, with Ashby's ultra-stable system (cybernetics) as the ideal (Figure 3), wants facts to be compared to planned outcomes. Measurement is central. It is rule-based. When those facts deviate too much from what was planned, an intervention from the top is initiated (a step-function; cut costs! increase prices!). In Figure 4, on the other hand, the task is to be on the lookout for signs that might indicate that the assumptions, under which the measurements of Figure 3 are taken, need to be changed. The rules of the game need to be re-framed (Goffman, 1974). This requires judgement as to the relevance and implications of the sign, a working through of what configuration of operational activities might be best suited for the organization to meet this new context, judgement of how a possible change may best be implemented.

It goes without saying that rules require a unity of command so that planned outcomes are set with authority, while standards require professional judgement as close to the situation as possible. One presupposes centralization, the other decentralization. **My claim is that management at the top of large organizations is a constant balancing of rule-based and judgement-based control under complexity and in changing contexts.**

To return to the introduction: The signifying property of Lennart Johansson is his desire to "see" the process he is judging – in real time. He does not want to work on the drawing board (in the abstract). The feed to his deliberation comes from detailed "real" observation and he builds solutions from the ground up, as it were. Jan Wallander, on the other hand, had a "guiding principle" to help him (and co-workers) sort solutions out by deduction and delegate decisions to responsible members close to the action. Both were highly respected and in continuous communication with their organizations, but from different perspectives.

Chapter 9
Working with words for a greater good – a new understanding of rationality required

Introduction

Jan Wallander and Lennart Johansson seem to have applied different logics in their work; one from details up to general principles, the other down from general principles to practical details. Both have accomplished a great deal, not least as negotiators. Lennart Johansson told me a fascinating story about Sweden's negotiations to join the European Union. One day he received a phone call from the chief Swedish negotiator, who wanted information about the consequences of the "*plafond*" solution for ball bearings (see Chapter 3), suggested by one of SKF's German competitors, that was on the table in Brussels. Åström, the deputy minister, thought Lennart's explanation was too complicated, and he asked Lennart to go to Brussels and sort the problem out with the EU negotiators face-to-face.

Jan Wallander managed to achieve an exemption for Handelsbanken from the Co-determination Act of 1975. That law prescribed that the unions must have two representatives on the board of large corporations. Due to the introduction of *Oktogonen* in the early 1970s, which provided that foundation with part of the amount with which Handelsbanken had out-performed the other major banks in the previous year, the foundation already had a considerable ownership in the bank and employees elected representatives on the board. This was accepted by the ministry (maybe the legislators had used the Handelsbanken solution as a template when formulating the law about board representation for employees). Jan Wallander himself did not talk about this but others did – with admiration. How did he accomplish this?

Håkan Samuelsson of Volvo Cars had a background as technical director at Scania and CEO of MAN when he was recruited to Volvo Cars. In our conversation, we arrived at the topic of whether management by objectives (MBO) was a method to reduce complexity. Not at all, Håkan exclaimed. Both MBO and bonuses tend to focus on minimum performance – what is required to get the bonus, no more – we want to do better than that! He then described how his favourite mode of control worked; he called it "management by means" (as opposed to objectives): It involved sitting down with a team of subordinates to discuss a problem. When you reached a common understanding of the problem and possible solutions, you simply provided them with the resources they deemed necessary and let them loose. The advantage of this approach was that you could follow up with just one question: "How are you doing?"

Reflection on "Doing the right thing"

What kind of rationality is described above?

The argument put forward in the previous chapter represents a large step compared to traditional economic theory with its "desires" and individual utility maximization, since the assumption that individuals are driven by their desires (and not by their free will) constitutes the very basis for economics calculation. It is also the basis for our conception of rationality (Searle, 1999, 2001). The problem is that we do not know (and cannot know, according to authorities like Adam Smith and Friedrich von Hayek) what these desires are. Still, we teach utility-maximization to our students and convince them either by claiming that when a person acts in a certain way he has revealed his preferences (i.e., desires) – whatever a person does is driven by desires – or by asking whether they'd rather have 5 USD or 10 USD (See! You have preferences!). We do not teach students about deliberation on the complexities of "doing the right thing" (Klamer, 2017).

A social science needs to take account of the meaning of "desire-independent" rationality, as Searle (2001) argues, because otherwise it is not possible to think in terms of free will (or even free markets). Freedom requires the individual to be able make up their mind out of free will. A responsible person and organizational member cannot be a slave to their desires! You often have to do the right thing, even if you would prefer to go golfing.

Searle's (2001) discussion concerns the problem "if not by desire, by what?" and his answer is "by commitment". Commitment is present when I make an assertion, and you accept it as valid in good faith. If I betray that good faith I can no longer be trusted and other commitments between us lose value. The organization is dissolved through loss of a common ideology (like that one should always tell the truth). Societies wither away into a Darwinian conglomerate of individual winners and losers.

Ideology is an interesting concept. It was first introduced by Count Antoine-Louis-Claude Destutt de Tracy (1796) during the French Revolution as a "science of ideas" – an extension of Locke's belief that human sensations are the only source of knowledge. Destutt added cognition and pointed to the four main realms of conscious behaviour - perception, memory, judgement and will – which make use of various combinations of sensations in verifying knowledge. Napoleon supressed the ideas of ideology from 1803 (because it threatened not only religious doctrines, but secular authority as well). In time, "ideology" came to be used pejoratively as an anti-thesis to "reason". Today, a common denominator of a definition would be:

> a set of beliefs, especially one held by a particular group, that influences the way people behave (Oxford Dictionaries)

In more detail:

- An ideology explains, more or less in detail, human experience and what the world consists of (ontology).
- It produces a relatively abstract programme for social and political organizing.
- It looks upon the implementation of this programme as a struggle.
- It not only seeks to convince those who are already believers but strives to recruit new loyal and committed adherents.
- It aims at a large section of the public but tends to provide intellectuals with a specific leadership role.

"Managers work with words" (Jönsson, 1983) was a rallying cry I used many years ago to argue for more detailed field studies of how managers (in fact) use and produce information in their daily work. Now, 50 years after I defended my PhD thesis, a large part of that time spent in the field observing and interviewing managers, and especially after the two sets of interviews (1990 and 2020) with industrial leaders this book is based on, I am more convinced than ever that the tools of management are words. When I asked those highly respected leaders about learning events that underpin the managerial principles they live by, they would tell stories about single observations – they would, wouldn't they, since they were asked about learning events – of deviations from the expected, finding explanations and initiating "ideological" discussions about improvement. Convincing colleagues that change is called for is a significant part of managerial work, and it seems to be an important basis for promotion.

Colleagues are often set in their routines and loathe to change them every time there is a slight mishap for which the close-at-hand explanation is that people have not been following proper procedures. These sceptics must be persuaded to join the crusade for improvement by good arguments, to abandon their departmental boundary work (Gieryn, 1983) and start a new venture on the available evidence. Ideology caps the case for that new venture by virtue of what is good for the organization – in the long term. Ideology serves as a "cap stone" in arguments for "bridging" between current and improved practices. When managers use the term "our business model" nowadays it is as an ideological expression.

Theory – again

Now, classical philosophy on rationality makes a strict distinction between facts and value. Given the facts and values, all rational decision makers will come to the same decision. (If they don't, economists will resort to explaining this by claiming that they have different desires, which is a void claim.) Searle (2001) has convinced me that it is not that simple – the language tends to get in the way. This insight came in the early 1900s with pragmatism, which was imported from the US (where Peirce and James were its best-known proponents) to Cambridge, where Ramsey, and to some extent Keynes, were persuaded; Russel, however, who was somewhat sceptical and rather vicious in his reviews, came around only to some extent. Wittgenstein, who had been in Cambridge to study under Russel (and had returned after the First World War), turned around completely; he renounced his earlier work in his *Philosophical Investigations* (1953) and initiated what has been called the "linguistic turn" in social sciences. Misak (2016, 2020) provides a detailed discussion of the process in Cambridge.

The focus of attention in pragmatic discourse is on the very first step in the scientific process: the observation of a surprising fact and the initiation of inquiry to find an "inference to the best explanation". In scientific discourse, such an "explanation" takes the form of a hypothesis to be tested (Popper, 1963).

In management, and in our daily life, actors cannot wait for a scientific process to run its course. Instead, fast thinking (Kahneman, 2011), where coherence rather than scientific proof is sought, is required. This, I would claim, is the very essence of market actor behaviour! The actor sifts through their experience for clues (Goffman (1974) would call them cues or keys) that could help build a coherent argument for action (now). (Goffman (1974) would call that re-framing.) However, a strict distinction between facts and values that becomes blurred when deliberation on coherence – here understood as consisting of mutually supporting arguments – is on the agenda. Multiple goals considered at the same time, politics, compromises, wishful thinking (Jönsson & Lundin, 1977), hope (Lear, 2006), and pessimism abound in complex situations when a team makes up its "mind".

When time is short and action is required, the option to postpone is not a valid proposal. The difficulty of upholding the distinction between facts (truth conditions) and values (conditions of satisfaction) ushers in the issue of meaning (and thereby Searle's (2001) "desire-independent rationality").

Searle starts from a rather severe critique of the Classical Model of Rationality

1. Rational actions are caused by beliefs and desires. (Not true! In general, most *irrational* action is caused by beliefs and desires.)

2. Rationality is a matter of obeying the rules of logic that define rationality. (Not true!)
3. Rationality is a separate cognitive faculty. (There is no such faculty distinct from language, thought, perception, intentionality.)
4. Akrasia (weakness of the will) can arise only when there is something wrong with the psychological antecedents of action. (Wrong! Weakness of the will is a common, natural form of irrationality, a consequence of the gap between thought and action.)
5. There are "desire-independent reasons for action". (Reference to Bernard Williams' (2012) argument about "internal" and "external" reasons.)
6. Rationality works only if the set of primary desires is consistent. (Wrong! Inconsistent reasons for action are common and inevitable.)

It is obviously a great challenge to take on the task of providing an alternative to the core philosophy of economics and other social sciences. Searle works in the frame of speech act theory. For analytical purposes, we can classify speech acts into different categories, such as an assertion, a promise, a command, etc. What does it mean to assert something? What constitutes an assertion? How do we understand the implications of an assertion? Searle points out, on his path to a conception of desire-independent rationality, that an assertion also includes a commitment to the truth of the claim. When I say, "It is raining" (bring your umbrella) it is not only a matter of checking whether my statement satisfies the truth condition that it is raining. There is also my commitment to that fact. I claim that it is raining, trust me! I assume responsibility for the wisdom in bringing an umbrella. There is a commitment in the assertion. Searle argues that the commitment emerges because of the imposition of conditions of satisfaction on conditions of satisfaction (p. 173). There is already a desire-independent reason for action in my assertion "It is raining!" (Bring your umbrella!) I mean that it is best to bring an umbrella if you want to avoid getting wet.

While an **assertion** says something about the state of the world now – which can be checked by observing the state of the world – a **promise** is a commitment to do something in the future – to change the world to fit the promise (turning up outside the cinema at 7 o'clock).

> (The) speaker stands in a special relation to his own assertions, in that he has created them as his own commitments. (p.176)

To see the significance of this, we need to note the meaning of "direction of fit"; an assertion has a direction of fit which is "language-to-world" (if the assertion does not fit the world, the only way to correct it is to change the assertion). A desire (or an intention, like a promise) has the opposite direction: "world-to-language" (the intention is to change the world to fit the speech act). Further, when I make a promise, I commit myself to change the world (do something) to fit the statement (You can rely on it!).

These are commitments that I make of my free will. The fact that my free will is involved (as opposed to coercion) commits me (this individual!) to do something. The others can rely on it because I am committed to live up to the promise. This has direct implications for my standing in the group participating in the conversation. Other members can construct their contributions on this basis. In that way, speech acts build an organization and members are obliged, by their commitments, to apply desire-independent rationality when engaged in the business of the organization. Over time, some of the required speech acts have been turned into standardized, formal language, such as when you sign a charter to establish a limited company, which, in turn, obliges you to apply desire-independent rationality in accordance with the Companies Act. The free will is no longer controlled by "brutish" desires, but by reason (and law).

You must give good arguments for action – you are "accountable"; for outcomes, as well as the truth, of your statements. You acquire a practical identity. A fair father will ask, "What have you got to say for yourself?" And if your account is accepted, you may be trusted to go out on your own again next week. The point is that you must provide good arguments that belong to your father's repertoire, no matter what mischief you plan for next week. Should your arguments be insincere and exposed as such, you end up in trouble. You must care for your practical identity to gain greater freedom of (responsible) action. Therefore, you apply desire-independent rationality of your own free will.

And so it goes on. Practices are enshrined in habits. When outcomes are the expected ones, habits are confirmed. Should they deviate from the expected, the underlying beliefs are made visible to the mind. I expected that outcome and it turned out to be this instead! Why? Is something wrong with my beliefs? The failed expectation initiates a search for a plausible explanation. In that situation, the actor may be open to dialogue. New ideas may be imported; ideas that contribute to a new understanding of why expectations failed. That understanding may be pieced together by bits and pieces of evidence. The criterion for accepting a new explanation is coherence (Kahneman, 2011); the pieces of evidence are "mutually supporting" – they make sense (Weick, 1995). Learning happens. Experience is expanded. Successful action based on a new belief, and related expectations, form new habits. It is in the situations when a new, surprising observation (fact) has been made that creative solutions and organizational learning are likely to appear. Such "appearances" constitute the bulk of the stories industrial leaders told me.

Furthermore, it is in such situations that the individual benefits from dialogue on possible causes. The creative opening towards new explanations comes from the realization that I (and my habits) did not cause this outcome. It was unexpected and so must have been caused by something other than my habit (my habit routinely produces/causes another outcome). I become aware of the possibility of other causes of the outcomes than my habitual action. I must find the best possible explanation for the surprising observation and go on from there. (I may also observe a change in context that could be expected to cause trouble (or an opportunity) and construct action on an assumption about future developments.)

Coherence and inference to the best explanation

To make sense of a surprising observation, one must construct a coherent narrative that accounts for available facts (necessary) and adds plausible assumptions to fill in the "blanks" to support a proposal for action. Cooren's (2000) canonical form, providing "blanks" to fill in, and police procedure oriented after "Motive, Means, Opportunity", provide a procedural guide, but there seems to be more to it than that.

The problem is that the "surprising observation" is an indicator of a failure, not only of expectations, but of the unreliability of the inductive method of prediction. That may not be a significant concern for the practising manager, but management is a matter of changing/improving the world by joint efforts in single cases. There are no laws of nature here, just people trying to do the right thing. That is a different human activity compared to scientific research to falsify a hypothesis (Popper, 1963). I expect that scientific research can find its way to support the work managers do; that will happen when it finds its proper place in relation to the complexities of management. It is unlikely to be achieved by emulating Natural Science ….. but what do I know?

So, we have a group of humans deliberating on whether to do something and, if so, what – here and now, under these specific circumstances and with these specific resources at hand? It is the group's duty to consider all available evidence and embark on a justifiable course of action. They are not doing it for themselves but for the organization. How can they know that now is the time to act (and expose themselves to the risk of being blamed for a failure.)? James (1907), the most well-known proponent of pragmatism, argues that the criterion of pragmatic truth is that one is willing to act on this information. That sounds reasonable, but what is the basis for that willingness?

Kahneman (2011) argues that it is a matter of coherence. Fast thinking is a "coherence machine". The pieces of evidence need to be aligned with the values that characterize the acting person's practical identity to form a complete narrative that constitutes an "inference to the best explanation" of the solution to the problem. A team will have a collective practical identity to serve as a compass in conversations. Korsgaard (2008) argues that this is a form of neo-Kantian constitution of agency. So be it. You need the arguments to justify action (Scanlon, 2014) that concerns other people (reason **p**, for agent **a**, to do **x**, under circumstances **c**)

Obviously, a "best explanation/solution" for the single situation at hand must consist of operational parts describing how the project can be carried out, integrated with the skills and competences constituting practical identity of the agent(s), and those operational parts will have been evaluated on several normative dimensions (sometimes contradictory). Coherence will be a property of the narrative (Manipulation, Competence, Performance, Sanction) describing the intended action. It is a narrative since it relates to the future, and it is intentional since it "commits" (Searle, 2001) the speaker/agent to action. Predictions can be used as arguments, but there is no room for measurement of consequences/facts in the future – unless the "world" (which this action intends to change) behaves law-like (and the project under consideration is likely to change "the laws" of the context in focus).

It seems to me that "the best explanation" will have to use standards as well as rules, but concurrently, to reach coherence. Williams (2012, orig. 1979)[1] discusses the difference between internal and external reasons, but here the difference is between the fact-finding (operational experience) and soul-searching (normative experience) orientations of deliberation. There are at least two logics in play here!

It seems reasonable to expect that a team that has worked together for some time will have established templates, applications of the canonical form (Cooren, 2000) mentioned earlier to use in sensemaking and in communication. Goffman (1974) would call it a "frame". They will, for instance, "frame" situations by filling in reasonable assumptions (from their common experience) in those parts of the template that lack current information. But could the same template be used in deliberation on "surprising observations"? That is, when we build our conception of "what should a person like me do in a **situation like this**?" Could "coherence" be measured by how well the account of the situation (including the surprising observation) fits the canonical form? Possibly, but fit in form only is not enough. The practical identity (a person like me) of the narrator (trust) comes in more tangibly. Remember that Cooren's (2000) template aims at the participants' understanding of what is said in a conversation, i.e., after it has been said. Here we are talking about

[1] Williams defines these two kinds of reasons by reference to the sentence as 'A has a reason to do X'. If first (internal), A has a motive that will be furthered by doing X and it turns out not to be the case the sentence is falsified. But second (external), if A does not have a personal motive to do X then the reason sentence will not be falsified.

deliberation ex ante. It is a project in the near future that must be judged. How do managers carry this out?

My respondents' life stories make me think that there is an element of ideology involved. The leader of the conversation in the team (or between mentor and mentee) inserts himself (or herself) as a capstone in the building of a bridge between "thinking" and "doing". Several of the respondents (speaking Swedish) used the expression "plunge into the cold water" (and start swimming) to describe what overcoming hesitation when facing uncertainty is like. Intellectually, the "push" must come from some ideological aspect of the project, say "for the common good". But as Frank Ramsey said in Cambridge 100 years ago, "language tends to get in the way". This is particularly troublesome when several areas of knowledge are engaged.[2] Here the statement by Searle (2001) above on the speaker's special relation to his own assertions (created as his own commitments) comes to mind. Assertions will be given different meanings from different areas of knowledge. Participants need experience in cross-area communication and the related compromising if they are to function well. (Assertion of power will not help, at least not much.)

To sum up: Complexity and lack of time put communication at the centre of deliberation. Several knowledge areas need to be engaged in attention, articulation, construction of creative solutions to detected problems stemming from surprising observations. One authoritative channel of communication is not enough. There need to be multiple channels and multiple nodes to accommodate creative problem solving.[3]

---

[2] For the social scientist, imagine a multidisciplinary team of researchers early in the research process who want to formulate a hypothesis to be tested by "proper methods".

[3] Simon (1996) is a useful reference for this chapter.

Enough of philosophizing for a while! Next, I will seek inspiration/ clues in an account of the institutional idea structure that I believe colours the management approach of the Swedish leaders I have interviewed.

Chapter 10
The "system" that selected the respondents for promotion to top jobs

Ingress: Who gets promoted?

One of the respondents in the first set of interviews (1990) said that there is no Swedish management culture, but there is an Atlas Copco culture. He is most likely right because the home market for Swedish industry is tiny. Most of the big corporations represented in the material have less than 5 % of their business and employment in Sweden. Still, when asked about the reason why Swedish industry has done so well internationally the answer was – especially in 2020 – 'that we respect other people and listen to their arguments'. (A mirror version: A small country like ours is not threatening.) Yes, yes... anybody could say that! Let me explain why I believe that there is something to this (Jönsson, 1995).

Some industrial history

One of the respondents in the first set of interviews told me about what happened when his company (STORA) was introduced on the New York Stock Exchange some decades ago. In the "road show" they would start by telling the story about STORA celebrating its 200 years' jubilee before America was discovered. The forestry industry has, thus, been around for some time, and it was focused on export early. This meant that young promising managers was sent abroad for extensive stays in other countries as part of their training. Thereby they came to see what life in enormous countries like Germany, France and Britain was like compared to the tiny Swedish business community. If you wanted to do business, you had to adapt to context. Impressing your own ways on context was not an option. You need to respect the other and adapt (within reason).

Iron ore and ingots gradually came to be value added by way of mechanical engineering – business to business – ball bearings, compressors, trucks…

Bellicose Sweden – at war with Denmark 30 times over the centuries – managed to keep out of war after the Napoleonic period. That included a "neutrality" policy during WWII that largely had the support of the Swedish people, but has been criticized by younger generations, especially in connection with Sweden's recent application for NATO membership. The benefit of that was that Sweden came out of the war period with its industrial capacity intact, which, in turn, allowed for the building of an advanced welfare state with a long social democratic rule, and a decent way to negotiate with well-organized unions. There was a rather severe strike among metal workers in early 1945, though. At that time Marxists had a strong say in unions, but from then on, the social democrats put great efforts into organising the labour unions. This set the stage for far-reaching agreements between unions, employers, and the state. To illustrate, take the agreement on economic development that has got Rudolf Meidner's, the legendary union economist and Gösta Rehn's, the Ministry of Finance economist, names attached to it.

The Meidner-Rehn-model was inspired by Keynes and meant that unions do not need to orient their wage demands toward the companies or industries with the lowest capacity to carry cost increases. Instead, economic growth could be enhanced by the least effective firms being pushed out of business. To compensate for the negative effects the state undertook to implement policies that would stimulate workers to move to the more effective, modern firms with more advanced technologies, stimulate investment in new firms and new technology, and implement active regional policies. Thereby the Swedish economy as a whole would become more competitive over time and able to carry the cost of the welfare systems.

This also cleared the way for centralized union-employer negotiations with local agreements geared to the standard set by the central one, with the state watching that the parties behaved. As it was seen to work reasonably well, trust between the parties grew into an institution. For several decades the social democrats held the majority in the Riksdag (Parliament) and, thereby, they could also shield the labour market from more Marxist-inspired movements. Sometimes it worked a bit too well; Gunnar Myrdal, the Nobel laureate, was Minister of Trade 1945 - 47. He came home from a visit the Soviet Union with a trade agreement that overwhelmed industries. Stalin's pet project then was to "electrify" the Union and the electricity generation equipment that Myrdal had promised him would fill the production capacity in ASEA (the main supplier) for decades. The company protested, there was a lot of business to be had elsewhere! Amendments were made.

So, Swedish industry enjoyed full capacity demand in most industries after the war, as Europe rebuilt its industry. But it also needed to invest in new machinery and automation as new technologies generated by the war effort could be adapted for industrial application. Growth was fast which resulted in the "Korea-crisis" of the early 1950s, whereby Keynesian economic policies were intensified. The state, industry and unions solved problems together – Sweden was a small but well-organized player in a large world.

The restructuring of the industry had started already after the First World War with a couple of banks active via closely related investment funds that allowed banks and their friends to reach majority positions or large ownerships in important companies, much like the German and, later Japanese "Hausbanks". In everyday economic debates one would talk about "bank spheres". Banks sometimes following their clients in their investments abroad. Most active here was the bank that is now SEB with its "owner family" Wallenberg. But Handelsbanken (SHB) (including Skandinaviska Banken from 1974) took up competition. The savings banks organized into Swedbank and the state set up its bank operations that is now part of NORDEA. These 4 banks played a central role in structuring industry. Managers tended to have their career inside the bank spheres, with Marcus Wallenberg (Sr) (Olsson, 2001) as a particularly active chairman of several corporations and recruiter of management talent. Wallenberg served the state well in trade negotiations during and after WWII and had a good standing in relation to the government. The Swedish Bankers' Association was the conduit for deals with the government concerning financial policies.

In this (corporatist) way a tradition, or if you prefer, an institution, of cooperation for a common cause - building an effective economy for competition abroad was established. This might be considered a conventional approach for most countries to follow, but one must remember that in the case of Sweden the domestic market is quite small. In daily conversations one would talk about Sweden as the "negotiated economy" (förhandlingsekonomin). One should also note the dominance of business-to-business firms in the Swedish industry. It used to be an engineers' economy, but in time – from the late 1980ies – neoliberalism, deregulated finance, and business educated managers came to the fore. The welfare state economy became **more complex**, not least by the growth of a new active institutional level in the form of a European Union, sustainability, financial crisis.

This institutional dislocation had effects on the careers of individual managers, while it was going on (and it continues to change) as well as after stabilization (not for long). This is mirrored in the "life stories" of the respondents in the strong tendency of their learning events being constituted by missions to deal with emerging problems in foreign places. The events that constitute the "life stories", like a string of pearls, are remarkably unique. The context that determined what tasks promising candidates would be selected for, was unstable. One cannot, really, prepare candidates for this by way of education. Of course, there is a basic level required. One of the respondent's told me a story about having studied a certain amount of thermodynamics; "enough to know when they (the R&D people) are 'bullshitting' me". But it seems fair to conclude that the respondents I talked to were promoted based on their "practical identity", i.e., competencies to get things done in teamwork under exceptional circumstances – to "see" how this new situation can be resolved. This is not a "natural selection" process of the Darwin kind (variety, selection, retention), but a more "managed" process in the sense that mentors and committees "select" a suitable candidate in a less wasteful way than Mother Nature does. Different talents are needed at different times. The respondents are different, the similarities are dwarfed by the differences. I have selected the life stories of Lennart Johansson, Jan Carlzon, Hasse Johansson, Dan Sten Olsson to illustrate this (above chapter 3). One should not generalize from the "properties" of those individuals but consider the "properties" of the context in which they were selected for important positions in large organizations.

Tempus fugit – time flies

In the old days when time did not fly but flowed like a majestic river (but be aware! Panta Rhei! According to Heraclitus around 500 BC)) it was rational to reduce the consequences of managerial action to cash flows (given a few assumptions) and discount them to a net present value that could be compared to the owners' objective. But now causalities ramify across several goal attributes and the world does not stand still long enough to justify assumptions over any more than a short time. We need to start anew with a conception of what management is all about (in the old days and in textbooks it is portrayed as "choice" among interesting alternative plans of action.).

The conception of what management is about has effects on how we conceive time. I would claim, and I expect most of the interviewed managers would agree, that management is about getting things done. If this is accepted the crucial moment is to take the step from "thinking" to "doing". First you contemplate action (deliberation), and then you act. When you act you expose yourself to scrutiny by colleagues and bosses. There is risk in acting, but it does not come as a probability distribution to be calculated. You have one try and you will be judged on the outcome, which is also dependent upon the efforts of others and counter measures by the competition. Once you have started action there is a lot you can do to adjust the plan to emerging contingencies.

The problem with action is that it can only be taken "now" – a tiny moment squeezed in between "history" (which you cannot do anything about (if our name is not Putin)), and "the future" (which you can only hope will be benevolent).

HISTORY > NOW > FUTURE

↑

Please act here!

When we act, we typically "read" how well we are doing in the reactions of others. This means that communication plays a significant part in management. Time becomes "cyclical" – actions – reaction – action – reaction. In modern "management speak" there is often talk about somebody being "process owner", which means that this person has been given the right to direct the action taken and correct deviations, but this is a matter of formal power.

It may reduce reaction time in situations where things are not going as one hoped for – when in doubt members know who to turn to. But, on the other hand a skilful member doing a central task may be the one in 'real' command. When many subtasks are done in parallel, time - as measured by the progress of each task – may be "split" as tasks vary in tempo. Monitoring the progress of the project becomes a multi-task one. The project may be scheduled as a series of sub projects, each with its "deadlines" and reporting in "stages", when estimated "target costs" are evaluated as well (Jönsson, 2004). The manager of the project (with all its sub-tasks) may have to serve like the conductor of an orchestra gesturing to get the different sections co-ordinated. Priorities and operational skill may be used to determine which sub-task should come first. "Timing" may at times be the essence.

Furthermore, time is a completely different phenomenon in planning as compared to the actual carrying out a complex process. In planning one can keep some variables constant while studying the effects of variation in one. But in action all variables (some previously unknown) may surprise the manager, requiring instant assessment of the situation. There is no time for analysis. Intuition steps in and the natural reaction is to try to get the process back on track according to plan, but there are also occasions when a skilful manager can capture the moment and improve on the plan with the help of a surprising discovery.

This feature of taking advantage of emerging opportunities appears rather frequently in in our respondents' "life stories". It is a matter of having a good enough conception of the plan to be able to "see" deviations and judge their significance. This requires attention – a couple of interviewees pointed out that organizations do not have enough attention to go around to be able to run a conglomerate structure properly like in the old days (they were thinking about management from the centre when they said that). Others argued that the only solution is to delegate to front line people. In that way the organization as such will increase its capacity to respond to a changing environment in its important details. But, even if this happens, a side effect of the thus "shattered" time component will be that the manner of management needs to adapt. It must let go of operational detail and focus on repeated (adapted) mission statement, trust in the judgment of colleagues, and control by coherence rather than against pre-determined single variable values.

Coherence, as a criterion for solutions, is a central feature in the other aspect that I have observed in the "life stories" of the elite managers I have interviewed. When dealing with complexity it is not reasonable to reduce problems and their solution to the value on one variable – not if you are responsible for the survival and prosperity of an organization.

Complexity – when you do not understand (completely) what you are doing

"High tech and horse-trading" was an expression used by one of the 1990 interviewees to summarize the nature of one of his first successful assignments abroad. The impression is that the "horse-trading" has no less part today even if the "high tech" part is more varied in terms of its anchorage in different and new knowledge areas.

In a large international corporation engaged in advanced technology products for many different markets and services related to the specific use by the individual customer, complexity is the normal. Demands for standardization in the name of production automation contradicts the relatively recent strategic decision to align more closely with the individual customer's value creation process. Solutions with modules and standard interfaces that allow combinations of components to suit varying demands are required. But a consequence of that may be extra logistical problems. Working in alliances may add complications as will the demands and regulations for improved sustainability of life on this planet. And it is not possible to "stop the world" while we adapt. Change is pervasive and imminent. These are problems that stem from complexity. Good arguments for different solutions will be presented from different perspectives and relating to different values – like sustainability that include social and economic processes beside environmental ones these days (Bebbington, 2001).

Time-out on rationality:
It is in this kind of context promising management talent is tested, and in which the "learning events" of the "life stories" of successful managers are set. One could say that this kind of system "selects" those that are promoted. What kind of rationality is at play here? Is it at all possible to be rational under such circumstances?

Since the beginning of time people have been taught that the guarantee for making the right decision is to base it on rational arguments and facts. Rationality is grounded in two shapes of logic: deduction and induction.

In **deduction** it is the form of reasoning that preserves the truth of the facts that go into the application of logic. This form of rationality suits machines and mathematicians. Given the premisses this is a true conclusion!

Induction always uses historical data and claims that its conclusion says something about the future (provided the world stays about the same). Artificial Intelligence uses this kind of logic (Larson, 2021), and finds "safety" in ever "Bigger Data". The grounding is in the assumption that the world is governed by laws of nature - individuals being driven by their "desires".

But there are other ways to reach conclusions that one is willing to act on – as discussed above.

In the first book (Doyle, 2014) on Sherlock Holmes – when Dr. Watson meets him and moves in with him to share an adventurous life – Holmes tells Watson about the difference in approach between detectives and scientists. While scientists analyse data to make predictions about the future (in the form of laws of nature), detectives look backwards – the murder has already happened and they seek facts (clues) that, together, corroborates an account of what happened, i.e., "explains" the murder. The one argues analytically and the other synthetically. It is synthetically true that "Snow is white" because you can check by looking, while it is analytically true that "Bachelors are unmarried" because of the meaning of the words (you don't have to check). Without going into the philosophical controversies around the analytic/synthetic distinction it is essential to point out its significance for economics and management.

When Searle (2001) argues that we need a conception of a desire-independent rationality (see the previous chapter) he stepped into a territory that economists, since 1871 (Menger, 1871), claim monopoly for. The only permissible basis for rational maximization of utility (McCloskey's (2006, 2010, 2016), "max-U") has been the individual's desire. It is so much easier for economists to analyse data to predict the future if they assume that individuals are controlled by their desires (not by "free will"). Rationality is a matter of choosing the best alternative given the goal (to satisfy desires – it is the desire that "causes" action). But, argues Searle (2001), most irrational action is caused by desire and belief! We must concern ourselves with people's acting with good reason.

The problem with complexity is that means and ends (desires) must be dealt with in the same process. One must build a justification for action that includes reasons for a specific goal being relevant here as well as the reason for why this set of operations best serve to reach that goal. The logic of fitting immediate goals together with immediate action with the help of a "cohesion" (Kahneman, 2011) criterion is not easily formalized or analysed. Searle (2001) uses "direction of fit" in conjunction with the speaker's "commitment" to build his case for desire-independent rationality. This puts a suitable "practical identity" (Korsgaard, 1996) at centre stage in judging whether a person's assertions are trustworthy as enough for promotion. When my commitment to the truth of a statement is verified by factual outcomes my "practical identity" is enhanced in the eyes of others – I can be trusted. The mirror image of my practical identity is constantly updated by the others. They need to be able to understand my intentionality (Searle, 1983) in their interpretation of communication in this particular "language game". The idea of language game starts with Wittgenstein (1953) and continues through Cooren (2000) and others. It is constituted by some commonalities in concepts, conceptions, and ways of speaking in a community (organization). If members follow the rules of that game, arguments will be, at least partly, compatible, and usable to build joint solutions. The point is that in this view of communication it is the receiver who determines the meaning of what is said. Therefore, communication in the immediate work team is important for promotion.[1] This was touched upon by a few respondents who complained that now they sit in personnel committees to take

[1] I have heard statements to the effect that nowadays careers are so fast that it is a waste of time to build communication skills that are locally anchored – you are soon going to be promoted anyway. I don't agree.

decisions on the basis of masses of "objective" HRM variables and tests – very tedious – while they themselves were promoted on factual accomplishments (and the fortune to make a good presentation to the right people at the right time). This dilemma concerning methods in promotion processes – measurement or judgment ("rule" or "standard" (Kahneman et al, 2021, 350ff.)) – takes on a new significance with the realization that dealing with complex situations is a more important task than before.

Cooren (2000) argues that people use a canonical form of a narrative in sensemaking, i.e., as a tool by which meaning, relevance and consequences are worked out (and tested) – to generate coherence. I have touched upon this template before (Table 1, p. 90) – it has been quite useful in coding the episodes of the "life stories" my respondents gave me – but I repeat it here to show how it can be used to deal with complexity (achieve coherence) when time is short. For that purpose, look at the "possible sub-narrative" part. Take a standard James Bond film for illustration:

1. **Manipulation**: M calls Bond to his/her office. SPECTRE is up to something again. (We all know about the devious plans of SPECTRE!). This time the first clue is in Venice, where we have lost an agent recently. Go there and find out! (Here it is possible to expand sub-narratives of serious threats to the entire world.)
2. **Competence**: Bond goes to Q and walks through the lab where several gadgets are demonstrated (showing how large the repertoire is). The things Q gives Bond turn out to be exactly what he needs later (proves his excellent foresight). Q's genius is borne out in the "Performance" moment of the narrative.
3. **Performance**: Bond's agility and competence in using gadgets in different scenes "on the run" confirm the sub-narratives of

the "Competence" moment. Bond has the skill, and the gadgets work as Q predicted.

4. **Sanction:** After all the gymnastics the main characters gather in M's office to celebrate having saved the world again. Bond gets a special greeting from miss Moneypenny

There are many "clues" in a Bond-story that allow us to construct the experience of seeing the film to our liking. It is constructed to allow framing variety. The tool for this is the "keys" we discover in the plot. (Poirot sees "clues" that we do not see until he, in the final scene with all members of the group assembled, tells the story of how the murderer must have carried out his deed – and we think: 'ah, yes, that is plausible!'). The different moments of the narrative support each other in linkages of "if-then". This is the same mechanism as abductive reasoning in pragmatism uses – in fact it is the foundational principle of pragmatism:

> *The surprising fact, C, is observed.*
> *But if A were true, C would be a matter of course.*
> *Hence there is reason to suspect that A is true"*
> (Quoted from Misak, 2016, p 41)

If there is a missing link in the emerging narrative, we fill the gap with a plausible "A" given our knowledge of the world.

The issue now is when to stop iterating. Clearly it is when we reach "reflective equilibrium" (Rawls, 1971, Scanlon, 2014) and are ready to act on this understanding. If we still are in doubt the inquiry continues (or is given up). If we accept the definition of management as "getting things done" this is what managers should do – **abductive reasoning**. Further, doing research on organizations in a changing and complex world, we, as responsible researchers, should work out new hypotheses in this way. Start from the unique observation of a manner of behaviour that needs to be explained.

Our age-old way to avoid confusion when market actors do not behave as expected is to refer to "revealed preferences". (Our standard assumption about subjective utility maximization was introduced by Carl Menger in 1871). Whatever people do it is controlled by their preferences, we are taught. If they do something else, it must be because they have changed preferences. This does not live up to basic scientific standards of falsifiability (Popper, 1963)!

But we might be wrong! Yes! In a social system, where individuals whom we respect have different opinions about what is right and effective, we may be wrong. People do change their minds because of good arguments. The check whether a good argument is good is the extent to which it can fit into a narrative built on as many facts as possible. Therefore, it is a better idea to listen to the arguments of the others to see if the narrative can be improved, than the age-old practice to reduce complexity by positing non-realistic premises for deductive reasoning (which yields true conclusions by definition – the world needs only to be fitted to the premises).

In social sciences we have competing theories "explaining" the same observations in different ways and very little of critical experiments to falsify theories. Thomas Kuhn (1962) was right, scientific revolutions are indeed rare, and this is explained by the unwillingness of "the old guard" to abandon the very platforms they built their merits on and start anew from scratch as it were. Instead, in social sciences we have "competing schools" combatting each other in the journals fervently until "the old guards" retire and let the new generation a freer space of choice of approaches. Maybe social sciences could get rid of its "physics envy" (trying to explain social phenomena as if they were the result of machine programs at work, or "Laws of Nature") by applying abductive reasoning in the hypothesis formulation phase. Thereby we could replicate the Darwinian mechanism for evolution also in social sciences (variety, selection, retention). But that requires a courage to go into action, first, with hypothesis generation based on facts to be explained ("surprising observations" in the field), and second, to "surround" the explanatory hypothesis with support and questions (Lakatos, 1965, uses the expression "protective belt"). This second process goes on until "reflective equilibrium" is reached, i.e., so long as doubt remains. In this way "theories" in social sciences about the everchanging social processes and related states develop piecemeal and rather slowly driven by a changing "desire" for the common good. This seems to be the way good managers of large organizations work with complexity and lack of time in a changing context. And skill in that communicative task provides ground for promotion.

Chapter 11
Is "management culture" possible?

Ingress

It was in the Electrolux interviews (1990) that we could detect something of a "culture" at the top of the organization. It was mostly in terms of the "vagueness" of control. (It was Hans Werthén who described Danish managers as "buccaneers" – the Dutch were still more difficult to deal with ("river pirates")). Gösta Bystedt displayed his attitude to the accounting system integration of new acquisitions by describing how he asked them to change anything they thought important (now) because this is the way you will report from now on (never mind product strategies). Anders Scharp came up the hierarchy by excelling in production automation in different contexts. Hans Werthén himself informed us that "you need to get yourself an opposition". The top management floor at the HQ in Stockholm (1990) looked like a coffee room surrounded by simple offices for the top managers (they were travelling a lot anyway). An Italian second tier manager described top management meetings as interesting discussions but "vague". One came out of the meetings with a blank notebook. When I confronted Gösta Bystedt with this "vagueness" he accepted the description and claimed that "good ideas" can "push through" while "bad ideas" tend to be "sorted out" by this vagueness. Don't you worry!

Michael Treschow (1990), CEO of Atlas Copco (later CEO of Electrolux) said that one cannot really talk about a Swedish management culture, but Atlas Copco has one. Leif Johansson (2020) (later CEO of Electrolux, Ericsson, and Volvo) gave an account of his early career when he was charged with "saving" the Husqvarna subsidiary, notably the motorcycle division, and did that by pushing out administrative managers and keep motorcycle enthusiasts. Hasse Johansson (2020) described how he was engaged in the design of an ignition system for the very large order the army had placed with Johansson's Husqvarna. They did not want motorcycles with batteries, so you must have a strong current from the kick-start mechanism. Ronnie Leten (2020) told me that he had been "Swedified" (at Atlas Copco) to the extent that he would probably not function in a Belgian company again.

Jan Carlzon (1990) no doubt managed to change the "culture" at SAS, from being an airline with traditional route scheduling and efficiency orientation, to a customer orientation with extreme decentralization (although he was very visible to employees, not least via the press).

Electrolux seems to have been an important training ground for many of our most respected top managers, but it is difficult to point to anything specific. (Beckérus & Edström, 1995). But can "vagueness" be a culture?

Culture?

Looking at the differences, if any, between the way "culture" was treated in the two interview series, it seems fair to say that earlier, in 1990, the leaders' persona seemed to play a larger role. I believe that it is the complexity of the management task that can explain some of that. Then - in 1990 - a well-trained engineer with adequate experience could respond to most emergencies with some confidence. Now, several areas of knowledge, like Law and IT, will be drawn into most inquiries and the centre of deliberation will be a group rather than one respected individual. One would assume that under such circumstances, "culture" would stand a greater, even if different, chance of rooting due to the multi-channel communication that complexity would imply. On the other hand, the opportunities/

temptations for competition between knowledge areas (like in a university) will abound. Finally, the communication problem will be greater since it must cover several (advanced) knowledge areas – there is a limit to simplification in communication if one wants to maintain trust. For Swedish corporations with their traditions of respectful negotiation it is anyone's guess whether "community" or "technological arrogance" (like when IT imposes its machine-adapted conception of what information is (Larson, 2021)) will determine the rules of the game.

It was not that times were less complex 30 years ago. In 1990 most of the big Swedish firms were in the middle of a wave of acquisitions to position themselves for meeting the emerging "inner market" in Europe. The acquired firms usually continued to run their own business as before, which meant that the corporations looked very much like conglomerates with a management problem that top management solved by intensive travelling. Percy Barnevik (1990) told me that he would gather 200 "national" managers in every country he visited, talk to them about the current campaign (like 'always ask an internal supplier first') and then take questions. He had a briefcase with overheads for every occasion and read reports all the time. He believed he could keep abreast of the development in his more than 5000 profit centres. I have written elsewhere (Jönsson & Strannegård, 2014) that I doubted whether Barnevik's successor could cope with that kind of information flow. Barnevik claimed to be "fanatic" about decentralization to the lowest possible level. In a sense he created a culture even if he had difficulties with the German part of the organization. Gardell (2020) of the financial firm (Cevian) that works according to a strategy of acquiring a large ownership in big corporations, demand a seat on the Board and argue for "simplification" of the company structure (selling out non-core business), argued that conglomerates are old fashioned. There simply is not enough attention available to manage a conglomerate from the centre. It is better to let "the market" do the job of keeping organizations on their toes.

There were some pronouncements of respect for the analytical work that Gardell & Co bring to the Boards they enter. But there was also critique of the tendency to leave the company when things have changed, and market values of the shares have increased. True that Gardell & Co enter companies that are "underperforming" according to their judgement, and that their entry is noticed by a market that expects forceful action and, thus, watch for signs of change that would justify an increased share value. This would be coupled with - as one respondent with experience of such an intervention told me – a "reduced" freedom of action for the CEO due to a downturn in key indicators.

Such activist interventions from "the market" will, no doubt, make the building of company culture more difficult. Several companies have witnessed the application of the most usual tactics by the interventionists – selling off non-core business – which is bound to have effects on the "community" of the corporation with a common history. Putting your money into an investment in the remaining (single) "core business" may look promising for a while, but if that business is made "leaner", and if it has a world leadership in a particular market, there are risks. With market dominance the possibilities to grow by acquisition are reduced as regulatory authorities become more watchful. Growth might only be possible to find by invention for new markets based in an excellent laboratory built for the core business. Any success in this respect will divert attention from the "core business" and introduce the conglomerate structure again….. back to square 1?

This core business idea seems to be the fashion in 2020 while internationalization by acquisition was in focus 1990. Then it was management by decentralization and 'trimming off' some non-core business (not too much). Now the catchword seems to be "consolidation" which means continued selling of non-core business and seeking extended cooperation with customers in improving their value-creation process. Supply-chain management could possibly be seen as a variety of that line of thinking. We see this trend in all kinds of business-to-business companies, and it has been there before even if it was not paid proper attention to in the 1990s. Looking back at the 1990 interview with Lennart Johansson about the strategic problems of SKF (ball bearings) I find an interesting account of how SKF struggled to gain orders to deliver "hubs" to the car industry, i.e., wheels with built-in (tightly sealed) ball bearings directly to the assembly line. Both Swedish truck companies (Scania and Volvo) have had success with built-in sensors that provide operating information to haulage customers that can be used to ensure that trucks earn money 24/7. Atlas Copco has a large part of its business in service contracts with automated production systems, etc.

A problem that has not been discussed in the 2020 interviews (but probably should have been) is the role of business models in today's "consolidated" structures. In the old days (1990) "the business model" seemed to serve well as a translation device between the diverse parts of the conglomerate and a central "financial" centre (Even if Percy Barnevik claimed that he read about 5000 profit/cost centre reports in ABB). But with a "consolidated" structure most of the diversity has already been eliminated and the strategic focus is to grow closer to the customers with all their particular details. The solution now – not much loved by those respondents that chose to comment – seems to be "integrated information systems. It might be that "company culture" gets lost in the process.

Chapter 12
What can culture do? Achieving ambidexterity

Ingress

Ronnie Leten, CEO of Atlas Copco, visited a distributor in the USA and was invited to dinner at the owner's house. It was a luxurious house! Ronnie felt curious and could not help asking "Where does all this wealth come from?" The answer was 'surprising'. "From Atlas Copco!" In my interview with him Ronnie exclaimed: "They were making more money than we did as producers!" The key was service (spare parts, repairs, maintenance). It was obvious, once you were confronted with the evidence, that Atlas needed to set up a service division. That would be a major undertaking! Acquisitions of importers and distributors, an inquiry with some customers in the mining industry suggested that there was a market for service contracts, especially in automated production ... one could build a case for a service division. The problems were to persuade the board that financing such a venture was profitable, and to shift the proud producer/engineering culture toward a customer service culture. The key to the first problem turned out to be the commissioning of a university study that showed that service is contra-cyclical in any economy. When sales of new machines are slow service increases as customers choose to keep the old machines running while waiting for better times. Changing the engineering culture was more of a long-term project.

Initiating or dealing with change

In complex and changing contexts one must be agile. This presupposes an ability to reconfigure standard or routine activities to meet surprising situations. (The non-surprising, e.g., "normal", situations are dealt with by these standards and routine activities.) For management such reconfigurations must be dealt with when surprises happen – or even before. When more than 90 % of your business is international - and in Business-to-Business – there will be surprises. Small and large ones!

Traditionally Swedish industry has solved the problem of adaption to changing local contexts by decentralization. That makes sense in a conglomerate. But when complexity increases and strong forces push toward information integration and supply management (to repeat: those respondents (2020) who mentioned "integrated information systems" (all) stated that they had not been of much use to them.), the problem of managing change seems to be different. The "perspective inside-out" and the "perspective outside-in" get more difficult to integrate. It is not immediately clear what a significant change in context will mean for operations. This is due to technological, informational, legal, social aspects that need to be considered.

When you are applying the "outside-in" perspective (market economics) you are likely to posit the changes in context as "facts", and the task is to work out the practical consequences for the inside (operations). Then, deliberation is a matter of "opening up" (Holmqvist, 2003) the idea (mental representation) of the organization to the possible impact of the observed changes (March, 1991 calls this 'exploration'). This task is made much easier (and riskier) if you reduce the number of aspects that are deemed worthy of consideration. It is therefore tempting to apply a reductionist perspective in a hierarchical structure – like waiting for the consequences to show up in financial reports. Large corporations with strong hierarchy will lose many opportunities and take defensive action too late because of this reductionist mechanism – to the extent that innovations happen in this reductionist perspective they era likely to emerge from a central laboratory (like in the 19th century). The problem in this "outside-in" perspective seems to be that possible opportunities abound, and to choose one before others will have to be done on limited factual grounds (hope… "take the plunge!").

If instead the "inside-out" perspective is applied (exploitation) there is a certain sense of security in that the initiative is "ours". We use our current technology, expertise, and knowledge to extend our business in "known" directions. The management culture is a given. Effort is more easily coordinated because of the ("natural") ego attribution. (Brunsson, 1976)

March (1991) discussed these twin activities of organizations – exploration and exploitation – in two (simple) models of organizational learning. One model assumes "mutual learning", the other assumes internal competition for resources and competences. His conclusion is that we should realize that exploration presupposes experimentation where outcomes are uncertain, distant, and often negative. Exploitation on the other hand often is, proximate and predictable.

> Thus, the distance in time and space between the learning and the locus for the realization of returns is generally greater in the case of exploration than in the case of exploitation, as is the uncertainty (March, 1991, p. 85)

March (1991) recommends a continuous influx of the "naïve and the ignorant" to promote organizational learning. Hedberg & Jönsson (1978) recommend "semi-confusing information" to promote questions (and answers). But order must be maintained even when the organization is adapting!

Consequences of a changing context for the design of control mechanisms

For a long time, management control has been modelled after Ashby's conception of the ultra-stable system (Ashby, 1960, p. 80 – 99) where (high frequency) signals between a controlling unit and the controlled unit are monitored by measurement of "critical variables". If the value of a critical variable falls outside control limits a "step-function" adjusts the way the controlling unit operates. This step-function adjusts until a stable state is reached. The mechanism will find stability if the interaction between the controlling and controlled units is much more frequent than the interventions from the step-function. This is how a thermostat works and it is how a budget-controlled department of our university works (or most other organizations). The system is ultra-stable. (Figure 3 above)

What I discovered in my interviews with business leaders, in 1990 as well as 2020, was that there is another type of monitoring that goes on in large corporations, and that this is a different philosophy/ logic in operation. Management teams monitor context to check whether the assumptions that form the basis for the current mode of management control are still valid. This is not an easy task since, as Bertrand Russel argued in an exchange with Frank Ramsey in the 1920s (Misak 2016), we often become aware of our beliefs only when they fail. (His example is a glass that seemed to contain beer but turned out to be a glass of tea. Blaahh!). This requires attention, and a sense of recognition of broken patterns. One is reminded of Goffman's (1974) "reframing", which is initiated by a" key" that helps the person understand a situation differently (Goffman's example is the child that thought the little otter attacked the big one, but sees the situation differently, when the adult says "They are playing"). "Semi-confusing" information (Hedberg & Jönsson, 1978) may cause questions that will demand explanations, and a better understanding emerges. This kind of monitoring does not use induction in explanations since there is usually no historical data to rely on – the observation of a new pattern is, after all, surprising. It is a matter of noting something new that seems relevant, but also that something is there that should not be there – it is worth a "second look" (Boltanski, 2011). This is the core of Pragmatism, "A surprising fact, C, is observed", and the search is on for "Inference to the Best Explanation". One could picture these two types of monitoring as the traditional management control idea of Figure 3 complemented with a monitoring in the form of context surveillance. These two together constitute the key to agility (Figure 4)

For the "surprising fact" to be registered as such the observer needs a trusted ally to ask, "Do you see what I see?", because the surprise that comes with this new observation raises risk (or opportunity) to new heights. Uncertainty is high, so one does not want to expose "brain ghosts" and "half-baked ideas" to people who will gossip. One might even consider talking to a superior too risky. A trusted person has demonstrated a sincere good will earlier and might also be deemed knowledgeable concerning the matter at hand. Over time that person may have been chosen as mentor in the task of finding the "Inference to the Best Explanation". The mentor and the mentee will probably use the tests discussed by Boltanski (2011) – truth, reality, existential tests – to verify hunches. When that explanation to the surprising fact is solid enough it is time to present arguments related to neighbouring "frames" (relevant knowledge areas, more distant colleagues, or even outsiders) – arguments that would provide "keys" that help the recipient reframe and embrace the new understanding. On that basis change will be initiated. Such change is likely to be experienced as a "step-function", i.e., a short circuiting that temporarily disrupts existing routines, since some old routines will be replaced by new ones. Learning new routines by habituation starts. It is this "short-circuiting" that makes agile adaption to the "surprising fact" possible. Such adaption also includes a conscious choice of a (possibly) narrower context to which learning is focussed.

Discussion

In complex environments and with not enough time - a situation described quite often in my interviews with industrial leaders - one can, at best, hope to set the organization on a new learning path. Such a new learning path presupposes increased attention and responsible response to emerging problems by front line managers, which, in turn, requires good communication. The problem I experience, which has grown more pregnant through the analyses of the interviews, is how does one chose, wisely, what path to embark on when information is uncertain in every conceivable dimension? In seminars we would talk about "brain storming" as a method to generate new ideas, but Mumford (2000) tells us that leadership based in extensive experience is the key in leading creative groups. An experienced leader can help the team avoid "cul-de-sacs" and encourage promising ideas.

The Pragmatists (Misak, 2016), argue that judgment should be grounded in the "practical consequences" of ideas. The agility of managerial action thus hinges on bridging the abyss between "great ideas" and "good practice". We can see, from studies of the refugee-crisis in Vienna 2015 (Kornberger et al, 2019) that bosses of different administrative units soon realized that they could do no valuable work from their offices. They had to go out to the "hauptbahnhof" and other places where the action was, and most of the time, "bless" the practices that were emerging. They could then "see" the practices and judge their fitness for the current purpose against relevant memory structures (and by listening).

The interview material is structured in the form of stories about many "learning events". It is not exactly like Flanagan's (1954) "critical incidents technique". His method of collecting stories from pilots about incidents where their competence was put to severe tests to build a basis for the design of improvements in pilot training programmes is closer to 'routine learning' of relatively new recruits than I have seen in my interviews. Furthermore, the respondents tend to tell me about successes that they have had in their career (rather than failures), and which represent management principles that they favour (good examples).

There were very few stories about failures. The teller of the story was also at the centre of events. There is almost nothing "objective" about them. But it is the narrative of the incident that gives it meaning, and that meaning can be abstracted to a principle of good management. A curious aspect of these stories about learning incidents is that they seem to have multiple "key" (Goffman, 1974) functions.

If the respondent talks about a modernization of the production system in an acquired US firm the solution will be "similar" in many respects to existing plants in Europe only transplanted to the US context – the "key" is a whole configuration of parts. But if the project is to build a service division by acquiring a large number of family-owned distributors with service functions (among other things), the number of "keys" may be numerous. Then part solutions that will be fitted together to form a proposition for a new strategy. It will be far more complex and need input of several competencies, each provided with appropriate "keys" This will elicit inputs from several knowledge areas in the collective construction of a pragmatic solution.

So, it is not because they are 'similar' to the current situation that keys become useful in deliberation about the problem, but because multiple "keys" emerge that can serve as building blocks in the construction of a fresh understanding, together, of the current situation – including the "surprising fact, C," that has been observed. In this way the century-old philosophy of pragmatism, hinted at several times above, (see Misak, (2016)) can serve as template for early phases of corporate re-orientation or as a more conventional agility-enhancing tool. (And I suspect it fits well into sustained sustainability development efforts as well.)

The critical factor when it comes to venturing into action based on this new understanding is a shift from "environment attribution" to "ego attribution". We discussed this extensively in the "Gothenburg school" – so named by Henry Mintzberg – when studying organizations in crisis in the 1970s (Hedberg & Jönsson, 1978, Jönsson & Lundin 1977, Brunsson, 1976). 'Environment attribution' signified the attribution of causes of the organization's success or misfortune to the context. This attitude generated a risk consciousness that fostered calculations, a need for more data, and hesitation about action, which in turn took energy and attention away from the actual carrying out of action.

'Ego attribution' on the other hand attributed success (and possible failure) to our own efforts. We are in control! It is up to us! The energy and attention applied in implementation helps to overcome doubt and mobilize team efforts. Yes, wishful thinking is involved, but the mobilization of effort compensates. The agile organization will fail sometimes – better not put all the eggs in one basket. But without the mobilization that generates a focus on the implementation of a common project at the right time agility will evaporate. The balancing of an "open up" attitude and a "focusing" attitude seems to be the crux of the management deliberation process that the successful managers I interviewed in 1990 and 2020 have in common even if the context was different (and changing). Let me illustrate:

Hans Werthén, the legendary leader of Electrolux, stated in the 1990 interview: "You have to keep an (loyal?) opposition" as a managerial principle. That opposition serves to improve the quality of team deliberations by exposing weaknesses in arguments that must be shored up and scrutinizing the logic in conclusions. Still, the criterion seems to be that the proposed action "makes sense". The courage to "take the plunge" and initiate action, despite some uncertainties, probably comes by training to act in new contexts. This is part of the mentoring that comes with being sent into diverse missions in the early career. Several of the respondents in the 2020 interviews – more so than in the 1990 series – stressed that they felt that this new assignment was beyond their competence, but somehow, they managed to cope – "swim in the cold water" as one said. Jan Carlzon (1990), as described in the summary above stated at the first meeting with employees (in the hangar) that he did not know much about the airline business and that they had to help him. He felt a "surprising" response, which probably set his later "obsession" with delegation of authority to the front-line people in motion at moment. Ronnie Leten (2020) (also as described in the summary above) "saw" the benefits of organizing a service division when a distributor told him that his "wealth" came from Atlas Copco. But Leten realized that he had to construct a convincing case for such a complex project to be presented to the board. It was a major and complex undertaking with significant risks. Too complex to present in one presentation. One must divide it up in suitable portions and apply the good old tradition of "soaking"[1]. Much of the stories about how to present a change proposal to the "principal" (the board, division head, target costing committees, etc.) seem to point toward the problems of communicating proposals for

[1] Leten seemed to like the Swedish word for it - "Blötläggning" (soaking) – preparing (in the old days) for the monthly "Big Laundry" by soaking the washing in big wooden vessels overnight. The legendary industrial leader, Marcus Wallenberg, seems to have coined the expression.

solutions under conditions of complexity. The easy way out, as mentioned, is to reduce the presentation to cash flow forecasts and key indicators – "trust me! I can deliver this!" – but one might reflect on an approach that may enhance the propensity to change in the mind of "principals".

I will first discuss a phenomenon brought up by several respondents, 1990 as well as 2020, mentoring, and then something picked up in literature about how the brain "works". Then it is time to return to pragmatism as the philosophy of it all.

Chapter 13
Mentorship, control structures, and changing contexts

Ingress

The once a conglomerate Hexagon has had a remarkable development. I have a special feeling for that company since it was one of the cases in my PhD thesis in 1971. There was a group of about 10 so called "Investment Development Companies" most of them initiated by banks. The business idea was to acquire family-owned firms where were problems with the generational change, develop them, and introduce them on the stock market. Focus was on the banks' customers and regional development. That was not a very workable idea since financing growth by loans at the same time as acquisitions were paid for new shares that required dividends that puts a strain on liquidity. One of these companies was Hexagon, a conglomerate of 30-40 companies, now (2000) in trouble, and owned by Melker Schörling, who was headhunting for somebody to turn it around. Ola Rollén, who had had a rapid career as trouble shooter in steel was invited to meet Schörling. It was a "nice" meeting, trust emerged, and Rollén was given a free hand to find the best way ahead. Rollén sold off most of the subsidiaries based on the principle that Hexagon must be "very good" on something. He acquired Brown & Sharp and focused that company on geo-measurement technology. Leica Geosystems in Switzerland was a big bite. Melker had to be persuaded about the "arrangement". Ola mentions a mapmaking company in Copenhagen and tells the story about how the police in one of the major cities in the USA uses the resulting system to direct and communicate with a large number of units patrolling the streets. He talks warmly about Melker's role of letting himself be persuaded, delegation of authority paired with responsibility, telling people what is wrong and allowing them to come up with solutions. Hexagon is, as far as I understand, a success story of daring leaps where several knowledge areas merge to joint solutions for customers. "Ego attribution" (We can do it! It is up to us!) compensates for uncertainty and complexity.

Normally one would think of mentoring as a kind of introduction to a job with the mentor being "appointed" by superiors to demonstrate and explain the operational aspects of the job. What I have described above is different. It is the mentee who chooses the mentor and the topic is support in deliberation, by questions, critique, and encouragement. There is a commitment to the wellbeing of the mentee in the relation and mutual trust.

There are several stories of trust relations – that kind of mentoring - between CEOs and large private owners. Relations that seem to release energy that is transmitted throughout the organization, and where further delegation of authority with appended responsibilities tends to reduce the need for detailed short-term reporting. (A phone call with "How are you doing?" will do.).

A different kind of mentoring, more frequent in the life stories, is the mentorship that young promising talent meets, and that helps in sorting out complex issues. That kind of mentor is a senior "speaking partner" to turn to with the eternal question "Do you see what I see?" and to work out new understandings of "surprise observations". This kind of mentorship stimulates cross-hierarchical communication, since young people in career progress will move between departments and postings while keeping in contact with mentors. I have come to believe, through working with the interviews, that these cross communications are more important for improvement work than I used to think. They are part of an "exploration" attitude towards the world (March, 1993), when the mind is open to new observations. Call this kind of exploration mentorship. The key seems to be the change in perspective that such cross contacts can offer.[1]

What could be meant by exploration mentorship?

The phenomenon in focus now is mentorship that supports the mentee in making sense of a "surprising observation, C" and constructing an action project that both "explains" the observation and designs a proposed solution. The dialogue between the two – mentor and mentee – encloses the shift from an "exploration" (open mind) attitude to an "exploitation" one (focus on the task ahead). That is the intellectual difficulty here.

When you ask people to tell you the story of their life with emphasis on learning episodes, you are bound to get singular narratives of situations where the respondent believe they learned something. Such narratives, interesting as they may be, do not constitute scientific evidence according to current doctrine. But I still remember learning about how markets work, in my first course in economics, by way of people's "utility maximization", thinking 'yes, that makes sense! So, it must be true!' I don't believe that "on faith" (that it makes sense) nowadays even if I have been on the lookout for solid evidence throughout my 50+ years of management research. Now McCloskey (2016) has shown, convincingly I think, that it was "just" rhetoric and ideas about bourgeoise dignity that drove the economic development in the late 19th century – that makes sense! What makes something "make sense" is that the arguments, based in facts and/or principles, hang together in mutual support. The "hanging together" comes from the narrative structure of the emerging proposition in question.

---

[1] The other kind, introducing the mentee to the routines of a certain job, with focus on these very routines, could be called "exploitation' mentorship.

Why this introduction in terms of arguments hanging together to make sense? Because I think that it is the essence of organizational (learning) life! – It is also the essence of the mentorship relations that criss-cross hierarchical structures in organizations, which in turn provide the seeds of change in relation to complex and fastmoving situations. That is why I have become convinced that mentorship is more important for organizations, especially big ones, than we (or at least I) have thought. Therefore, I have looked closer at the life stories in the 1990 as well as the 2020 interviews. The references to mentors are usually not very detailed – like that the mentor encouraged the respondent to take the job that seemed too demanding - but the fact that the respondent mentions them seems significant. These are my arguments for a new interest in mentorship and the dynamics of the mentor-adept relationship in a deliberation mode of management. My ambition at this stage can stretch no further than to show that they "make sense."

Definition: Mentorship[2] is to assume co-responsibility for somebody else's career, experience accumulation, and development of half-baked ideas. It is conducted by dialogue and a genuine interest from the side of the mentor to listen to, understand and advise the protégé.

Mentorship is, obviously, built on a trust relation and a difference in experience between the two parties. In a sense it transfers social capital between them. The most obvious benefit from mentorship is that adept is given an opportunity to discuss "half-baked" ideas and observations without risking "public shame" for thinking 'out of the box'. The mentor may look upon the adept as a project to be prepared for more complex tasks. Let me point to a few effects on

[2] The word stems from the legend that Odysseus left his son in the care of the goddess Athena who assumed the shape of Odysseus' friend Mentor.

(exploration) mentorship in a context where management as deliberation is in focus:

Mentorship provides "resonance" for individual managers who are in a process of building "practical identity"

Practical identity, defined as

> a description under which you value yourself, a description under which you find your life to be worth living and your actions to be worth undertaking, (Korsgaard, 1996, .p. 101)

should be understood as the "compass" whereby the individual, as a member of an organization, deliberates, speaks, and acts to justify membership and find self-esteem. The problem, as speech act theorists tell us, is that we cannot get to know who we are – our practical identity – until we act and see how others react to our action. There is a risk of negative reactions. We prefer to do our first probes of uncertain proposals with people we know wish us well, like a mother or a mentor. When we are in doubt, as we usually are when new ventures are considered, a show of interest and the right questions may encourage the protégé to develop the project further.

Mentorship stimulates an application of desire-independent rationality

As mentioned earlier, Searle (2001) argues for the need of a "desire-independent" rationality in social sciences. His arguments also apply to real organizations where members, by the very fact that they are members, are expected to act for the good of the organization. The solution Searle argues for relates to the fact that when we make a promise, statement of fact, or other "speech acts", we automatically include a **commitment** to the veracity of the statement. Without such a commitment social structure cannot be built and maintained. The person who speaks confirms his or her sincerity in being a member. If the statement turns out to be false that member loses in trustworthiness, and consequently, social capital. The use of lies is destructive to organizations because it eliminates meaning in communication. How should one understand the statement like "I am a liar!" – true or false? Other members cannot act with confidence on such "information" and are well advised to assume the worst. Mentorship builds on trust and, thus, is part of the foundation of organization. Mentorship may, and probably should, criss-cross the formal structure of the organization.

Mentorship provides opportunities to develop "reasons" à la Scanlon (2014)

He argues that a reason has the form of a relation - P is a reason for agent A to undertake action X under condition C. R(P,A,X,C). The components must "hang together" (make sense). This means that P is a well-formed argument, if A is a competent actor, X is an effective set of operational activities, and C are circumstances that are favourable to a successful outcome (including overcoming problems and obstacles). Most of the time this kind of reason, R, has the form of a narrative that shows how the components of R support each other. It serves justification (Boltanski & Thévenot, 2006).

By asking questions of clarification a mentor can direct the protégé's attention toward "missing links" in the first descriptions of newly discerned phenomena (threats or opportunities)

The first product of attention to the details of a situation is to notice that this is worth a "second look". By asking questions the mentor may help the protégé to take a "second look" at the links between arguments to come back with fully developed reasons. The mentor can push for coherence (Kahneman, 2011), which, in turn, is a criterion of "clarity of thought" (Misak, 2016)

Mentorship helps the protégé to bridge the gap between "thought" and "action"

Going into action is a singular event that includes a risk of failure, there is a need for an element of "passion" (Cooren, 2011) to take "the jump into the cold water" (as one respondent expressed it). By getting "positive feedback" from the mentor, the protégé can find the enthusiasm that generates enough energy to initiate action and succeed (Brunsson, 1976, Jönsson & Lundin, 1977).

Mentorship helps the articulation of a good explanation

As mentioned earlier (sorry for the repetition), the core issue in Pragmatism is this:

> The surprising fact, C, is observed.
> But if A were true, C would be a matter of course.
> Hence there is reason to suspect that A is true.
> (Quoted from Misak, 2016, p 41)

This translates to seeking an "Inference to the Best Explanation" (McCain & Poston, 2017), which is a current version of pragmatism that relates well to mentorship. The mentor engages in helping the protégé to find the Best Explanation. With management understood as "getting things done" every manager will face the question about what to do now all the time – the situation is complex, and time is short. Managerial experience (and promotion prospects) has to do with the work of forming a coherent conception of the situation – now. Complexity stems from the presence of multiple goal dimensions that must be dealt with simultaneously – not sequentially as standard rationality would have it. Inference to the Best Explanation is deliberation on means and ends simultaneously. The protégé will start the process by asking "Do you see what I see?" and when the observation of a factual C is ascertained the work of inferencing the Best Explanation may start.

Mentorship builds social capital

Mentorship builds social capital in the form of trust and good will in the joint evaluation of successful ventures which also discerns causal patterns. Mutual generosity in praise, and praise coming from others, is the raw material of trust. With trust, critique may even be appreciated. But the relation is vulnerable to breaches of trust, like when ideas are stolen, or power games played. Good will accumulates as expectations based on Best Explanations are confirmed by outcomes.

Mentorship in crises

When crisis strikes and an organization needs to find new ways to deal with its context such change may require that hierarchical structures are "short-circuited". In that case mentorship may be a route through which good ideas are relayed and developed. In general mentorship is likely to serve creative purposes as mentors/leaders, due to their more extensive experience, will be able to advice against (likely) "cul-de-sac"s, and encourage first steps in a promising direction (Mumford, 2000)

Mentorship and abductive reasoning

Mentorship provides a suitable environment for abductive reasoning in the pragmatic tradition (Misak 2016) as a method to deliberate on what to do now. Abductive reasoning is a risky business since it is likely to generate false starts, stupid proposals, and frustration. Just like when scientists construct work hypotheses and related tests and their required measurements of variables at the start of a scientific project. The advantage of abductive reasoning is that it generates constellations of variables that may provide "the best explanation" ("reflective equilibrium" (Scanlon, (2014), Rawls (1971)), which can thereafter be tested. I have claimed that one can only act "now" (true), but in reflecting together with a mentor (deliberation) prior to action one may, for example, "split" the concept of time while discussing what part of the set of acts that constitutes action should come first. In the same manner complexity, which is constituted by means as well as ends (at the same time) may also be "split" into constituent parts (in deliberation).

Team as collective mentor

It seems obvious that mentorship is different in the top management team where the CEO is the centre and members work as a kind of collective mentor, as compared to earlier stages in a career. The "team spirit" that can be found in a group of "equals" may be the expression of collective mentoring. For a younger person in an early career one may expect a stronger emphasis on trust in one chosen mentor, and possibly the relation reaches (and should reach?) across administrative orders.

If we accept that management is about getting things done, we also must accept that we should do the right thing. In view of complexity, which stems from the need to deal with several organizational goals at the same time under changing circumstances, management becomes a genuinely deliberative task. A deliberative task includes thinking, prioritizing in a particular situation, going into action, communicating, justifying, and being responsible for the consequences. In complexity nobody can claim access to all relevant information, so deliberation must mean dialogue with trusted others. This is where mentors fit in. They are not just there for introducing new recruits to the job, they need to be there in complex situations with uncertain consequences in judgment of what options there are and in justification of the chosen path (exploration mentorship). We need to know more about the role of mentors in complex problem solving through the career of managers. It is not so much, that they know better than the mentee, but that they provide "resonance", often in the form of questions that need answers, and that they are trusted (not to gossip about the crazy ideas of the mentee).

Chapter 14
Pragmatism: The essence of getting things done

Ingress

While Electrolux had its standard management control system at the centre of the integration and management of new acquisitions and it worked pretty well for home appliances, Leif Johansson had a different task when charged with the job of turning the Husqvarna motorcycle business around. It was an odd acquisition that had come as an extra together with the chain saw business that Hans Werthén fancied. It was necessary to reduce costs as well as finding a market niche. So Leif Johansson reduced the standard administrative staff and engaged motorcycle fans. The organization was "tuned" to discussions with qualified customers and the breakthrough came with the large order for battery-free motorcycles for the army.

For Dan Sten Olsson (DSO) social process aspects of the real estate business have been in focus for some time. He wants to help stabilize "exposed areas" (neighbourhoods with mostly rental properties, crime, bad school results, heavy social service demands, "resource-weak" immigrants). It is not just for social compassion, but because it is good for business. DSO knows that a stable area does not have as high a turnover as the exposed areas, which reduces cost, there is less repair work and general maintenance. If people are happy and stay, business will flourish. So he has stories to tell about outreaching activities, like partnering with the municipality to set up and run youth clubs, support schools, football fields etc. The effects are long term and indirect, setbacks occur, but DSO keeps arguing for acts oriented toward improving the context of the housing projects. He hinted in the 2020 interview that he was thinking about investing in schools (Mark! "Not to make money!") to improve neighbourhoods for those living there.

These two examples illustrate activities oriented toward the contexts – hands on, pragmatic – to improve the prospects, long term, for the business. To carry such things out, even with temporary setbacks, the organization needs people dedicated to effects beside the "bottom line". Pragmatic people who judge by the "practical consequences" as the new philosophical school, pragmatism, argued some 100 years ago (Misak, 2016)

The core of (scientific) pragmatism

The common understanding in Europe and large parts of the USA in the 19th century was that a scientific approach is built on induction, which means that you collect (historical) data and make pronouncements about the future on that (statistical) basis – given that the world will behave in the same way as before. That is a reasonable position to take concerning those parts of the world where laws of nature apply. It is less evident that it could apply also to those parts of the world where creative humans work hard to "beat the system" by offering a better choice to fellow humans than the one they had yesterday – or, for that matter, read the newspaper every day and behave accordingly.

The foremost philosopher in Cambridge at the turn of the century was Bertrand Russel. He was dead set against the idealists on the continent who argued that philosophy was about how to analyse ideas once they have entered the mind, and wanted to show that the realist approach, where the analysis was directly connected to reality and facts by direct access to reality via a non-distortive picturing of facts into the mind. In that way philosophers could give good advice to scientists. Wittgenstein was on the same track with his *Tractatus*

(1922) He had come to Cambridge in 1911 to study under Russel's guidance. Another important actor, beside John M Keynes, the economist who wrote a Treatise of Probability in 1921, was the young mathematics student, Frank Ramsey, whom we shall hear more of in the following account based on Misak (2016, 2020).

Pragmatism came to Cambridge in the 1920s

The philosophy of pragmatism travelled from Cambridge USA to Cambridge England primarily by way of the young mathematic/economist/philosopher Frank Ramsey "discovered" the foremost (but troublesome) American representative of the philosophy Charles Sanders Peirce. Peirce's only and short academic employment (lecturer in logic) was at John Hopkins university. He held the position for only 5 years. During that time, he had students like Dewey and Veblen. He was dismissed on the grounds that he had lived together with another woman before his divorce had been confirmed. Frank Ramsey was a busy person who assisted Bertrand Russel in getting his proofs right, translated Wittgenstein's *Tractatus* to English, and criticized Keynes for his "principle of indifference" (if there is no evidence to differentiate between outcomes, we should consider them equally probable). He died at the age of 27, a great loss to several academic disciplines. Here we will concentrate on his reasoning around "degree of belief".

The core idea of pragmatism in Peirce's version is that deliberation/ analysis starts from a (surprising) observation in search of a rule or a hypothesis that explains it. In evaluating candidates to such an explanation, the inquirer should consider the practical consequences of accepting that explanation. (For the academic researcher this amounts to considering what variables need to be included and how they must be measured.) This way of drawing (tentative) conclusions from an observation to a more general rule or hypothesis is called abduction. It differs from the more standard ways of logic, deduction, and induction, in that it allows new ideas. A problem here is how and why a person makes a "surprising" observation. Russel provides a solution in his suggestion that it is a matter of expectations failing. Expectations being based in beliefs, most of which are not present in our conscious mind most of the time but become "visible" to us when they fail. (Blaahh! I thought that glass of tea contained beer!)

Cambridge (England) was preoccupied with probability in the early 1900s. Keynes, Russel and Ramsey participated. Moore, the ethics professor, wrote about what is the meaning of "good". Keynes and Russel started from the question: "What is a good reason to believe that a proposition is true?" But they soon switched to the world view that probabilities are properties of nature that one can measure (in the form of frequencies). Pragmatism can be said to have started from that same question but stopped with the view that probability is more like the degree of belief (of the individual) that the proposition is true. Therefore "clarity of thought" was required, which meant using logic and facts and assume responsibility for the consequences of asserting that something is true. For Peirce the assertion that something is true is not only to say it, but also to do it (assume responsibility). Therefore, one must collect evidence <u>and</u> arguments. For him any doubt as to the truth of a belief is an irritation that prompts us to further investigation.

For Peirce a belief has three properties:

1) It is something that we are conscious of
2) It removes the irritation stemming from doubt
3) It established a disposition to act in our mind

Missing a (true) belief or a habit, given that you care about the matter, you have reason to inquire further about the issue (Misak, 2016, p 20ff).

What is this? A belief is something that we can and should reflect upon. If we feel doubt when doing so, we must, as responsible persons, make further inquiry until we have good reasons for our belief. If we are convinced that we have good reasons, we commit ourselves to act accordingly. Belief, thus, has a direct link to responsibility.

How do these abstract ways of thinking effect our conduct of our life in the real world – as researchers, leaders in organizations or investors? Well, a "belief" does not try to "define" the truth of that belief by further abstract propositions but is oriented toward **elucidation** (clarity of thought) by way of the relations that the belief has to facts and arguments, i.e., by inquiry. The ambition to elucidate aspects of the belief then becomes a driving (causal) factor in our pragmatism. We may claim that successful action based on that belief may become the basis for a rule of action (or habit) that we adopt while we accept responsibility for the consequences of our actions. We are ready to give an account of our actions. We cannot get access to "The Truth", but our beliefs can be sharpened and execution more effective by testing our beliefs in action. In the final analysis it is successful action (practical consequences) that confirms our beliefs, which, in turn, is the foundation of the set of rules that we call "good practice" (praxis).

We pre-test our beliefs by inquiry into their parts and relations against the background of a situation or a context we are facing. The parts are usually facts (observations) or relations between facts. In "economic" deliberations we often 'translate' these facts with the help of assumptions about the world (like "U- max", McCloskey, 2006) – assumptions that we seldom question – and guard ourselves against critique by adding "ceteris paribus" (other things unchanged) to our conclusion.

Take, as an example, the so-called marginal utility theory that was introduced by Menger (1871). This theory claims that markets reach equilibrium because individual actors continue to 'make deals' until they can no longer find ways to improve their utility by deal-making. In such a situation the marginal utility of further transactions is zero (or worse). Schumpeter (1954), who provided us with a history of economic analysis, points to the fact – with a certain irony – that in equilibrium, reached with the help of Smith's "invisible hand," there are no reasons for further business – the economy grinds to a halt. Yes but, we say, then somebody with a good idea about how to improve our life appears and demand increases again. We have another disequilibrium to set us in motion. But what was it that moved that creative individual to invent that good idea? Is there a "marginal utility" in not yet invented ideas?

Chandler (1977) pointed in his path-breaking book, "The Visible Hand," to the fact that the management structures that emerged in large corporations more than 100 years ago fundamentally changed the way large parts of the market economy works. There has been a "managerial revolution" that is hardly at all considered when economists make their calculations based on statistics gathered in accordance with the historical model of how the entrepreneurial economy functions.

Testing your own beliefs

We need, as responsible persons, to question arguments and test facts on which our beliefs are based – clarity of thought as Peirce advised. Boltanski (2011) provides some tools for that inquiry. Different approaches are needed depending on what the suspected problem (doubt) is. To see those differences, we need to distinguish between "the world" (out there, immense, and largely unknown) and "reality" (those parts of the world that we can describe and analyse with our current knowledge, concepts, and vocabulary. A phenomenon appears before us as understandable to the extent that we apply concepts and relations to it. (No! That is not a bullfinch! It is a robin singer. Look at the amber colour on its breast. Bullfinches are brighter red and robin singers have a narrow beak!)

Let me comment somewhat on the description of the bird just given. This is what troubled Wittgenstein when he was on his way to embrace (kind of) pragmatism in 1929-30 (Waismann & McGuinness, 1979). His original position had been that there is a perfect language (a first language) that philosophers use in their analysis of propositions by way of logic and symbols. But now, under criticism by Ramsey and others, he was on his way to conclude that our everyday language is the only one needed, because of its references to the world. Abstract analyses of propositions stated in the perfect, first language, do not lead anywhere, because they have been disconnected from the world. Hypotheses now should be understood as statements about the future that have not yet been proven true or false, but they are still with us. Hypotheses construct expectations that "work" or do not work. This can be tested.

Back to the testing of our own beliefs. Remember that the world is everything out there. Most of it unexplored and un-explained (like how we can feel "pain" or "happiness" (galia) as an emergent property of the "firing" of millions of neurons in out brain). If we are about to go into action, it is a good thing if our thoughts are "realistic". We need to put (translate) our beliefs into a language that helps us become aware of whether our expectations are "working" or not to focus on what it takes in terms of operations to carry out our emerging plan so we can learn.

A first step in testing that we, or rather our thoughts, have the proper connection to the world is Boltanski's (2011):

- "Truth test" which serves to confirm that something is correctly described and measured (a fact). Repeated application of that test confirms that there is a norm to be guided by. (Testing, now and then, of whether the norm is still valid is recommended.)
- "Reality test" is a test of relevance. It comes to use in situations where there are differences of opinion. It serves the purpose of comparing what "is" with what "should be". This test is notable because it distinguishes between the norm by which value is generated and judgment whether the activities under that norm really live up to the norm.
- "Existential test" deals with the issue of whether a part of "the world" which is so far not part of our "reality" should be included in "reality", and thereby be subject to rational analysis. (Rational arguments can only exist in "reality" as it is defined by our concepts, conceptions, tools of analysis and out language). The problem here is that for that part of the world that lies outside out current understanding of "reality" it is not possible to use "rational" arguments. So, the arguments for inclusion in our deliberations (in "reality) have to be value-based (ideological, emotional). One area where this is increasingly visible is in "sustainability", not because sustainability arguments are irrational in themselves, but because they have not been part of managerial discourse before. They must be entered into the discussion by, e.g., arguments of justice – we cannot allow ourselves to ruin the life conditions of future generations.

Closure

When the test confirms our understanding that the object of the test is indeed a fact (or a relevant value) we have closure, and further steps of inquiry can be taken. If the result of an existential test is that the "non-rational" argument has merit the whole line of reasoning will be re-evaluated against this background. Arguments will be re-aligned – and "gaps" identified. Doubt will initiate further inquiry. For this to be possible in an organizational setting, and when management is driven by the ambition to "get things done", it is necessary to abide by a desire-independent rationality (Searle, 2001). Only with such a communicative team rationality is it possible to insert new values or goal proposals in the deliberation. Such insertions will often be required when several knowledge areas are engaged in deliberation. The tool for achieving closure ("reflective equilibrium" (Rawls, 2001)) is the canonical form of a narrative (Cooren, (2000), table 1 p. 90 above). It is the willingness of the listener to fill in "gaps" in the emerging narrative with plausible assumptions that is promising for team-based deliberation. Also, the fact that the first and last part of the canonical form – "manipulation" (want to/have to) and "sanction" (reward/ punishment or commendation/critique) are the parts that accommodate value statements (or ideology). When a team (or someone in authority) sanctions a plan of action it also means a commitment to the reasonableness of the proposed action in this context. Members of the team (or the person in authority) with a practical identity as responsible persons, commit their reputation as worthy members. Social capital, part of the organizational culture, is at risk or stands to be enhanced (Hope vs anxiety). (Share-holders stand to lose money, but they are outsiders at this moment of deliberation.)

"Closure" does not relate to "truth" as much as to the (free) will to act. When we have good reasons to believe that this is the right thing to do, we act. To illustrate the meaning of this statement I return to my early youth:

As a kid I borrowed a book at the library called "Science for Children" or something like that. In it there was a story about Dr

Einstein and the Theory of Relativity. Dr Einstein was on his way home from his job at the Patent Office in Geneva. He entered the back of the tram going down the (straight) Main Street and looked back at the clock on the church tower. It was 4 o'clock. Now imagine that the tram travelled at the speed of light. If that was true, then the hands of the clock would show 4 o'clock for ever. The light showing the movement of the hands of the clock would never reach the tram! So, the truth of measurements is dependent on the conditions under which they are taken. Wow! I had (sort of) understood the Theory of Relativity! It was the narrative that made that understanding possible – not mathematical formulas. Not that it had much effect on my football game which was the important part of life at that time.

In a modern corporation the members of the board represent the owners and this balance between reasonable hope and considered risk applies to them as representatives. Their role will normally be to let themselves be persuaded (or not) by the presentation of the management team, ask questions of clarification, set off time for further inquiry, and then assume responsibility – inside-out – for the consequences of the proposed action plan. In this sense the board assumes responsibility for the first and the final part of the narrative ("manipulation" – we want to/have to, and "sanction" – this is commendable action). The middle part of the narrative ("competence" and "performance") is taken on trust that the management team will be able to carry out the project with available resources. (one should note that it is the intangible properties of the proposal – "hope" (Lear, 2006) and "passion" (Cooren, 2011) - that carry the project across the abyss between "thought" and "action").

To complicate things one step further we should contemplate the shift in "intentionality" that takes place when we go from thought to action. Searle (1983) discusses the differences between the Continental conception of "intentionality" and the British one. In the Continental conception attention is focused on the immediate action.

If I want to scratch my nose I watch the movement of my arm, hand, and finger directly so my mind can guide action towards the nose. In the British conception attention is on purpose and goal. British thinking and Continental doing. If I have understood Searle's description correctly there will be plenty of causes of misunderstandings between Continental and British philosophers! Ideally, the crossing of the abyss between "thinking" and "acting" mentioned above must include a shift from the British conception (keep focus on purpose) to the Continental one (keep focus on doing what is required to fulfil purpose). To take that "plunge" is described in many ways in the "learning events" of the life stories of my respondents (1990 and 2020).

The pragmatic aspect of deliberation

Imagine that we have a resolution that this is worth doing (Korsgaard, 1996, Klamer, 2016). What then? As mentioned, Peirce, argued that we must consider the practical consequences when judging what is appropriate action, and that doubt drives (causally) further inquiry. Ramsey, who was engaged in the discussion on truth and probability in Cambridge at the time, picked up the thought that "degree of belief" has effects on inquiry as well as action (Misak, 2020). It seems to me that the disagreement in Cambridge about what is meant by "belief" or "truth" generated unnecessary debate. A metaphor about a walker that arrives at a crossing with no road sign and nobody to ask for direction, will illustrate. Peirce (1893, in Collected Papers (1931 – 1958), no 4, p. 57) was first to use it. Should the walker turn right or left? His solution is that the walker can chose either way as a provisional hypothesis but be on the lockout for somebody in the fields that she could ask for direction[1]. Russel (1921) saw this as an unacceptable confusion of

[1] James (1907) had understood "belief" as true if the practical consequences of having that belief are good.

the fact that action originates in the hypothesis and the belief in the truth of the hypothesis. That something "works" does not mean that it is true! Keynes (1921), who had argued that probability should be looked upon as a reason to believe that a statement is true pointed out in a letter (1926) that he had found reluctance among students to abandon "some variant" of frequency theory, and that he would not be surprised if they proved right. Ramsey's (1926) solution to the problem of action under vague or probabilistic knowledge was to require that that degrees of belief should be consistent. This consistency requirement between degrees of belief - given available evidence – a heritage from Thomas Bayes a clergyman whose theory of probability was published posthumously in 1764 – is the key. If, and when, new evidence becomes available, the practical man should re-assess his beliefs (under the law of consistency).

When a person has re-assessed his beliefs under the law of consistency, she or he has reached a kind of saturation that late Kantian philosophers (Rawls, (1971, 2001), Scanlon (2014)) have called "reflective equilibrium". There he or she stands with an understanding of the situation based in available evidence and arguments that are deemed relevant. Now it is time to make up one's mind. Hirschman (1970) offers three options:

Exit which means that "membership" is abandoned, which is discrete in the sense that one does not have to provide any reasons for breaking up the relationship. In the complex environment of a large company "exit" (with a lower-case e) may simply mean that a specific aspect of the company's business is not relevant to consider due to the current priorities (reduction of complexity by way of ignoring certain values).

Voice, according to Hirschman (1970), is to criticize and point to needs for improvement. In the case of analysis of a prospective acquisition it may be argumentation for further investigation. Is there some aspect of this that we have not yet analysed? Are there other sources of information?

Loyalty is a kind of satisfaction with the situation even if one could wish for something better. Some aspects of a proposed solution may be so promising that it is worth to "endure" bad values on some variables. A member has so much "invested" in the company that he or she decides to stay. There is a time aspect in this. Hope that a temporary setback will be followed by good times may justify a decision to "stay on" for now.

Deliberation by communication

Faced with uncertainties like the ones describe above – complexity and lack of time – one needs help from friends. I have mentioned mentors, but there is also a need for input from other areas of knowledge. To establish connections between areas of knowledge we need narratives that provides "keys" between frames of reference. Thereby mutual re-framing can be achieved. One's partners in communication concerning the meaning of a surprising observation will ask questions of relevance to them until a plausible narrative about the situation and the action required is achieved (reflexive equilibrium). My own experience from participant observation (Jönsson, 2004) is that this "understanding" can be quite different for different members, due to their different areas of expertise. But the "common understanding" is tolerable also for those who are not very enthusiastic about it. They can act to support the common project because they feel they are in control of their own part of the project ("ego attribution") – and trust others to do their part. In this way the practical identity/internal reasons connect to the common endeavour. There is a narrative for the common project and a personal narrative on how the personal practical identity participates (competently) in it.

On that basis action will be initiated. The change is likely to be experienced as a "step-function", i.e., a short circuit that temporarily disrupts existing routines, since some old routines will be replaced by new ones. Learning new routines by habituation starts. It is this "short-circuiting" that makes agile adaption to "surprising observations" possible. Shifts in intentionality from internal reasons (practical identity) to implementation of plans (external reasons), from an exploring mode to exploitation (March, 1991, Jönsson & Lundin, 1977) occurs. This "toggle" between internal and external reasons (Williams, 1979) is sometimes visible in my respondents' shifts in logics as they give their account of the event.

The ultimate challenge – Sustainability/stewardship

In the interviews there was a marked increase in the mention of sustainability issues in the accounts. In the coding of the accounts sustainability in a broad sense was noted by references to all three context dimensions (environmental, social, economic) in the same account. However, the entry points to sustainability differed.

I have already mentioned how Dan Sten Olsson provided an elaborate set of arguments about the relations between the dimensions in his account of how resources spent on the environment, social activities (youth clubs), schools, encouraged tenants to stay and help stabilize the area (and lower costs related to tenant turnover and maintenance).

Lennart Evrell, CEO of Boliden, gave an interesting account of the plans for the restauration of the site after a gigantic open-pit copper mine (Aitik) is going to be closed (current application has set that time to 2046). The sustainability department has a plan that includes turning the pit into a (deep) lake, hiking routes for leisure time activities like fishing and camping. When the plans were presented to the regional city council the chairman asked how long it will take for the pit to fill up into a lake. The answer was. "About 200 years"..... 'And if we lead the nearby stream into it?' "150 years". This illustrates the shift in time perspectives that are needed in deliberations about improvements of the environment. Carina Hansson, CEO of Estrella (chips) talked about being keen to hire immigrants from the neighbourhood to work in production, but it was necessary, for safety reasons, that they had adequate knowledge of Swedish in a largely automated production system. Support of the school and a nearby half-way house, and other activities was part of the cooperation with the municipality. However, the differences in logics, time perspectives, and the meaning of words – tend to get in the way of orchestrated action toward sustainable communities.

The discourse on sustainability is chiefly based in a thought model of natural science. Climate change, how to save electricity now that Russian gas does not flow into Europe[2] any longer, wildfires, declining fish populations, are debated in media. The experts are scientists who point out that, according to the latest predictive model, the target set in the latest climate conference will not be met in time. Stronger measures in the form if laws and regulations are required. It is abstractions like "government", "industry" or "tourists" that should change its/their ways. This is a complex area of regulation where "experts" (in one knowledge area) claim a right, by their expertise, to regulate large parts of society – much like economists and jurists have worked indefatigably to regulate free trade and capital movements since the 1930s (Slobodian, 2018). But

---

[2] In Sweden we do not use much natural gas since we have plenty of hydroelectric power, but nowadays our electricity grid is connected to the European one and "the market" determines prices. When they go up in Germany people in southern Sweden will be hit by price hikes not included in their budget. Not so many decades ago people in the north complained that the southerners did not pay enough for the electricity produced by the northerners..... Then the government decided to close nuclear plants (like the Germans) most of them located in the south.... So, we look out the window every morning to see if the windmills will stabilize the price today … it's a mess.

there is a long distance from abstract (even if urgent) principles down to practical action on the ground.

There is hardly any "discourse" on stewardship. The occasional article in media occurs about what "you" can do to help saving the climate, but little about the moral aspects of individual conduct. A steward is, according to Oxford dictionaries, somebody who is charged to care about something on behalf of somebody else. The very definition of the concept brings in the long term, Humanities and arguments about how to be a good citizen. There are the matters of "free will" and responsibility, and the matters of competence, resources and know how – and there is the matter of "desire-independent rationality" (Searle, 2001). A steward must be a steward out of free will, and judge action in view of the benefits for the principal (the community). He or she must be competent in judgment concerning the complexities of the problem and should be provided with adequate resources to carry out her or his duties. (Mark that stewardship to a large extent deals with duties.)

The logics are, thus, different in arguments about sustainability and stewardship respectively. They do not mix well. Participants in the debate tend to relate to power. Few are persuaded. Well… it is not difficult to understand that the climate is getting worse, but somebody else should do something about it. As mentioned Kahneman et al (2021, chapter 28) points to two basic approaches to regulation of an activity area: standards and rules. If rules are used, focus is on measurement. If we want to reduce "reckless driving" we define this road as a 50 km/hour road, put up a sign, and the police can focus on measuring speed (rather than whether the driving was actually reckless). With standards as the regulating device there is a law saying that reckless driving is not accepted, and the police is charged with judging whether the driver was reckless under the circumstance (which is difficult). The problem with that approach (standards) to "reckless driving" is that the courts (another area of knowledge) demand proof and apply precedent, which pushes regulatory practices toward "rules" – words get in the way of collective and individual judgement since they are given meaning in context.

But there remains the option to "switch" between incompatible logics by way of communication that can relate to more than one logic. A precondition is that we (partly) abandon our preference for **concepts** in favour of **conceptions**. This because with a 'conception' – an understanding of the situation to which a concept may apply – it is possible to change one's mind by reconfiguration of that understanding. A concept is, by way of its definition, a premise for deductive (or inductive) reasoning. It cannot be changed without invalidating the analysis. In a complex problem area, stable definitions are rare.

When we work under a particular academic discipline, part of our competence is to know the definitions of the variables, how to measure properly, and the forms of calculation. The definition of concepts is at the heart of analysis.

When we work with practical matters – getting things done, like weeding in the garden – action is always taken in context. The circumstances determine, to a large extent, what can be judged as meaningful or successful action. A conception is the understanding of this situation in this context. It points to action in that context rather than a formal calculation or deductive logic given definitions and formal rules.

The "switch" between logics through communication is likely to come by "re-entry" of narratives cast in the respective frames of the participants. The narrative of each side will contain "keys" for reframing on either side. Such "keys" will connect to the other participants' narratives and build bridges toward common understandings. After some back-and-forth – it is not primarily "feedback" but rather" re-entry" of adapted narratives - a seemingly pragmatic resolution is arrived at oriented toward successful action.

What does it take to "switch" between logics, language games, communities of learning, discourses, etc?

After pondering all these "life stories" told by prominent industrial leaders I believe that it is possible. Some of my respondents were obviously symbols of the culture of their organizations (Jan Wallander, Jan Carlzon, Percy Barnevik, Hans Werthén, Lennart Johansson, Leif Johansson, Dan Sten Olsson, Ola Rollén). Some were part of the 1990 series of interviews, some were from 2020. Over those 30 years much has changed – I summarized this as an increase in complexity and a compression of time – and there is an increased tendency in 2020 to include constellations of people in accounts of "learning events". Most conspicuously there are examples of pairs of leaders (large owner plus CEO) where it seems like the holder of the role of the owner is to let himself be persuaded by the CEO, and, when that happens, give the project his blessing. This is probably not a particularly unusual situation – as thesis advisor to many Ph.D. students over the years (with a lead principle to let the study be the student's project) I have often assumed the role to be the one to persuade.

Sometimes there are more than two participants in deliberation, which opens further dimensions, like attention directing, dealing with multiple values, as well as a changing operational technology. One wonders how it is possible, intellectually, to manage effectively under such a regime. In academia we attack complex problems by reducing dimensions and variables to something that fits our calculative practices. We formalize to such an extent that it guarantees that our conclusions are true (given the premisses… which we tend to forget after a while). But that does not work in a "get-things-done" setting where you act towards an "unreduced" world. In such a world "surprises" will happen, and they will have to be explained to correct the premises on which previous deliberations were founded. I will try to give an account of what comes to mind when pondering what is required to cope with changing complexity in organizations. Organizational culture may be seen as a carrier of its coping capacity, much like consciousness serves the individual. The problem is that consciousness as well as organizational culture must be considered emergent properties of the body in question. "Emergent" means that the phenomenon comes about as a result of interaction between many variables in context, but is not reducible to those variables.

Speculating about how organizational culture is initiated and grows I have been inspired by the comments by Searle (2001) on Edelman (1992). Searle is obviously impressed by Edelman's admittedly speculative reasoning about how consciousness is possible, but he is somewhat disturbed by a lack of clarity in Edelman's text at times.

The problem that philosophers and neurobiologists debated was the matter of "qualia". Searle (p. 97ff) gives an example to illustrate what qualia is: Do the experiment to pinch the skin on your left forearm between the thumb and forefinger of your right hand. What happens? First the pinch sets up a series of neuron firings beginning with the sensory receptors of your skin, that go up through the spine via a region called tract of Lissauer, and then into thalamus and other basal regions of the brain. The signal then went into the somato-sensory cortex and perhaps other cortex regions. A few hundred milliseconds after the pinch something else happened – something you don't need neurobiologists to know. You felt a mildly unpleasant pain. It is purely subjective (others cannot feel your pain), and it is ontological (It is there! You don't have to learn what it is). The feeling of pain is a subjective (first-person) experience, while the mode of existence of the firings up through the nerve system to the brain have an objective third-person existence that can be mapped by others. That feeling of pain is an example of the "qualia" that remains to be explained.[3] Nagel's (1974) "What is it like to be a Bat?" is standard reading in philosophy.

It is obvious that the feeling of pain (consciousness) needs to be explained by the workings of the real parts of the body, but how does "qualia" emerge from those firings of neurons? Is my satisfaction with understanding Searle's text the same as somebody else's? Probably not. My knowledge of philosophy is limited. (Like most philosophers I have read seem to have little knowledge of management in large organizations). Edelman (1992) lists the requirements that must be met for a biological system (like our nerve system) to produce consciousness – I bring this up because I believe that something similar could be said about "organizational culture" (if we think about it as a "brain" that must detect and respond to a complex and changing environment):

1. It must have a memory, which in Edelman's version is an active memory able to re-categorize against the background of previous categorizations.
2. It must have a system for learning. For Edelman this includes not just memory but also value – an ability to value some stimuli over others.
3. It needs to be able to distinguish self from non-self.
4. It must have a system for categorizing successive events in time and for forming concepts.
5. There must be ongoing interactions between the system under 4. and the systems described above (points 1 – 3)
6. Most importantly, there must be a set of "re-entrant"[4] connections between the special memory systems described

[3] In economic texts the term we often use is "intrinsic"

[4] This is a concept often used in computer science to signify a function that can be used for more than one task concurrently.

in points 1 – 5 and the anatomical systems (eyes, ears etc) that are dedicated to perceptual categorizations.

With these points (as summarized by Searle, 2001, chapter 3) we might have "primary consciousness". This is a necessary pre-condition for developing higher-order consciousness that not only feels and perceives but also is able to make the self-nonself distinction. This latter ability can only come from social interaction. A tall order, indeed!

Edelman arrives at the conclusion that science cannot tell us why warm feels warm. The problem of "qualia" is unsolvable for science with its requirement for generality because no two people will have the same qualia. (This is so because one of Edelman's premises is that the group of neurons (millions) dealing with one task, say recognition of green, is established by **selection** rather than by design. The groups of neurons that do not come to use are – in time – eliminated.) Individuals will differ.

I believe organizations can develop a "culture" that is partly like "consciousness" because the "re-entrant" pathways that Edelman (and Searle?) post as necessary conditions for higher order consciousness, and that it can be traced in an organization and thereby managed (at least in a longer perspective). The re-entrant pathways could run through mentorship relations, beside the ordinary hierarchical routes of communication (couldn't they?).

If so, every member of the organization should have a mentor and be a mentor! While hierarchical communication builds on authority or power, the mentor-mentee communication is based in trust. The hierarchical boss is likely to suspect conspiracies among mentor networks but will overcome these suspicions by also being a mentor/mentee. With mentorship built into the "practical identity" (Korsgaard, 1996) of each member, communication in that network will assume an ethical dimension that is essential for the organization's dealing with complexity and lack of time because values and operational aspects must be dealt with simultaneously. (Note that I place "practical identity" at centre stage here!)

Some leaders have taken extra measures to foster good communication, and thereby avoiding misunderstandings, by writing down statements about the values this organization is supposed to live by (I am not talking about the "value base documents" that many organizations produce and publish nowadays, not least our university, which are worked out by communications experts and seems to serve PR-purposes rather than ethics.). Three respondents discussed such documents explicitly. Jan Wallander (interviewed 1990) went public in 2002 (Wallander, 2002) with the principles he lived by during the reformation of the company culture in Handelsbanken from the early 1970s, with its stress on personal responsibility and matching mandate to take decisions. Since then, I have learned that there is a booklet of principles that is edited now and then, especially when a new CEO is appointed and is given an opportunity to endorse the culture as well as make statements about his/her own reform ambitions. Percy Barnevik brought up his "bible" spontaneously and promised that I would get a copy (against a pledge to keep it to myself), but he did not deliver (it was, after all an oral promise in an evening interview with an overly busy executive (Jönsson & Strannegård, 2014, Chapter 13). He, as well as Wallander, was a great believer in decentralization and local mandates to act on local information under personal responsibility. One should note, however, that he was also an ardent reader of the latest periodic reports of the more than 5000 profit or cost centres (at the time of the interview, kept in the briefcase always with him. After the interview (2020) with Dan Sten Olsson I have learnt that he keeps a "White Book", that he edits now and then, with principles he pledges to live by and expects other managers to do as well. At the interview itself

Olsson said that he strives to build a "forgiving" organization, meaning that people are encouraged to take reasonable risks in their daily (responsible) work. Jan Carlzon (1986) has written a best-selling book.

From the interview context it is clear to me that those texts (and others that have not been brought to my attention) serve to establish accountability in the sense that membership in the organization includes a readiness to give good reasons for one's own action, and the principles of those texts also bind the principal in the same way. It is a commitment that becomes part of a person's "practical identity".

Part III

Concluding remarks

Chapter 15
What does this mean for management as deliberation?

The driving force of management as deliberation is laid down in the practical identity of the organization's members. Membership carries with it a duty to act for the good of the organization (stewardship). Membership also requires an alignment of the individual's persona with the aims, culture, and regulations of the organization. This sounds "foreign" in an era of individualism and neoliberalism. Individualism (these days) is closely related to egoism. This status has been reached over decades of emancipation since the Enlightenment period (Modernism). That conception is a necessary building bloc in the construction of "economic man" since the time of the Austrian microeconomics more than 100 years ago. But it is at odds with the descriptions I got in both sets of interviews. The most common answer to the question on what has made Swedish corporations so successful in international competition has been "we respect the other person; we listen to the other". Confusing to an economist who has 'unity of command' as load star! How else could a company be "entrepreneurial"? React to price signals? Maximize utility?

When one hears "respect for the other" as an explanation for success, one can, of course, dismiss such statements as "propaganda" or "self-delusions", but when they are uttered by people in leading positions in industry with distinguished careers one should pay attention. One comes to think of Hayek, the influential neoliberal economist. He did not go well together with the people in the Economics Department at Chicago University who strived to form conceptions of economic problems that allowed analysis and mathematical models. Hayek turned increasingly to metaphors as "proofs" of his arguments after his opus on "the Constitutions of Liberty" (1960). He stuck to his conviction that the market is "unknowable" by the actors. Market actors react to "price signals" in order to 'survive' rather than to maximize utility (Slobodian, 2018, chapter 7). This made the metaphor of a 'shoal of fish' quite useful. None of the individual fish in the shoal knows what it is doing and why, but they still move in concert to avoid hunting predators. They have learnt to move at a given distance from their neighbour. It is routine and it serves them reasonably well.

Given, as I have repeatedly claimed, that increased complexity and lack of enough time has made management more difficult and that communication is the probable solution, individualism must be redefined. It must be something like the "practical identity" Korsgaard (1996) discusses. When my respondents point to Swedish managers' willingness to listen to the other as a major cause of their companies' international success one should listen and think. That kind of individualism – respect for the individual – (not a winner/looser conception) can be expected to steer toward a value-based economy (Klamer, 2017). With increasing complexity, the need for tools to differentiate between important values and less important ones increases. The more powerful the technologies at hand, the more important to do "the right thing" when we apply them. The more we realize that many knowledge areas must be engaged in managing things the more important to listen to the other and apply reason (in the real world). That kind of individualism - respect for the other – links to loyalty to the good of the organization via mentorship understood as communication with others having different experiences and knowledge bases, and membership.

Such communication presupposes trust in the good will of the other, which facilitates the use of mentorship relations across hierarchical structures (multi-channel communication).

	TRUST	
INDIVIDUALISM	MENTORSHIP	LOYALTY
	MEMBERSHIP	

Figure 1 (again). *The dimensions of "Practical Identity"*

The individual's dilemma as member of an organization is to combine "individualism" (being a person) with "loyalty" (being true to the organization's aims), while deserving "trust" from other individual(-s) as well as maintaining membership of the organization. In this balancing act mentorship is likely to play a central role throughout the career, but with changing content as the career progresses (from introduction to professional work to strategic reasoning in complex situations). In sum: to build a "practical identity" (a competent and responsible member of the organization) the individual is dependent upon resonance from one or more mentors. To a large extent mentorship will be in the form of reactions to the mentee's (proposed) interpretations and actions, which is communicative in nature and given meaning in narrative format.

Part of the increased complexity stems from the **changing context** (beside direct competition). To deal with this, managers must devote a large part of their attention to discern and give meaning to such changes ("lo and behold"). This is a difficult problem even to discuss since the neoliberal crusade, since the early 1930s, has been very successful in persuading us that the solution to all the institutional problems that burden the global economy is free trade and the free movement of capital. Therefore, the regulation of these aspects of our life should be handed over to economists and their partners, the jurists. In recent years it seems like the jurists have gained an ever-greater role. The idea of "the rule" of "the rule of law" is commanding more attention in the pertinent "epistemic communities" who feel they have an obligation to steer the global economy right by supra-national regulation. The vicissitudes of democratically elected governments of sovereign nations should not stand in the way of global economic growth. The problem here is that people, including economists and jurists, realise that economic growth is not the solve-it-all solution that it has been hailed as – even if the problem of re-allocation of wealth to those less fortunate that economists refer to in their "cost-benefit" analyses could be realized in real life (DeMartino, 2022).

If we accept the claims of Adam Smith and Friedrich von Hayek that markets are "unknowable" – without the appended belief that the "invisible hand" will solve all problems if we let it be free – everything is turned upside-down in our world view. The free-market solution is deeply ingrained in society. Hayek's explanation that the actors in the market do not maximize utility (which would require vast amounts of knowledge) but act "to survive" turning markets into something like "schoals of fish", does not take us very far (even if it saves the market economy as the design goal). Now we (increasingly?) realize that it is the phenomenon of "economic growth" that drives us toward destruction of the planet we live on. The next step in thought – at least to me – is that the economy must be "managed". That places a host of scientific, moral, ethical, societal problems before us. I have, for example, noted the extensive literature on the lack of knowledge about the management of large corporations that actors (in general) on the financial markets are burdened with. The laws surrounding property rights do not help. They give owners the power to control but not the knowledge. Chandler (1977) discussed a "managerial revolution", but that revolution happened over many decades and was not very revolutionary (except for those who believed that markets have wisdom). After analysing and thinking about the life stories given to me in 1990 and 2020, I have come to respect the intensive training and selection process that promising talent goes through in a managerial career of dealing with "surprising observations, C". Such 'surprising observations' "drive", to use Ramsey's (Misak, 2016, chapter 6; Misak, 2020) expression, their deliberations "causally", albeit "vaguely", which result (sometimes) in improvement initiatives, that, when successful, provide "learning events". One type of such observations may be what others (e.g., competitors) are doing. The mutual adaptation between companies that follows could well be described by Hayek's metaphor about the "schoal of fish". The adaptation initiatives can be understood as a more benevolent context for a Darwinian evolution (variety, selection, retention) inside a large organization. That context provides an interesting training ground for future leaders.

The complexity will generate 'surprising observations' that are in themselves complex to work out the "practical consequences" of. Multiple sources of knowledge will come to use in such "Inferences to the best explanations". Mumford's (e.g., 2000) work will be more relevant here than classical economic micro theory, and Habermas 1981, vol I and II) will provide an "ideological" background.

I believe that this "capstone" function of managerial deliberation deserves closer study "on site" – obviously in the form of case studies. A striking thing in my own efforts (Jönsson, 2004) of this kind is the sheer amount of background information that is needed to begin to understand what is said and meant in such management team meetings. A memory for life is when we stumbled into the consequences of the 9/11 terrorist attack in New York on an engine components producer for the aeroplane industry. A virtual stop in new orders. We were supposed to study the work on integrating a new acquisition but got this opportunity (surprise) to follow the problem-solving related to 9/11 as extra topping. We recorded all top management meetings over an 8-month period in 2002 but chose to refrain from reporting on the effects of the 9/11 crisis (Jönsson et al, 2004).

The scientific dilemma in that case was partly ethical but the consequences of the terrorist attack on those directly hit as well as all who lost their jobs in a far away country (at least temporarily) also made us think carefully about the role of scientific research in cases like this. My comment on our experience then as well as on the life stories of my respondents is that the topic was "meaning" rather than "truth". The management team (and we) could see that 9/11 grounded a large number of aeroplanes that just stood there waiting for air travel to pick up again, but the management team also "saw" that in the meantime engine development in the pipeline would make those grounded planes obsolete due to their limited fuel efficiency. There would be a new "take-off" in a couple of years and this supplier had to prepare for this although the order book was empty for the moment. The discussions in the management team included people we never had heard of in the early part of the case. What could "plasma-welding" have to do with 9/11? They discussed the **meaning** of the 9/11 crises for their company rather than the **truth**, which was plain enough. This is also a characteristic of the 'learning events' in my interviews – meaning rather than "truth". The team (sometimes only mentor and adept) work out an understanding (and its practical consequences) of attention-grabbing, surprising events. The condition of satisfaction is meaningfulness rather than "truth" (Searle 2001, p. 170 ff.). Meaningfulness relates easier to action due to its normative content (values and duties) because it is cast in narrative form. The problem is that one cannot get articles about "stories" published in a scientific journal. There are too many details to account for to fit the article format. You have to write a book (or several ones)!

When one acts in the role of manager the main duty is to get things done – the right things. That means that the objective is to change the world to better suit the intended organizational activities in a future "normal" production of value. Therefore, the criterion should be "meaningfulness". The manager (or team) constructs an intentional core to the project and sets the stage for what counts as good arguments in the implementation phase. All the time with the recipients of the communication in mind. In that way they make it possible for members to judge their own contributions to the emerging project. That is why these "stories" 1) come in narrative form and 2) have multiple "keys" that members can connect their specific experiential horizon to. They (the stories) are not possible to subject to complexity reduction by application of "general" theory. Too much information would be lost. Consequently, the ambition of the writer of a book about such stories should load it with multiple "keys" for readers to construct meaning against their own experiential background.

There is a "culture" dimension to managers' attention to improvement opportunities in large organizations. At times one can feel a kind of nostalgia about the "direct contact" with the world of the events they told me about. That is not easy to achieve in large organizations when your position is at the top. Therefore, central leaders must cultivate "close presence by proxy" by frequent reaffirmation of ethical principles (not the ones worked out by PR people), by frequent travel for "direct" contact with areas of change, being a champion of "learning from mistakes".

"Finding the right people" was a theme in several interviews, often in connection with comments on the problems with assessing, in committee, a large number of variables and tests provided by HRM systems. There was a kind of nostalgia about the (good?) old days when "people" were judged for promotion directly on performance and persons. One could argue that information systems, (integrated or not) can only produce the information the machines or models are programmed to produce, given the proper feed of measurements. But if an important part of the manager's job is to judge "surprising observations" and initiate action under conditions of complexity and uncertainty, the crucial problem is to get those "surprises" in sight and understand their implications - not even AI can do that (Larson, 2021)! A culture of "presence by proxy" might help.

The longing for "direct" contact with local processes cannot easily be satisfied in large organizations. Those in top positions must reach out by proxy. This requires frequent travelling to confirm and re-confirm the main points that guide deliberation on "surprising observations" (one respondent (1990) pointed out that it is somewhat difficult to maintain enthusiasm when you have told the same story a dozen times).

Further on "proxy", there was not much talk about the role of consultants in the interviews even if they seemed present in the background in many cases. In the 1990 interviews two consultants were included, one CEO of the most prominent Swedish firm at the time, and one "ideologue" of the development department of the main industrial association. Both were well known in business circles for their preaching of decentralization and team work close to different processes at the time (Japanese management was in vogue). They talked much about their role as speaking partners, even mentors, to leaders. Reading about the success of the most prominent consultancy firm (Bogdanich & Forsythe, 2022) one realizes that there must still be a market for advice out there.

When a crisis is upon the organization time is extremely short and uncertainty is maximal. Then it is difficult to find "keys" toward a stabilizing solution. We can see, from studies of the refugee-crisis in Vienna 2015 (Kornberger et al, 2019) that agency bosses soon realized that they could do no valuable work from their offices. They had to go out to the "Hauptbahnhof" and other places where the action was, and most of the time, "bless" the practices that were emerging. They could then "see" the practices and judge their fitness for purpose by listening to description of the current situation. One way of dealing with crisis is to shift position close to the action. When that is not possible one can arrange to have several look-out points and perspectives. Hans Werthén, the legendary leader of Electrolux, stated in the 1990 interview: "You have to keep an (loyal?) opposition" as a managerial principle. Again, communication becomes even more crucial.

The variety in situations described by the respondents is great and it seems only possible to grasp their meaning by reflecting on the implications of each aspect that comes up. The "learning events" of the life stories have multiple "keys" also to academic fields of inquiry. There are good reasons to question the validity of any effort at summary conclusions.

Chapter 16
Life stories and their "moments-of-truth" – on the validity of these findings

As mentioned, the interview material is structured in the form of stories about many "learning events". Planning to analyse them as a common illustration of managerial principles in action one comes to think of Flanagan's (1954) "critical incidents technique". His method of collecting stories from pilots about incidents where their competence was put to severe tests. The purpose was to build a basis for improving pilot training programmes. But then conclusions will be close to 'routine learning' of relatively new recruits. This is not what I have seen in my interviews. The respondents tend to tell me about successes that they have had in their career, events that represent management principles that they favour (good examples).

There were very few stories about failures. The teller of the story was at the centre of events. There was little "objectivity" about them even if the stories themselves were convincing. It was the narrative of the incident that gave it meaning. That meaning can be abstracted to a principle of good management. A curious aspect of these stories about learning incidents is that they seem to have multiple "key" (Goffman, 1974) functions. They provide material for several kinds of reflection based in different academic knowledge areas. That is their nature – to connect to different fields of experience.

For example: If the respondent talks about a modernization of the production system in an acquired US firm the solution will be "similar" in many respects to existing plants in Europe only transplanted to the US context – the "key" is a whole configuration of parts. But if the topic is how to build a service division by acquiring a large number of family-owned distributors with services functions the number of "keys" will be large as each acquisition is unique and part of a larger solution. Parts will be fitted together to form a proposition for a new strategy that is far more complex and in need of input from several competencies. Hence, the existence of many "keys" and difficulties in coding the narratives into categories.

I have chosen to present some of the material from the interviews in the form of reflections on the meaning of a phenomenon (surprising observation?) discovered in the narratives. This means, admittedly, that the conclusions of this study are rather vague. A critic might argue that the data I have gathered (and analysed) are only a specific kind of "hearsay". But my respondents have, seriously and engaged, told me about important learning experiences ("moments-of-truth") in their career. Failures are almost absent. A few have stressed the importance of learning from mistakes, but overwhelmingly it is the success stories that "makes the man". It seems like my respondents have been constructing a "practical identity" through these experiences that justifies promotion to high positions of trust. I find that very interesting.

Conclusions

I will focus on some "discoveries" that are new to me and evaluate their validity[1]:

1. **"A surprising fact, C, has been observed".** This core observation of Pragmatism and its abduction process has been present in more than 50 % of the 684 learning events that were gathered through the interviews. It took a while to realize the significance which is that, with a "surprising observation", one realizes that

[1] Some of these "discoveries" will be trivial for readers with more and better knowledge than I have. If they are trivial or self-evident, I should be pleased since I have learned something that everybody already knew – or because I managed to present them in a way that makes them appear self-evident.

one's expectations have not been met and that is likely to be caused by faulty beliefs/assumptions. The logical consequence of this insight is that deduction or induction are not readily useful tools since the premises are disqualified. The "repair work" starts from one fact, C, which needs an explanation. Inference to the Best Explanation necessarily is a **constructive exercise** since the only thing that is certain is that the old assumptions about the world do not hold (except the observed fact C). One would expect the first thing to do would be Boltanski's (2011) "truth test" and "reality test" (whether C is really a fact, and relevant). Then the construction of an explanation to C can start. The problem here is that available operational data have suddenly become uncertain. "Truth" beyond the realization that the observed fact, C, is surprising, is not easily available. The first ambition therefore must be to give "meaning" to the surprise. The Best Explanation will be to find the A - which might be a constellation of facts and values – that would make C follow "as a matter of course".

2. **Reducing uncertainty by abduction.** This is the core nature of Pragmatism – to reduce uncertainty when facing a need to do something about the consequences of the surprising observation. The confusion caused by the realization that one or more of our beliefs (assumptions about the world) is not valid may cause action paralysis. The rational thing to do then is to start from the fact at hand – the surprising observation C – since the usual analytical tools, deduction and induction, must be reduced to auxiliary logical work, working out consequences of newly constructed assumptions. The problem then is to keep "clarity of thought" in the construction of a new thought model (Best Explanation) that can serve as a basis for action, i.e., in giving meaning to the situation and the possibilities contained in it. (To

find "the truth" is of course welcome, but the "surprise" dimension of the situation makes that less likely.)

We must remind ourselves here that "action" is defined by the presence of an actor who is driving events. This means that values come into the deliberation process, and we know that there is no rational way to choose what value to pursue (use as a criterion). Furthermore, in an organization a justification (judged by other members) must accompany the action plan, which itself must be operationally coherent. Among analytical philosophers in Cambridge, who were focused on "the truth" of conclusions given the (true) premises, the proposition of Pragmatism (Peirce and James) was unacceptable. Ramsey gid not agree, by battling with Wittgenstein about the meaning of his (1921) *Tractatus,* he had become convinced that "words get in the way" – facts cannot enter directly into the Mind for analysis since words always include interpretation. That happens when deliberating about action. The famous wanderer who arrives at a crossing with no signpost and nobody to ask could choose either way since they are equally probable to lead to the destination given the current information, they said in Cambridge. Yes, Ramsey said, but added that the task now was to be on the lookout for somebody to ask for direction while walking. Deliberation includes re-constructing the problem to become "which way is more likely to provide me with somebody to ask about direction? (Is that a house over there?)"

3. **Rationality in an uncertain situation.** Uncertainty is a condition where there is little reliable information – yes, we have the "observation of the surprising fact C", but little more, at least not in analysable form. But we have Searle's (2001) observation that a speech act always contains a commitment by the speaker to the veracity of what is said. Lying is not a sustainable strategy in

organizational communication. To be a reliable member of an organisation means to tend to one's "practical identity". Communication with a trusted member confirms membership. This kind of confirmation is more needed with increasing complexity of issues. Since it is of little use to start building trust relations when the crisis is hot it is rational to tend to them when times are "normal". A trusted member (team or mentor) has some operational competence and established communication habits. In uncertain situations it is rational to turn to such members that seem to "fit" the problem at hand (or could contribute knowledge that seems required).

Due to the uncertainty generated by the "surprise" and the situation's complexity the character of problem solution will be "constructive" in the sense that arguments and facts will be built into coherence around the "explanation" to the surprising fact C. Rationality assumes the form of "meaning" contained in a narrative of a proposed improvement project to be implanted into the body of otherwise "normal" business. In constructing an explanation to the observed (deviating) situation contributions may be solicited from various sources of knowledge (preferably inside the team) by way of "re-entry" (Edelman & Tonioni, 2000; Searle, 1997) where the same (kind of) information is taken up by different knowledge holders and serves as "keys" (Goffman, 1974) in parallel framing/re-framing of conceptions. Coherence "emerges" – nobody can specify in advance what is required since the situation is "surprising" (i.e., expectations have failed).

4. **When the deliberating team is approaching action,** the significant addition is the intentionality aspect (Searle, 1983). The very definition of action includes intention – there is someone (or something) that drives events towards some end, otherwise it would be – just events. So part of the attribution of meaning to the emerging project is to provide it with intention and

competence – to use two of the moments of the narrative template (Cooren, 2000). With the addition of intention, the commitment of the leader is made public to all (attentive) members. With the commitment follows responsibility as well as accountability (in a wide sense). The project is made "social" in the sense that all members are obliged to participate. This role of being an active member is described as *"courage d'esprit"* (courage in the face of responsibility) by Clausewitz (1832). It is not the courage shown by the soldier in the trenches when facing the risk of bodily injury, but the social courage required when one faces the responsibility. It is a communicative phenomenon that builds social capital. A good presentation (narrative) of the project must strike the right balance between making members aware of the risks of failure, while at the same time mobilizing the necessary "courage d'esprit" to carry the project through - with necessary corrections under way.

The problem emerging in comparing the 2020 interviews with the 1990 ones is that with an increased closeness to the customers' value creation process – and the related local problem-solving activities – the communicative distance between local and central members of the organization increases. The variety in operational information (this possible solution to this particular problem) becomes too great to handle by normal channels of communication (and "normal" information systems). The rational solution is further delegation to positions closer to the action, which in turn, places a greater responsibility to communicate the intentions of the organization clearly. The temptation to reduce information transfers in both directions to cost and profit figures, is likely to increase the risk of loss of sustainability for the organization.

The issue of whether it is "rational" to spread a general sense of "intentionality" by communication to larger segments of the organization, or to "dress" messages in local context in more focused communication, is a matter of research. But there seems to be no doubt that delegation of authority is a necessary move for a large organization to be able to respond effectively to local customers' particular demands stemming from their specific value generating process.

Sum: Managerial deliberation in a large organization will (normally) take place in a context of delegation of authority to make local decisions. With increasing complexity and lack of time this dimension assumes increased strategic relevance.

5. **A counter argument here is** that organizations strive to exploit their "competitive advantage" (of course they do!) and should focus their attention on what competitors do. This line of thought stems from economics and had its breakthrough at our business schools with Porter's (1980) book. Strategy became a hot topic. It is easy to teach due to its close connection with microeconomics. Instructive modelling could be done without much data. Wernerfelt (1984) pointed to the opportunity to analyse firms from the "resource side" rather than the "product side". Petraf (1993) draw together a large number of assumptions (heterogeneity, imperfect factor mobility etc.) necessary to do a "proper" analysis of the competitive advantage of a business firm and we all realized that this approach had yet a long way to go.

Two things deserve comment when comparing learning events in the two-interview series (1990 and 2020);

1) I found virtually no traces of the "competitive advantage" vocabulary in the interviews. There are a couple of learning

events that can be classified as being about competitive advantage. The most prominent one is Jan Carlzon's account (1990) of the change in market approach by SAS, from a view of cost efficiency, capacities, and routes to an approach that stresses "passengers in the driving seat" (which means that customers are treated as individuals and persuaded by "front line" individuals to become regular customers). But even in this account there is little mention of what competitors do. Percy Barnevik (ABB), also 1990, explained the internationalization strategy (ASEA used to be an exporting company) in terms of acquisitions, first in the Nordic countries, then in Europe, and finally the USA and ASIA. One could understand that the key is the effort to gain a strong market position in selected areas, a competitive strategy. But even if the targeted companies were subject to analyses, it was as targets of acquisition rather than as competitors, and how they could be integrated (which would require changes). In the only interview with a leader of fast-moving-consumer-goods (FMCG; snacks), Carina Hansson, the competition was present as a background, but the learning events accounts were largely about developing new potato varieties for the chips, logistics, social neighbourhood support, integrating immigrant workers – in short, the company in its wider context.

The large majority of accounts (especially in 2020) were coloured by the fact that Swedish industry is a business-to-business industry. The accounts were about getting closer to the customer, solving problems together with the customer, using (IT) technology to improve the offer to the customer. There was mention, though, in 1990, of Finnish forestry industry investing in better production technology, while Swedish firms invested more in local market presence –

which could be understood as a statement of "competitive difference" rather than "advantage".

Of course, one could understand the frequent use of a "strong market position" argument as a variety of "competitive advantage". But if that position is gained by acquisitions rather that marketing strategies, the managerial "handicraft" involved differs from that proposed by economists.

3) The "roots" of competitive advantage. I have already discussed (chapter 8 above) how a neoliberal view of the world economy established itself from the 1930s and onwards. A common trait in that discussion was that every nation (and every company?) could find some aspect (farming) that it could be exploited to advantage. An agricultural nation should perfect and export its agricultural output and import to cover other needs – all for the best of everybody. The proofs were in the form of geometry (given the assumptions) with different slopes of demand curves etc – both Wernerfelt (1984) and Petraf (1993) use geometry in transferring the same kind of reasoning to the firm level/markets. But Slobodian (2018) points out that the starting point for the policy application of the idea of competitive advantage was the existence of an extensive system of tariffs that impeded competition in the name of the need to protect the national economy after the First World War. Mises and Hayek were deeply involved in the efforts to find ways to make the newly created nation of Austria (one of the 6 nations that were created when the empire of the Habsburgs was dissolved). Mises realized that in order to become competitive Austria would have to invite investment from abroad and that required that workers accepted a

substantial cut in wages. But he also saw that the empire of Austria-Hungary had been quite successful in managing all the nationalities of the empire by a certain amount of self-government while keeping trade and capital allocation inside the empire free. To break the protectionist tendencies based in each nation's efforts to re-start its economy after the war it was agreed among economists that supranational regulation to achieve free trade and free capital movements was necessary. Each nation is too egoistic, looking after its own (narrow) interests. All would be better off if every nation focused on its own competitive advantage in accordance with the Heckscher-Ohlin theorem and the advice of professional economists. Exploitation instead of exploration, to use March (1991) terminology. This goes on to this day. "En route" economists have increasingly engaged jurists, but again and again met resistance from sovereign nations with elected governments who re-wrote all the agreements to give nations the final say on their own economy. (Maybe this has served to somewhat reduce the speed with which Mother Earth's resources are depleted?). In the process thoughts about international regulation seen as an order of "constitutions" with some leeway for elected governments to do what they were elected for has emerged. There was also the minor incident with Piketty (2014), who claimed that the main argument for nations to allow "capitalists" to remain wealthy – the wealth "seeps down" to everybody – if anything it seems to "seep up". The battle for "equality" goes on and the resulting international regulations add to the complexity managers of large companies are facing.

6. **On top of this** there was an increasingly rapid development of IT applications in all areas of business, including unexpected (?)

influences via social media on society, and the intensifying debate on sustainability. One can safely claim that increased contextual complexity of the management task is the important change over the last 30 years. The sense of lack of time was there also in the 1990 interviews, but my impression is that it is more pronounced under complexity conditions of 2020. After all, management is about what to do now.

Summary: Management and complexity

The first reaction to complexity is to try to reduce it. The most conspicuous effort close to managers is the application of the idea that "the market" is the best allocator of resources. This idea has given birth to different forms of "corporate raiders" who mobilize financial resources to buy a large swath of a company's shares, claim a seat on the Board and promote a policy of concentration to the "core business" by selling off non-core activities. When their intentions become publicly known share prices increase, and when sell-offs are announced they increase further. Raiders cash-in and move to the next target company. There was not much comment on this phenomenon; people from the financial sector in some cases argued that it is a good thing that top management is subjected to this kind of "shake-up" now and then. From CEOs there were comments to the effect that "when you have low performance you lose some of your freedom of action". The argument from some that the Board has little chance to grasp the full complexities of the consequences of selloffs is a repetition of what has been known since Berle & Means (1932). There is no reasonable chance for a board member to keep abreast of the developments that are relevant for management even with full time engagement.

So, our hope for a better future rests with the management of our leading companies. A summary of what overwhelming complexity means for the management task has to start from the communicative task of providing organizational members – and others – with reasons for acting in a certain way (embark on a promising path):

Reason-giving

A problem that follows from increased complexity is that it is more difficult to provide good reasons for a certain line of action. I have adopted Scanlon's (2014) claim that a reason is a relation, R(p,a,x,c). (**p** is a reason for agent **a** to do activity **x** in situation **c**). This is not easy to communicate. When pressed from the outside world a manager might resort to concepts like "share-holder value" and the like, but that is not useful for internal communication because it easily disconnects from operational facts. If we instead look upon reason-giving as loading a plan with intentionality, it seems necessary to look upon the reason giving as an exercise in narrativizing plans. We know from the development in linguistics that it is the receivers of a message that determine its meaning. Narratives tend to have a "canonical" form that people use in interpretation.

Reason-giving in context

When we give reasons, we give them in context. Under these circumstances it is the right thing for me (and you - us together) to do x. A good friend will ask whether we have the skill and competence to succeed, and when the team has reached "reflective equilibrium" they will sanction the project. Basically "getting things done" means changing the world to fit the promising result (word). "Direction of fit" is at play (promises/values = world-to-word; statements of fact = word-to-world). In complex situations there will be "surprising observations", which by their own logic reveal that our expectations have failed and that the beliefs on which those expectations were based have been wrong. The primary managerial task for leaders of large organizations then is to construct an "Inference to the Best Explanation" with all available help. To elicit such help in re-framing the meaning of the situation the emerging narrative/explanation needs to exhibit "keys" (Goffman, 1974) that provide "entry points" for relevant knowledge areas. **This means that the most important insight from this study is that management, seen as deliberation (on how to get things done), is a matter of giving meaning to the project.** ("Truth" is nice, but here different knowledge areas, and hence, many "truths" are in play.)

Individuals giving reasons

When we communicate arguments to serve as reasons, we also communicate **commitment** to the truth, relevance, or intention conveyed. All those commitments go into a memory box called "practical identity" which is a "description" (Korsgaard, 1996, p 101) under which we value our acts and build our social capital. Being true to oneself amounts to being true to one's commitments. Organizations live by it. Membership, trustworthiness, organization is about individuals being true to their commitments (in the eyes of themselves as well as the others').

When one of my respondents describe his favourite form of control as sitting down with a team, discussing a problem, reaching an agreement on what the solution might look like, give them the resources, go, and follow up by asking "How are you doing?" (He called it *management by means,* if I remember correctly), the meaning is management based on the team members' commitment.

Management as setting the stage for reason-giving

In Sweden there is an old public sector tradition concerning the procedures for decision making sometimes referred to as "General Director in Plenum". The head of a state agency (General Director) could take a decision (alone) in the meeting with his closest subordinates (the heads of the various bureaus of the agency). This form had the advantage that the General Director could present his reasons (pros and cons) for the decision in plenum, which could then guide future decisions in the bureaus on similar matters. At the same time, it placed responsibility with the general director, who would have to justify the decision again if there was critique from Parliament or the public. In this way precedents are established without much procedural delay. The General Director set the stage for future reason-giving. A rather clever method.

We need more of this kind of "stage-setting" the more complex the situations management deals with. Several knowledge areas get engaged, delegation to those close to the situation will be increasingly necessary, and the leader will have to focus attention to setting the stage for the giving of good reasons by members of the organization. Those members need to be well aware of their "practical identity", which is in focus when trust, membership, individualism (in terms of respect for the other) is allocated.

References

Ashby, Ross, (1960), *Design for a Brain*. London: Chapman & Hall

Batson, C. Daniel & Laura L. Shaw, (1991), Evidence of Altruism: Toward a Pluralism of Prosocial Motives. *Psychological Inquiry*, vol. 2, pp 107 – 122.

Bebbington, Jan, (2001), Sustainable development: a review of the international development, business, and accounting literature, *Accounting Forum*, Vol.25, No.2, pp.128-157.

Beckérus, Åke & Anders Edström, (1995), *Den Europeiska Rockaden – Svenska Företag väljer ny strategi* (The European Castelling – Swedish Corporations choose new strategy). Stockholm: Svenska Dagbladet.

Bennis, Warren, (1989), *On Becoming a Leader*. Boston: Addison-Wesley

Berlinski, Claire, (2011), Five Myths about Margaret Thatcher, The Washington Post, 22 December.

Bergenek, Anders & Richard Sahlsten, (2020), *Stenability – The Story of Stena Roro.* Gothenburg: Breakwater Publishing.

Berger, Peter L. & Thomas Luckman, (1995), *Modernity, Pluralism and the Crisis of Meaning.* Gütersloh: Bertelsmann Foundation Publishers

Berle, Adolf A. & Gardiner Means, (1932), *The Modern Corporation and Private Property*. Piscataway, N.J.: Transaction Publishers

Bernard, Thomas J., (1983), *The Consensus – Conflict Debate.* New York: Columbia University Press.

Bjursell, Cecilia, (2007), *Integration through framing – A Study of the Cloetta Fazer merger.* Dissertation. Linköping University

Bogdanich, Walt & Michael Forsythe, (2022), *When Mckinsey Comes to Town: The Hidden Influence of the World's Most Powerful Consulting Firm.* London: Bodley Head

Boltanski, Luc, (2011, original 2009), *On Critique – A Sociology of Emancipation*. (transl. Gregory Elliott.). Cambridge: Polity Press.

Boltanski, Luc & Laurent Thévenot (2006, original 1991), *On justification – Economies of Worth* (transl. Catherine Porter). Princeton: Princeton University Press

Bourdieux, Pierre, (1977, orig 1972), *Outline of a Theory of Practice* (transl. Richard Nice). Cambridge: Cambridge University Press.

Brown, Andrew D. & Thompson, Edmund R. (2013). A narrative approach to strategy-as-practice. *Business History* vol. 55, pp. 1143-1167

Brown, Étienne, (2018), Kantian Constructivism and the Normativity of Practical Identities. *Dialogue: Canadian Philosophical Review*, No 3, pp 571 – 590

Brown, Peter, (2015), *The Ransom of the Soul – Afterlife and Wealth in Early Western Christianity*. Cambridge, Mass.: Harvard University Press

Brunsson, Nils, (1976), *Propensity to Change – An Empirical Study of Decisions on Reorientations*. PhD Dissertation. Business Administration, Gothenburg University

Butterwick, Richard, (2020), *The Polish-Lithuanian Commonwealth – Light and Flame*. New Haven: Yale University Press

Buttny, Richard, (1993), *Social Accountability in Communication*. London: Sage

Carlzon, Jan, (1986), *Riv Pyramiderna!* (Tear down the pyramids!) Stockholm: Bonniers

Chandler, Alfred D. Jr, (1962), *Strategy and Structure: Chapters in the History of the American Industrial Enterprise*. Cambridge, Mass.: MIT Press

Chandler, Alfred D Jr, (1977), *The Visible Hand: The Managerial Revolution in American Business*. Cambridge, Mass.: Harvard University Press.

Clausewitz, Carl von, (orig.1832/1998), *On War*. (Orig. Vom Kriege), Paret ed. Princeton: Princeton University Press

Cooren, Francois, (2000). *The Organizing Property of Communication*. Amsterdam: Benjamins

Cooren, Francois, (2011), *Action and Agency in Dialogue - Passion, incarnation and ventriloquism*. Amsterdam: Benjamins

Czarniawska, Barbara, (2011), Performativity in place of responsibility? *Journal of Organizational Change Management,* vol. 24, no 6, pp 823 - 829

Dante, Alighieri, (1472/many translations), *The Divine Comedy.* Florens

Darwin, Charles, (1859/2019), *On the Origin of Species*. Richmond (UK): Alma Books

DeMartino, George F., (2022), *The Tragic Science – How Economists Cause Harm (even as they aspire to do good).* Chicago: Chicago University Press

Destutt de Tracy, Antoine-Louis-Claude, (1796), *Éléments d'idéologie: Première partie - Idéologie proprement dite*. Paris: Didot

Dewey, John, (1922), *Human nature and Human Conduct: An Introduction to Social Psychology.* New York: Holt

Dierickx, Ingemar, & Cool, Karel, (1989), Asset Stock Accumulation and Sustainability of Competitive Advantage. *Management Science,* Vol. 35, pp 1504 – 1511.

Doyle, Conan, (2014), *A Study in Scarlet.* London: Penguin Classics

Duggan, Lisa, (2019), *Mean Girl – Ayn Rand and the culture of Greed.* Oakland: University of California Press.

Edelman, Gerald, (1992), *Bright Air, Brilliant Fire: On the Matter of the Mind.* New York: basic Books

Edelman, Gerald, & Tononi, Giulio, (2000), *The Universe of Consciousness: How Matter Becomes Imagination.* New York: Basic Books

Engwall, Lars (ed), (1985), *Föregångare inom Företagsekonomin* (Pioneers in Business Studies). Stockholm: SNS

Ezzamel, Mahmoud, (2012), *Accounting and Order – Evidence from the Ancient* World. London: Routledge

Feulner, Edwin J., (1999), *Intellectual Pilgrims. The Fiftieth Anniversary of the Mont Pélegrin Society.* Washington DC: Heritage Foundation

Fisher, W.R. (1987), *Human Communication as Narration.* Columbia: University of South Carolina Press.

Flanagan, John C., (1954), The Critical Incident Technique. *Psychological Bulletin,* vol 51, no 4, pp 327 – 358.

Fleurbaey, Marc, Olivier Bouin, Marie-Laure Salles-Djelic, Ravi Kanbur, Helga Novotny, Elisa Reis, (2018), *A Manifesto for Social Progress – Ideas for a Better Society*. Cambridge: Cambridge University Press.

Forester, John, (2012), On the Theory and Practice of Critical Pragmatism: Deliberative Practice and Deliberative Negotiations. *Planning Theory,* no 1, pp 1 – 18

Friedman, Milton & Anna Schwartz, (1963), *A Monetary History of the United States 1867 – 1960.* Princeton: Princeton University Press

Garfinkel, Harold, (1984), *Studies in Ethnomethodology.* Cambridge, Polity Press

Geertz, Clifford, (1973). *The Interpretation of Cultures. Selected Essays.* New York: Basic Books

Gergen, Kenneth J. & Gergen, Mary M., (1983), Narratives of the self. In T.R. Sarbin &K.E. Scheibe (esd), *Studies in Social Identity,* pp. 254 – 273. New York: Praeger

Gergen, Kenneth J. & Gergen, Mary M., (1988), Narratives and the Self as Relationship. *Advances in Experimental Social Psychology,* vol 21, pp 17 - 56

Gieryn, Thomas, (1983), Boundary work and the demarcation of science from non-science: Strains and interests in professional ideologies of scientists. *American Sociological Review,* vol. 48, no 6, pp. 781 – 795.

Gigerenzer G, Brighton H. (2009), Homo heuristics: why biased minds make better inferences. *Topics in Cognitive Science.* No 1 pp 107 – 43)

Goffman, Erving, (1974), *Frame Analysis – An Essay on the Organization of Experience.* Boston: Northeastern University Press.

Greenfield, Liah, (2001), *The Spirit of Capitalism. Nationalism and Economic Growth.* Cambridge, Mass.: Harvard University Press

Grice, H. Paul, (1989), *Studies in the Way of Words.* Cambridge, Mass.: Harvard University Press

Haas, Peter, (1992), Introduction: Epistemic Communities and International Policy Coordination. *International Organization,* vol. 46, no 1, pp 1 – 36

Haberler, Gottfried, (1936), *The Theory of International Trade with its Applications to Commercial Policy*. London: W. Dodge

Haberler, Gottfried, (1961), A Survey of International Trade Theory. Princeton University: Special Papers in International Economics, No 1, July 1st.

Habermas, Jürgen, (1981/1984), *Theory of Communicative Action, Volume I: Reason and the Rationalization of Society* (transl. Thomas McCarthy). Boston: Beacon Pres

Habermas, Jürgen, (1981/1987), *Theory of Communicative Action, volume II: Lifeworld and System: A Critique of Functionalist Reason*. (transl. Thomas McCarthy. Boston: Beacon Press.

Hayek, Friedrich von, (1944), *The Road to Serfdom*. London: Routledge

Hayek, Friedrich von, (1945), The Use of Knowledge in Society. *The American Economic Review*, vol. 35, pp 519 - 530

Hayek, Friedrich von, (1960), *The Constitution of Liberty*. Chicago: Chicago University Press

Hedberg, Bo, & Jönsson, Sten (1978), Designing Semi-confusing information systems for organizations in changing environments. *Accounting, Organizations and Society*, vol. 3, pp 47 – 64.

Heritage, John, (1984), *Garfinkel and Ethnomethodology*. Oxford: Polity Press

Hirschman, Albert O. (1970), *Exit, Voice, and Loyalty: Responses to Decline in Firms, Organizations and States*. Cambridge, Mass.: Harvard University Press

Hobsbawm, Eric, (2002), In*teresting Times – A Twentieth-Century Life*. London: Penguin

Ireland, Paddy, (2009), Financialization and Corporate Governance. *Northern Ireland Legal Quarterly*. Vol. 60, No 1, pp 1 – 34.

Holmqvist, Mikael (2003). A dynamic model of intra- and interorganizational learning. *Organization Studies*, vol 24, no 1, pp. 95–123.

Ims, Knut J., (1987), *Leder i dialog (The leader in dialogue)*. PhD Dissertation, Business Administration, Gothenburg University

James, William, (1907), *Pragmatism – A new Name for some old ways of thinking*. London: Longmans Green & Co

Janik, Allen & Toulmin, Stephen, (1996), *Wittgenstein's Vienna*. Chicago: Ivan R. Dee

Jensen, Michael C. & Meckling, William H., (1976), Theory of the Firm: Managerial Behavior, Agency Costs and Ownership Structure. *Journal of Financial Economics*, vol. 3, no 4, pp 305-360

Jönsson, Sten & Rolf A. Lundin (1977), Myths and wishful thinking as management tools. In "Prescriptive Models of Organizations". (Nystrom & Starbuck editors). *TIMS Studies in Management Sciences*. Volume 5, pp 157-170.

Jönsson, Sten, (1983), Relate management accounting research to managerial work! *Accounting Organizations and Society*. vol 23, no 4, pp 411 - 434.

Jönsson, Sten, (1988), *Accounting Regulation and Elite Structures – Driving Forces in the Development of Accounting Policy*. Chichester: Wiley.

Jönsson, Sten (1995), *Goda utsikter – perspektiv på svenskt management* (Good prospects – perspectives on Swedish industrial management). Stockholm: Nyrenius & Santerus (reprint 2021 Göteborg: BAS)

Jönsson, Sten, (2004), *Product Development – Work for Premium Values*. Malmö: Liber

Jönsson, Sten, Rovio – Johansson, Airi & Kokk, Gary, (2004), Articulation of principles on the micro-level – observing argumentation in a merger process. GRI-Report 2004:1. School of Business, Economics and Law, Gothenburg University

Jönsson, Sten & Lars Strannegård (eds.), (2014), *Ledarskapsboken* ("The Leadership Book"). Stockholm: Liber.

Jönsson, Sten, (2019). *A Comparative History of Bank Failures – from Medici to Barings*. New York: Routledge

Jönsson, Sten, (2021), *När Molnen Hopar Sig – Svensk Företagsledning Förr och Nu.* (Gathering Clouds – Swedish Management then and now). Göteborg: BAS

Khalili, Laleh, (2022), In Clover. *London Review of Books,* vol. 44, No 24 pp 13 - 16

Kahneman, Daniel, (2011), *Thinking, Fast and Slow*. London: Penguin Random House

Kahneman, Daniel, Sibony, Olivier and Sunstein, Cass R. (2021), *Noise – A Flaw in Human Judgment.* Lodon: William Collins

Keynes, John M. (1921/1973), *A Treatise on Probability*. Reprinted in "The Collected Writings of John Maynard Keynes", Vol. 8. London: MacMillan

Keynes, John M., (1936), *The General Theory of Employment, Interest and Money.* London: MacMillan

Klamer, Arjo, (2017), *Doing the Right Thing – A Value Based Economy.* London: Uniquity Press.

Koppl, Roger and Richard N. Langlois, (2000), Embeddedness, Organizations and Language Games. Paper presented at the SCANCOR conference on "Crossing Boundaries: Economics, Sociology and Organization Theory, 30 September, Stanford.

Kornberger, Martin, & Anders Enberg – Pedersen, (2019), Reading Clausewitz, reimagining the Practice of Strategy. *Strategic Organization,* vol 19, no 2, pp 338 – 350.

Kornberger, Martin, Stephen Leixnering, Renate E. Meyer (2019), The Logic of Tact: How Decisions Happen in Situations of Crisis. *Organization Studies,* Vol. 40, No. 2, pp 239 – 266

Korsgaard, Christine M., (1996), *The Sources of Normativity.* Cambridge: Cambridge University Press.

Korsgaard, Christine M., (2008), *The constitution of agency: Essays on Practical Reason and Moral Psychology,* Oxford: Oxford University Press.

Kuhn, Thomas S., (1962), *The Structure of Scientific Revolutions*. Chicago: Chicago University Press

Lakatos, Imre & Musgrave, Alan (eds) (1965), Criticism and the Growth of Knowledge: *Proceedings of the International Colloquium in the Philosophy of* Science, *Vol. 4*. Cambridge: Cambridge University Press

Langholm, Odd (1979), *Price and Value in the Aristotelian tradition – A study in Scholastic sources.* Oxford: Oxford University Press

Larson, Erik J., (2021), *The Myth of Artificial Intelligence – Why Computers Can't Think the Way We Do*. Cambridge, Mass.: Harvard University Press

Lear, Jonathan, (2006), *Radical Hope – Ethics in the Face of Cultural Devastation.* Cambridge, Mass.: Harvard University Press

Lewis, Michael, (2018), *The Fifth Risk – Undoing Democracy*. London: Penguin

Lui. Glory M., (2022), *Adam Smith's America: How a Scottish Philosopher Became an Icon of American Capitalism.* Princeton: Princeton University Press.

Madrick, Jeff, (2011), *Age of Greed: The Triumph of Finance and the Decline of America, 1970 to the Present.* New York: Knopf

Magnusson, Lars, (1999), *Merkantilismen – Ett ekonomiskt tänkande formuleras.* Stockholm: SNS

March, James. G., (1991), Exploration and exploitation in organizational learning. *Organization Science,* vol. 2, no 1, pp. 71–87.

March, James G., and Johan P. Olsen, (2008), The Logic of Appropriateness, in *Oxford Handbook of Public Policy,* edited by Martin Rein, Michael Moran and Robert E. Goodin, Oxford: Oxford University Press.

McCain, Kevin & Poston, Ted (eds), (2017), *Best Explanations: New Essays on Inference to the Best Explanation.* Oxford: Oxford University Press

MacLean, Nancy, (2017), *Democracy in Chains – The Deep History of the Radical Right's Stealth Plan for America.* London: Scribe Publications.

McCloskey, Donald N., (1990), *If You're so Smart: The Narrative of Economic Expertise.* Chicago: University of Chicago Press

McCloskey, Deirdre N., (2006), *The Bourgeois Virtues – Ethics for the Age of Commerce.* Chicago: Chicago University Press.

McCloskey, Deirdre N., (2010), *Bourgeois Dignity – Why Economics can't Explain the Modern World.* Chicago: Chicago University Press.

McCloskey, Deirdre N., (2016), *Bourgeois Equality – How Ideas, not Capital or Institutions, Enriched the World.* Chicago: Chicago University Press.

Menger, Carl, (1871), *Grundsätze der Volkwirtschaft.* Wien: Baumüller

Mirowski, Philip, (2013), *Never Let a Serious Crisis Go to Waste – How Neoliberalism Survived the Financial Meltdown.* London: Verso

Misak, Cheryl, (2016), *Cambridge Pragmatism: From Peirce and James to Ramsey and Wittgenstein*. Oxford: Oxford University Press

Misak, Cheryl, (2020), *Frank Ramsey – A sheer excess of power*. Oxford. Oxford University Press

Mises, Ludwig von, (1912/1953), *Theory of Money and Credit.* New Haven: Yale University Press

Mises, Ludwig von, (1920), Die Wirtschaftrechnung im sozialistischen Gemeinwesen. *Archiv für Socialwissenschaften und Sozialpolitik* vol. 47, pp 86 – 121.

Mumford, Michael D., (2000), Managing Creative People: Strategies and Tactics for Innovation. *Human Resource Management Review,* pp 313 – 351.

Myrdal, Gunnar, (1931), Om penningteoretisk jämvikt (On monetary equilibrium). En studie över den "normala räntan" i Wicksells penninglära. Ekonomisk Tidskrift, no 5/6, pp 191 – 302

Nagel, Thomas (1974), What is it Like to be a Bat? *The Philosophical Review,* vol 83, pp 435 - 450

Nagel, Thomas, (1996), *Universality and the reflective self.* (chapter 7 in Korsgaard (1996)) Cambridge: Cambridge University Press

Nelson, Janet L. (2019), *King and Emperor – A New Life of Charlemagne.* London: Penguin

Nkrumah, Kwame, (1965), *Neo-colonialism: The Last Stage of Imperialism*. New York: International Publishers

Ohlin, Bertil, (1933), *Interregional and international trade*. Cambridge, Mass.: Harvard University press

Olsson, Ulf, (2001), *Att förvalta sitt pund ("to manage one's pound")– Marcus Wallenberg 1899 – 1982*. Stockholm: Eklids

Östling, Leif, (2020), *I Backspegegeln – Min tid i Scania, Volkswagen och Wallenbergsfären*. (In the rear mirror – My time at Scania, Volkswagen and the Wallenberg Sphere). Stockholm: Ekerlids

Paciolo, Luca, (1494), *Summa de arithmetica, geometrica. Proportioni et proportionalitat*. Venice

Peirce, Charles S., (1931 – 1958), *Collected Papers of Charles Sanders Peirce*, 8 volumes. Cambridge, Mass.: Belknap Press

Pentland, Alex, (2015), *Social Physics: How Social Networks Can Make Us Smarter*. New York: Penguin Books

Petraf, Margaret A., (1993), The Cornerstone of Competitive Advantage: A Resource-Based View. *Strategic Management Journal*, vol 14, pp 179 – 191.

Piketty, Thomas, (2014), *Capital in the Twenty-First Century*. Cambridge, Mass.: Harvard University Press

Pistor, Katharina, (2019), *The Code of Capital – How the Law Creates Wealth and Inequality*. Princeton: Princeton University Press

Platon (c. 375 BCE), *The Republic*.

Polanyi, Michael, (1958), Personal knowledge: Towards a Post-Critical Philosophy. Chicago: Chicago University Press.

Popper, Karl R., (1945), *The Open Society and its Enemies*. London: Routledge

Popper, Karl R., (1957), *The Poverty of Historicism*. London: Routledge

Popper, Karl R., (1963), *Conjectures and Refutations: The Growth of Scientific Knowledge*. London: Routledge

Porter, Michael E., (1980), *Competitive Strategy: Techniques for Analyzing Industries and Competitors.* New York: Free Press.

Ramsey, Frank, (1926/1931, also reprinted in Ramsey, 1990, pp 34 – 51), Truth and Probability (selections read to the Moral Science Club in 1926)

Ramsey, Frank, (1931), *The Foundations of Mathematics and Other Logical Essays,* (R.B. Braithwaite (ed.), London: Routledge &Kegan Paul.

Ramsey, Frank, (1990), *Philosophical Papers* (D.H. Mellor (ed.)). Cambridge: Cambridge University Press

Rawls, John, (1971), *A Theory of Justice.* Cambridge, Mass.: Harvard University Press

Rawls, John, (2001), *Justice as Fairness – A Restatement* (edited by Erin Kelly). Cambridge. Mass.: Harvard University Press

Robson, Keith, Willmott, Hugh, Coper, David & Puxty, Tony (1994), The Ideology of Professional Regulation and Markets of Accounting Labour: Three Episodes in the recent History the UK Accounting Profession. *Accounting, Organizations and Society,* vol. 19, no 6, pp 527 – 553.

de Roover, Raimond, (1963*), The Rise and Decline of the Medici Bank,* 1397 – 1494. Cambridge, Mass: Harvard University Press (1963).

Rosenblatt, Helena, (2018), *The Lost History of Liberalism – From Ancient Rome to the Twenty- First Century.* Princeton: Princeton University Press

Russel, Bertrand, (1921), *Analysis of Mind.* London: Allen & Unwin (Gutenberg eBook 2008)

Sacks, Harvey, (1963), Sociological Description. *Berkeley Journal of Sociology,* vol 8, pp 1-16

Sarbin, Theodore R. (Ed.). (1986). *Narrative psychology: The storied nature of human conduct.* New York: Praeger

Scanlon, T.M., (2014), *Being realistic about reasons.* Oxford: Oxford University Press.

Schmahlenbach, Eugen, (1919), Grundlagen dynamischer Bilanzlehre. *Zeitschrift für Handelswissenschaftliche Forschung*, vol. 13, pp 1 – 60 and 65 - 101

Schumpeter, Joseph, (1954), *The History of Economic Analysis.* London: Allen & Unwin

Scott, Marvin B., & Lyman, Stanford M., (1968), Accounts. *American Sociological Review*, vol 33, pp. 46 -62

Schön, Donald, (1983), *The Reflective Practitioner: How Professionals Think in Action*. New York: Basic Books

Searle, John R., (1983), *Intentionality: An Essay in the Philosophy of Mind.* Cambridge: Cambridge University Press

Searle, John R., (1997), *The Mystery of Consciousness.* London: Granta Books

Searle, John R., (1999), *Mind, Language and Society – Doing Philosophy in the Real World.* London: Wiedenfeld & Nicolson.

Searle, John R., (2001), *Rationality in Action.* Cambridge, Mass.: Massachusetts Institute of Technology.

Simon, Herbert A., (1996), *The Science of the Artificial.* Cambridge, Mass.: MIT Press

Sjöstrand, Sven-Erik (2016), *Rethinking Corporate Governance. The Forming of Operative and Financial Strategies in Global Corporations.* Cheltenham: Edward Elgar.

Skinner, B. Frederic, (1971), *Beyond Freedom & Dignity*. Indianapolis: Hackett

Slobodian, Quinn, (2018), *Globalists – The End of Empire and the Birth of Neoliberalism.* Cambridge, Mass.: Harvard University Press

Smith, Adam, (1776), *Wealth of Nations.* Chicago: Chicago University Press

Soufian, Mona, William Forbes, and Robert Simon Hudson, (2013), Adapting Financial Rationality: Is a new Paradigm Emerging? *Critical Perspectives in Accounting,* vol 25, no 8, pp 724 – 742

Streeck, Wolfgang, & Schmitter, Philip C., (eds.), (1985), *Private Interest Governance: Beyond Market and State.* Beverly Hills: Sage

Taylor, Frederick W., (1911), *The Principles of Scientific Management*. New York: Harper

Thomson, J. A. K. (1955). *The Ethics of Aristotle: The Nicomachean Ethics*. New York: Penguin Classics.

Waismann, Friederich & McGuinness, Brian (eds), (1979*), Ludwig Wittgenstein and the Vienna Circle. Conversations recorded by Friedrich Waismann*. Oxford: Basil Blackwell

Wallander, Jan, (2002), *Med den mänskliga naruren – inte mot!* (With Human Nature – not Against!) Stockholm: SNS

Wasserman, Janek, (2019). *The Marginal Revolutionaries – How Austrian Economists Fought the War of Ideas*. New Haven; Yale University Press.

Watson, Graham, & Seiler, Robert M. (eds.), (1992), *Text in Context – Contributions to Ethnomethodology*. Newbury Park, Ca.: Sage.

Weber, Max, (1930), *The Protestant Ethic and the Spirit of Capitalism*. London: Unwin

Weber, Max, (1922/2019), Economy and Society – A New Translation (edited and translated by Keith Tribe). Cambridge, Mass.: Harvard University Press

Weber, Max, (2020), *Charisma and Disenchantment – the Vocation Lectures* (Reiter & Wellmon, eds.). New York: New York Review of Books.

Weick, Karl E. (1995), *Sensemaking in Organizations*. Thousand Oaks, C.: Sage

Wernerfelt, Birger, (1984), A Resource-based View of the Firm. *Strategic Management Journal*, vol. 5, pp 171 - 180

Williams, Bernhard, (2012, orig. 1979)), Internal and External Reasons (in Setiya & Paakkunainen eds., *Internal Reasons – Contemporary Readings*). Cambridge, Mass.: MIT Press

Wittgenstein, Ludwig, (1922), *Tractatus Logico-Philosophicus*. London: Kegan Paul

Wittgenstein, Ludwig, (1953). *Philosophical investigations. (Philosophische Untersuchungen)*. New York: Macmillan.

Zajonc, R. B. (1960). The process of cognitive tuning in communication. *The Journal of Abnormal and Social Psychology, vol. 61,* pp. 159–167.

Zuboff, Shoshana, (2019), *The Age of Surveillance Capitalism. The Fight for a Human Future at the New Frontier of Power.* London: Profile Books

www.ingramcontent.com/pod-product-compliance
Lightning Source LLC
LaVergne TN
LVHW102009210926
848483LV00010B/231